TO LIVE
IS
CHRIST

The Emerging Church

*the story of the Roman Catholic Church
from its beginnings to the present*

Ronald J. Wilkins

Wm. C. Brown Company Publishers
Dubuque, Iowa

This edition of *The Emerging Church* has been submitted for ecclesiastical approbation. Teachers' comments will be appreciated.

EDITORIAL CONSULTANTS:

for Sacred Scripture—Very Rev. Brendan McGrath, Professor of Theology, Loyola University, Chicago, Illinois; Past President, the Catholic Biblical Association of America

for Adolescent Religious Education—Mrs. Ruth Cheney, Program Services Associate for the Youth Ministry of the Episcopal Church; Chairman of the Screening Committee of the International Christian Youth Exchange

for Adolescent Psychology—Dr. William D. Wilkins, Professor, School of Leadership and Human Behavior, United States International University, San Diego, California; Consultant for the Office of Economic Opportunity, Washington, D.C.

for Social Sciences—Dr. Raymond Polin, Professor of Political Science, Graduate School, St. John's University, Jamaica, L.I., New York

ADVISORS:

Mr. Armand Bertin, Director of Catholic School Programs, Archdiocese of New Orleans

Mr. Thomas Zimmerman, Author; Former Teacher, St. Scholastica High School, Chicago

Fully aware of religious education as a key factor affecting human relations, the editors invited a Protestant and a Jewish scholar to review material presented in these books as it bears on their respective faith communities. These are Dr. Edward Zerin, Rabbi, and Dr. Martin E. Marty, Editor, *Christian Century*. While their personal views and religious beliefs obviously must differ from some of the views presented in these books, both feel that the content has been so handled as to increase intergroup understanding.

Excerpts from *The Jerusalem Bible*, copyright © 1966 by Darton, Longman and Todd, Ltd. and Doubleday and Co., Inc., used by permission of the publisher.

Excerpts from *Today's English Version of the New Testament*, copyright © American Bible Society 1966, 1971, are used by permission of copyright owner.

ISBN 0-697-01650-1

Fifth Printing, 1977

CONTENTS

Christianity is an event: the coming of Jesus Christ (who Christians believe is the Son of God) into the world of people. The Christian Church is an assembly of people who give living witness to the present reality of this event in their lives. *The Emerging Church* is the story of Christianity as it was expressed, first, in Roman Catholicism and continues to be expressed there.

The Emerging Church is not written as a defense of the Roman Catholic Church, and it is not an exposition proving that the Roman Catholic Church is the one true Church. It is a brief account of how the Christ-event found expression in the lives of people who experienced the meaning of Jesus for people, as this meaning has ever been understood by the Roman Catholic Church and expressed in its doctrines, liturgy, and laws designed to help people fulfill themselves through their Roman Catholic Christianity. It is a book that presents, in capsule form, the story of the Roman Catholic Church as it attempted to be the instrument through which Jesus continued to live and be effective in the world of people from the time when he no longer lived among them in his three-dimensional body.

The Emerging Church is written to serve both as background for and a springboard to in-depth study and discussions of the role of the Church as the body of Christ. Its purpose is to help the reader understand what the Church is and what its role is in this moment of history (the only moment that counts) through a study of what the Church believes itself to be and how it lived this belief in history. It is hoped that through a deeper understanding of what the Church is and through an appreciation of how it lived out its mission in history that those who are searching for the meaning of the Church in their own lives will capture the significance of the meaning of the words that Jesus spoke to his disciples during his last visit with them. "Lord," they said to him, "are you going to restore the rule to Israel now?" "The exact time is not yours to know," Jesus replied. "The Father has reserved that to himself. You will receive power when the Holy Spirit comes down on you; then you are to be my witnesses in Jerusalem, throughout Judea and Samaria, yes, even to the ends of the earth." (Acts 1:6–8). *The Emerging Church* presents the history of the fulfillment of that mission as it is carried out in the Roman Catholic Church.

PART ONE

The Church Views Itself

"All men are called to . . . union with Christ," said the bishops of the Roman Catholic Church in their Constitution on the Church *"who is the light of the world, from whom we go forth, through whom we live, and toward whom our whole life strains."* (November 21, 1964)

If the Church did not believe this, it would have no reason for existence. The Christian Church, like other religions, presents a religious interpretation of the world as they experience that world. Unlike other religions, however, the Christian Church is not based only on a philosophy, an ethical code, or an interpretation of history. It is founded on the acceptance of Jesus as God's Son who, Christians believe, became a human being to bring Divine Life to creation.

Most of the three billion 700 million people in the world practice some form of religion or other. There are over one billion Christians, of whom more than 550 million are Roman Catholics. How could a faith that began with the belief that a man rose from the dead grow from its insignificant beginnings in an enslaved nation in a "God-forsaken place" to become the faith-community of so many? The answer is at once simple and complex.

It is simple because of what Catholics believe the Church is. It is complex because, given the limitations of human nature and the diversity of the people who are Christians, there are many reasons for (and against, of course) the growth and continuity of the Church. Catholics believe that it is through the grace of God: they believe that it is part of God's plan for the salvation of people.

This belief that God is directing things naturally to their natural end is an essential aspect of Christian belief in God. It is derived from the Jewish belief in a saving God. It is best illustrated, perhaps, by this incident recounted in *The Acts of the Apostles.*

Then the High Priest and all his companions, members of the local party of the Sadducees, became extremely jealous of the apostles [who were preaching about Jesus with great success]; so they decided to take action.... [They] called together all the Jewish elders for a full meeting of the Council; then . . . they brought the apostles in and made them stand before the Council, and the High Priest questioned them. "We gave you strict orders not to teach in the name of this man," he said; "but see what you have done! You have spread your teaching all over Jeru-

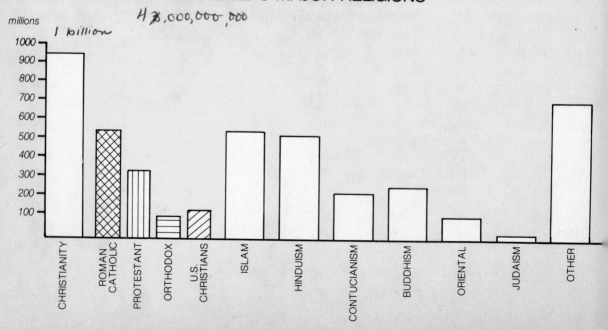

THE WORLD'S MAJOR RELIGIONS

4 8,000,000,000

millions

1 billion

1000 — 900 — 800 — 700 — 600 — 500 — 400 — 300 — 200 — 100 —

CHRISTIANITY · ROMAN CATHOLIC · PROTESTANT · ORTHODOX · U.S. CHRISTIANS · ISLAM · HINDUISM · CONTUCIANISM · BUDDHISM · ORIENTAL · JUDAISM · OTHER

salem, and you want to make us responsible for his death!" Peter and the other apostles answered back: "We must obey God, not men. The God of our fathers raised Jesus from death, after you had killed him by nailing him to a cross. And God raised him to his right side as Leader and Savior, to give to the people of Israel the opportunity to repent and have their sins forgiven. We are witnesses to these things—we and the Holy Spirit, who is God's gift to those who obey him."

When the members of the Council heard this they were so furious that they decided to have the apostles put to death. But one of them, a Pharisee named Gamaliel, a teacher of the Law who was highly respected by all the people, stood up in the Council. He ordered the apostles to be taken out, and then said to the Council: "Men of Israel, be careful what you are about to do to these men. Some time ago Theudas appeared, claiming that he was somebody great; and about four hundred men joined him. But he was killed, all his followers were scattered, and his movement died out. After this, Judas the Galilean appeared during the time of the census; he also drew a crowd after him, but he also was killed and all his followers were scattered. And so in this case now, I tell you, do not take any action against these men. Leave them alone, for if this plan and work of theirs is a man-made thing, it will disappear; but if it comes from God you cannot possibly defeat them. You could find yourselves fighting against God!" The Council followed Gamaliel's advice.

Acts 5:17–18, 20, 27–39

We believe that the grace of God is the force behind the growth and continuity of the Church. If this is our belief, how does God operate in the real world of human limitations and the diversity of people who are the Church?

As you know, God operates in His creation according to His nature; that is, through the ordinary factors involved in the growth dynamics of His creation. In people, God acts through the minds He has given them to enable them to perceive, through the power of choice He has given them to enable them to select, and through the talents He has given them to enable them to achieve. (God's will, or purpose, is not automatically achieved in free beings, of course, for people are not things responding blindly to physical or chemical forces, and they are not animals responding to instinct or training alone. They are human. They are created free. They act and react to a complex of forces which causes them to do now one thing, now another, depending on their capabilities, the circumstances of time and place, and the aspects of prior training and previous choices. As far as the Church is concerned, Christians believe that God enabled the apostles to perceive themselves and those who joined them as the body of Christ in the world, as the new people of God "on pilgrimage here on earth," and as a social institution organized to carry out the work of Christ in the world. They believe that God gave them extraordinary help so that their choices and their talents were directed to the accomplishment of His plans for His Church.

Why the Church views itself as the body of Christ and as the new people of God is the subject of the first chapter. How the Church carried out the work of Christ in history is the subject of Part Two of this book.

Structure of the Church
1. Pope
2. Cardinal
3. Arch Bishops
4. Bishops
5. Monsieneur
6. pastor
7. priest
8. deacons
9. Nuns
10. Lay People

3

The Church as the Body of Christ

1

There is no doubt of the effect that the presence of Jesus had on the people of his time. But Jesus knew that if he was to be equally effective in the lives of people after he was no longer present to them in his physical body, he had to be present to them in some way other than in a general, historical sense.* He knew he had to be present to them in actuality. Catholics believe he chose to be so present in several specific ways. They believe this because of what he said.

First, Christians believe that Jesus is present in them through their baptism. ("If anyone loves me, he will keep my word, and my Father will love him, and we shall come to him and make our home with him." *John* 14:23) Then, they believe that he is present among them and in them when they are gathered for a religious purpose. ("Where two or three meet in my name, I shall be there with them." *Matthew* 18:20) Also, they believe he is present to them and in them in their liturgical celebrations. ("Then

---

* Persons who have gained a place in history are "present" to people after death through their being remembered, through the influence their lives have on people, and through what they said or did during their lifetimes. This is not what is meant by the presence of Christ in the Church.

NC PHOTO

he took some bread, and when he had given thanks, broke it and gave it to them, saying, 'This is my body which shall be given for you; do this as a memorial of me.' He did the same with the cup after supper, and said, 'This cup is the new covenant in my blood which will be poured out for you.' " *Luke* 22:19, 20) And, they believe Jesus is present in them, and through them to the world, as his disciples.

Father, I want those you have given
  me
to be with me where I am,
so that they may always see the glory
you have given me
before the foundation of the world.
Father, Righteous One,
the world has not known you,
but I have known you,
and these have known
that you have sent me.
I have made your name known to
  them
and will continue to make it known,
so that the love with which you have
  loved me
may be in them,
and so that I may be in them.
As you sent me into the world,
I have sent them into the world,
and for their sake I consecrate myself
so that they may be consecrated in
  truth.
I pray not only for these,
but for those also
who through their words will believe
  in me.

John 17:24–26; 18–20

There are other presences of Christ in his Church, of course, such as the Real Presence of Jesus in the Blessed Sacrament and the special presence of Christ in the souls of the just. We are concerned with the presences mentioned above because they bear directly on the point we are discussing: the Church as the body of Christ.

Why the Church Believes It Is the Body of Christ

According to their own testimony, the apostles did not really understand the role of Jesus in God's plan for the world (see *Acts* 1:6) nor why they had been selected as his followers until the Holy Spirit came to them at Pentecost. Only then did they begin to understand the meaning of Jesus for the world and their own role in making this

ROHN ENGH, PINE LAKE FARM

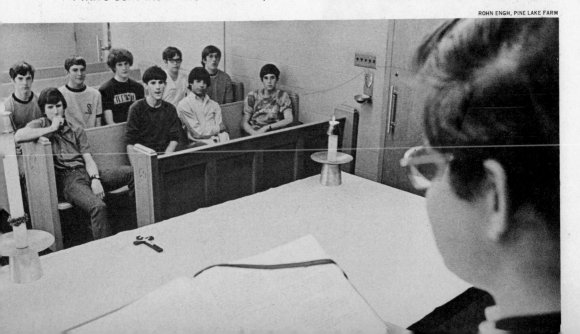

5

meaning known. They remembered that Jesus had said:

> . . . You will receive power when the Holy Spirit comes on you, and then you will be my witnesses not only in Jerusalem but throughout Judea and Samaria, and indeed to the ends of the earth.
>
> *Acts* 1:8

> Go, therefore, make disciples of all nations; baptize them in the name of the Father and of the Son, and of the Holy Spirit, and teach them to observe all the commands I gave you. And know that I am with you always; yes, to the end of time.
>
> *Matthew* 28:19–20

In other words, they understood that they (and those who accepted Jesus as savior) were to be the instruments through whom Jesus would express himself to the world after his ascension. They were, in effect, the "new" body Jesus had chosen in order to be present to people throughout history.* St. Paul expresses this understanding in one of his letters to the Christians of Corinth to whom he wrote:

> Just as the human body, though it is made up of many parts is a single unit because all these parts, though many, make up one body, so it is with Christ. In the one Spirit we were all baptized, Jews as well as Greeks, slaves as well as citizens, and one Spirit was given to us all. . . . Now you together are Christ's body; but each of you is a different part of it.
>
> *1 Corinthians* 12:12–13, 27

---

* For Christians, the Church as the body of Christ is reasonable and perfectly understandable. They know that just as the Son of God chose his particular physical body to express his Divine Personhood in a particular place for a limited time, so he could select his followers to be the visible means to express himself for all time.

But the apostles were (and Christians are) the body of Christ not because they preached about Jesus, acted in his name, and did the things Jesus did. *They were his body because he constituted them his body, making them alive with his Spirit.* They had an organic life proper to their role as Christ's body in God's saving plan. They were bound together by more than mission, fellowship, goal, desire, companionship, and dedication to a common cause. They were bound together, as one body, through their union with Christ who lived in them (as he had promised) just as he had lived in his physical body. They were, indeed, a true body whose head was Christ. "Now the Church," said St. Paul in his letter to the Colossians (1:18), "is his body; he is its head."

Because the Church is the body of Christ through which he expresses himself to the world, Christ is present in his Church. That is, Christ is acting when the Church is acting as Church (as distinct from the individual activity of one of the members of the Church). Thus, for example, the preaching of the gospel is not simply a recounting of the historical events in which Christ acted; it is Christ at work in the word being proclaimed. When the Church is gathered for the Eucharist, it is not simply a group recalling and celebrating a past event; it is Christ celebrating the Lord's Supper with his followers and inviting them to eat his flesh and drink his blood, which is present to them as it was present to the apostles at the first Lord's Supper. When the Church baptizes, forgives, confirms, is present at weddings, consoles the sick, or designates ministers, it is Christ who is so doing in the present. And when the Church cares for the poor, the sick, the suffering, the frightened, the lonely, the discriminated against, and the disenfranchised, it is Christ acting in the present as he did in the past when he was physically present to people in his own land. And when the Church sends missioners to preach Christ to those who do not know him, it is Christ announcing the Good News of God's kingdom.

It is this consciousness of itself as the body of Christ acting in the present which is the driving force of the Church to fulfill its mission as it sees it at any given moment in its history. It is attempting to make Christ present to people in their own historical lives. It is, in reality, the social expression of Christ in history.

7

The Church as the People of God

The Church as the body of Christ was constituted by God for a purpose: to be the expression of Christ in history in order to carry out the salvation mission of Christ. As such, the Church is a sign of God's saving acts and an expression of the reality of Christ himself.

As a sign of God's saving acts in Christ, the Church is a "sacrament."* It is a living witness to God's saving actions in Christ, and a means to salvation designed by God to make His saving actions visible, accessible, and efficacious. In this sense, the Church instituted by Christ is a sacramental community of persons constituting a people selected by God to make His creation holy. As St. Peter said:

> But you are a chosen race, a royal priesthood, a consecrated nation, a people set apart to sing the praises of God who called you out of darkness into his wonderful light. Once you were not a people at all and now you are the People of God . . .
>
> *1 Peter* 2:9–10

* A sacrament is a visible sign instituted by Christ to signify and be God's saving action in a specific case.

This designation of itself as the people of God is not an expression of self-glorification, and it does not arise from religious pride or a false sense of spiritual elitism. It is, rather, an expression of the Church's awareness of its origin and purpose and of its consciousness of the awesome responsibility of its mission. It is the reason behind its liturgical, sacramental, moral, pastoral, social, and ascetical life. The Church knows what it is and why it is, and attempts, however inadequately at times because of the normal human limitations inherent in any human endeavor, to be what it is supposed to be.

What Does the Term "People of God" Mean?

When the Church speaks of itself as the people of God, it does not use the term "people" in a general, indiscriminate way to designate simply a gathering of persons, as you might when you say, "many people showed up for the game." And it does not use "of God" to imply that it is a gathering of religiously inclined people who believe in a God, as distinct from people who do not believe in a God. It uses the term "people of God" to signify a specific group of people who form a particular community of believers possessing four characteristics.

First, everyone who has accepted Jesus as savior and been baptized belongs to the Church. No distinction is made among them, and no one or no group is more the people of God than any others. As St. Paul said in his letter to the Galatian Christians:

> . . . and you are, all of you, sons of God through faith in Christ Jesus. All baptized in Christ, you have all clothed yourselves in Christ, and there are no more distinctions between Jew and Greek, slave or free, male and female, but all of you are one in Christ Jesus. . . .
>
> *Galatians* 3:26–28

There are, of course, different ministries, services, and functions within the Church to serve the entire people of God, but there is no elite group that can call itself, or be considered, the Church. Some are more religious than others, some with special offices, some following particular life-styles, it is true, but they are members within the entire commu-

RELIGIOUS NEWS SERVICE

nity. All in the community have been called equally by God to faith in Christ and to respond to his commands in love. So it is not the measure of response which makes a person a member of the people of God; it is the response to God's call in Christ itself. This does not mean, of course, that the degree of response to God's call is not important. It simply means that all persons baptized in Christ are the people of God.

Second, all people are called to be members of the people of God through God's invitation. The invitation is not made to particular individuals or to specific racial or ethnic groups. There are no predetermined criteria for selection. No one has to qualify to receive God's call. The invitation is not a privilege or an honor given to a select few because of their qualifications, making the Church a kind of exclusive club or a private religious group to which a person is admitted because of some merit of his own. All people are God's, and He invites all of them to number themselves among "His people."

Third, people belong to the Church through their own free choice, and it is they who are the Church. The Church is not something that exists over and above people,

or an institution existing apart from and distinct from the people who are its members. It does not have an existence all its own as some kind of suprahuman or supramundane entity. It is the people who make up the Church. If it is God who calls all people to salvation, it is people who respond: it is the responding people who are the Church.

If the Church really is the people of God, it is impossible to see it as a quasi-divine hypostasis between God and man.* This would be a . . . misconception which would dissociate it from the real people who make up the Church and make it into something in its own right . . . a suprapersonal institution mediating between God and man. Certainly the Church is always more than the sum of its individual members; but it is and remains the fellowship of its believing

---

* *Quasi* means *variously resembling* or *seemingly* or *partially* but *not actually* or *wholly*. Here *hypostasis* means a union of two things resulting in a third which has an existence all its own.

members whom God has gathered into his people. There can be no Church without this people of believers. *We* are the Church—not God, not Christ, not the Holy Spirit. Without us and outside us the Church has no reality. . . . There can be no faith, sacraments, and offices, nothing of an institutional nature, without men, they cannot precede or be superior to men. All these things exist in the fellowship of believers, who *are* the Church; it is this fellowship, which is identical with the new people of God, which constitutes the *basic structure* of the Church.*

If the Church is people responding to God's invitation and is not something apart or distinct from people, it is affected by and reflects the real economic, political, social, cultural, and historical lives of the people who are the Church. In other words, the Church is in history and is affected by history.

In addition, even though the people of God have been infused with new (that is, divine) life, they still have the human limitations and weaknesses that are a part of their earthly existence, they still feel the impact of the human drives which incline them away from the self-denial of the gospel, and they live in a sinful world that sometimes lures them from the principles of their faith commitment. Their expression of Christianity will reflect the tensions they experience from their own natures and the pressures they feel from the world in which they live.

And the Church will reflect the individuality of the members who are the people of God, whose physical and intellectual equipment, emotional and psychological responses, and dedication to an ideal are as varied as the individuals themselves. Some are deeply religious, some are only mildly so; but most are somewhere in between.

Some are strong and some are weak; but many vacillate between strength and capitulation. Some are totally dedicated, some use Christianity for their own ends; but most are trying their best, given their abilities and capabilities, and the circumstances and pressures they face. Some are rich, and some are poor; some are healthy, and some are sick. Some are bright, some are not so bright; but most are rather average. Some are hyperactive, some are lethargic; but most respond to the demands of Christianity to a greater or lesser degree depending on their personality, temperament, prior training, understanding of the demands of Christianity, and on their age, health, and ability to respond to God's grace present to them.

Because the Church as the people of God includes all people of every age, and includes in its membership every kind of people and every kind of individual, it is transhistorical

---

* *The Church* by Hans Küng, C. Verlag Herder R. G., Freiburg im Brusgau, 1967, English translation C. Burns and Oats Ltd., 1967, Published by Sheed and Ward, Inc., New York, p. 130.

and transcultural even though it expresses itself historically and culturally at any given time and in any given place. Because this is so, the Church is not dependent upon history nor tied to a particular culture, even though it affects history and culture and is affected by them.* This is its fourth characteristic.

Understanding this interaction between what the Church is and how it expresses itself historically and culturally, is central to understanding the history of the Church because the Church is a living community of believers who express their Christianity culturally.

The history of any people is the history of the interaction of the economic, political, and cultural forces which have shaped that history; hence, the history of the Church is the history of the effect that Christianity has had on culture and culture upon Christianity.

For example, the first culture into which Christianity moved was Judaism. Christianity has its roots in Judaism because Jesus was a Jew, a product of the Judaism of his time, and the Church's first leaders and members were Jewish. Both he and they thought, talked, and acted as the devout Jews of their day thought, talked, and acted.

When the first Jewish Christians moved outside of the spheres of Jewish culture and were confronted with Syrian, Egyptian, Greek, Roman, and African cultures, they found that they had to express their understanding of Jesus in terms that were intelligible to people with non-Jewish language forms, philosophies, outlooks, and habits. As the Christian sphere of influence broadened, it moderated and improved the culture of the people it influenced; it, in turn, was affected by the culture into which it came. The same exchange of influences occurred in succeeding ages of history.

This interaction of Christianity and culture explains why the Church expresses itself as it does today, and why it will express itself in the future in terms of the society in which it will survive. As various cultures blend and are modified by contact with each other, and as the world moves more and more toward a planet culture and away from purely regional cultures, the Church will continue to be the social expression of Christ in history but in the terms of the planet culture that will emerge. And, as ethnic, cultural, regional, and national differences begin to meld into each other and become less and less distinct, the people of God will become more and more a "catholic" people. They will truly be universal.

Therefore, although Christianity is more than a cultural force of human making, it must express itself culturally. This is at once its strength and its weakness. Because it is not dependent upon a particular culture, it can express itself in a variety of ways, each of which is authentic Christianity as long as it remains faithful to its mission. But, because it must express itself culturally, it will exhibit the limitations of its cultural expression. Hence, it will never reach its ideal state as long as the created world as we know it exists.

There will always be a condition of tension between the real and the ideal. When you understand this, you will understand the dynamic nature of Christianity and its constant need for change and updating. You will begin to understand why the bishops at Vatican Council II referred to the Church as a "pilgrim Church in exile from the Lord," and why the title of this book is *The Emerging Church*.

---

* For example, even though modern Africa is moving toward Christianity in great numbers (see page 247), its move is not without problems. In January, 1975, Zaire's President, Mobutu Seso Seko, banned the teaching of religion in all schools as part of his "Africanization" program. What effect this will have on the nearly 12,000,000 Catholics in Zaire is yet to be seen.

3 The Church as a Social Institution

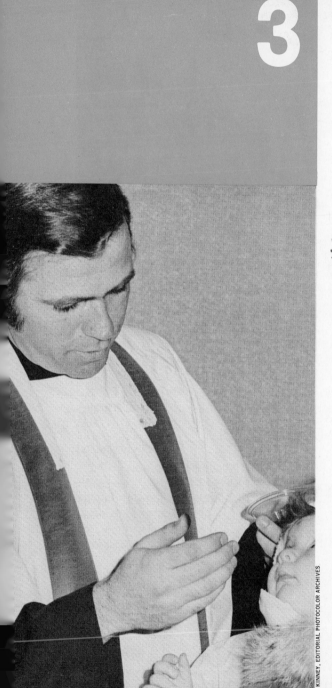

The Church, reflecting on what it is, sees its mission to be the same as Christ's: to preach the good news, to honor the Father, and to promote peace among people.* In other words, the Church exists in people for people: it is a social institution. It is, in reality, the social expression of Christ in history.

Everything we have said about the dignity of the human person, and about the human community and the profound meaning of human activity, lays the foundation for the relationship between the Church and the world, and provides the basis for dialogue between them. . . . presupposing everything which has already been said by this Council concerning the mystery of the Church, we must now consider this same Church inasmuch as she exists in the world, living and acting in it. . . .

Christ, to be sure, gave His Church no proper mission in the po-

---

* The Church preaches the good news through proclaiming the gospel, honors the Father in its worship, chiefly the Eucharist, and promotes peace among people through its social and moral services.

litical, economic, or social order. The purpose which He set before her is a religious one. But out of this religious mission itself come a function, a light, and an energy which can serve to structure and consolidate the human community according to divine law. As a matter of fact, she can and indeed should initiate activities on behalf of all men, especially those designed for the needy, such as the works of mercy and similar undertakings.

Moreover, since in virtue of her mission and nature she is bound to no particular form of human culture, nor to any political, economic, or social system, the Church by her very universality can be a very close bond between diverse human communities and nations, provided these trust her and truly acknowledge her right to true freedom in fulfilling her mission. For this reason, the Church admon-

ishes her own sons, but also humanity as a whole, to overcome all strife between nations and races in this family spirit of God's children, and in the same way, to give internal strength to human associations which are just. *

※ 3 ways

Because the Church is people organized to carry out the mission of Christ in the world, it has the characteristics of any human social organization. Like any human organization, it is structured to fill a need. Like any human organization, it grew and developed as time went on, and divided itself into functional parts to fulfill its purpose. Like any human organization, it has its strengths and weaknesses, its major and minor divisions, its obsolete departments and functions, its dedicated personnel and its

* "The Church in the Modern World," *The Teachings of the Second Vatican Council,* (Westminster, Maryland: Newman Press, 1966), nos. 40, 42.

functionaries. Like any human organization, it changes slowly, reacts to situations and social conditions with what seems to be ponderous slowness, and acts with caution stemming from a deep sense of tradition and purpose. *Unlike human organizations, however, the Church is not structured for business, social, or political purposes; it is organized to fill a religious need.* In other words, the Church is a human organization fulfilling a social need, and it is a religious organization fulfilling a divine command.

What Is the Social Mission of the Church?

Christ did not organize the Church as we know it now, nor give it its present structure. He gave it a mission. The organization and structure of the Church, as we know it, grew out of an evident need that arose as the number of believers increased.

Some time later, as the number of disciples kept growing, there was a quarrel between the Greek-speaking Jews and the native Jews. The Greek-speaking Jews said that their widows were being neglected in the daily distribution of funds. So the twelve apostles called the whole group of disciples together and said: "It is not right for us to neglect the preaching of God's word in order to handle finances. So then, brothers, choose seven men among you who are known to be full of the Holy Spirit and wisdom, and we will put them in charge of this matter. We ourselves, then, will give our full time to prayers and the work of preaching." The whole group was pleased with the apostles' proposal; so they chose Stephen, a man full of faith and the Holy Spirit, and Philip, Prochorus, Nicanor, Timon, Parmenas, and Nicolaus from Antioch, a Gentile who had been converted to Judaism. The group presented them to the apostles, who prayed and placed their hands on them.

Acts 6:1–6

It is evident that the Church, from the very beginning, understood its social mission

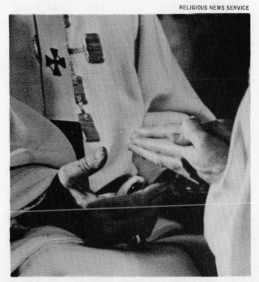

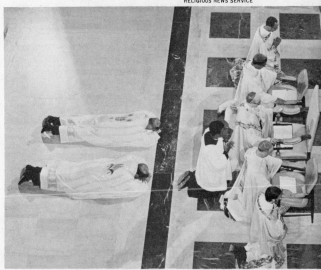

to have two distinct aspects: preaching about Jesus and praying, and serving the material needs of the community. The former role was to be undertaken by someone special "who has been with us the whole time that the Lord Jesus was traveling round with us, someone who was with us from the time John was baptizing until the day when he was taken up from us—and [who] can act with us as a witness to his resurrection. . . . to take over this ministry and apostolate." It was then that Mathias was listed as one of the twelve apostles." (*Acts* 1:21–22; 25–26) For serving the material needs of the community, persons were chosen who were "filled with the Holy Spirit and with wisdom." (*Acts* 6:3)*

As we have indicated, as time went on and the number of Christians increased, various other ministries were added to the Church for practical reasons. For example, to assist the bishop in his *liturgical* function (the official worship of the Church), certain persons were selected and ordained; Catholic Christians call them priests. To assist the bishop in other service functions, other members of the Church were selected to fulfill special needs of the Church, like teaching, caring for the sick and the poor, administration, and the thousand and one other jobs associated with any kind of social institution. As St. Paul said in his first letter to the Corinthian Christians:

---

* This distinction in community services remains to the present day. In the Catholic Church certain persons are selected by the Church to fulfill the apostolic mission (that is, the mission of the original Twelve) of the Church. These are the bishops, whose primary function is to be the chief pastor of a particular community of Catholic Christians united to the universal body of Catholic Christians. This unity is signified by the bishop's union with the successor to St. Peter, the bishop of Rome, called the Pope.

HAROLD M. LAMBERT

RELIGIOUS NEWS SERVICE

HAROLD M. LAMBERT

There are different kinds of spiritual gifts, but the same Spirit gives them. There are different ways of serving, but the same Lord is served. There are different abilities to perform service, but the same God gives ability to everyone for all services. Each one is given some proof of the Spirit's presence for the good of all. The Spirit gives one man a message of wisdom, while to another man the same Spirit gives a message of knowledge. One and the same Spirit gives faith to one man, while to another man he gives the power to heal. The Spirit gives one man the power to work miracles; to another, the gift of speaking God's message; and to yet another, the ability to tell the difference between gifts that come from the Spirit and those that do not. To one man he gives the ability to speak with strange sounds; to another, he gives the ability to explain what these sounds mean. But it is one and the same Spirit who does all this; he gives a different gift to each man, as he wishes.

1 Corinthians 12:4–11

People are the Church

Though in the Catholic Church the visible organization is highly structured, the structure is not the Church. The people are. The structure of the Church, like the structure in any human organization, is designed to serve the purpose of the Church. Its government is directed to fulfilling its mission—preserving the thrust of the gospel message through its doctrinal statements, its liturgical practices, its canonical and moral laws in a particular time and a particular place and its social messages. All this has but one purpose: to enable Catholic Christians to be Christ to the world in which they live.

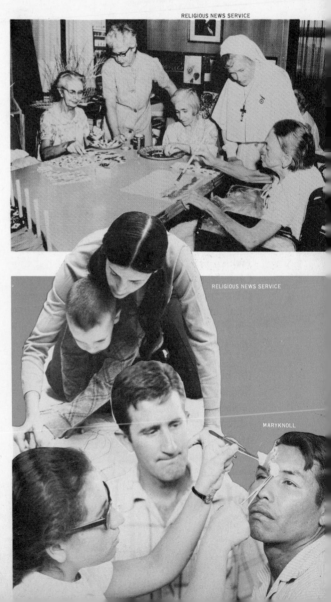

RELIGIOUS NEWS SERVICE

RELIGIOUS NEWS SERVICE

MARYKNOLL

MARYKNOLL

The Church as Pilgrim

4

CONTEMPORARY CHRISTIAN ART, INC.

Keenly aware of the role of Jesus in God's creative plan, Christians have always tried to understand their role as a body of people in the world. They have attempted to describe their role as they understand it in phrases given them in the New Testament which, they believe, is God's revelation to them concerning the Church. As we have seen, for Christians, the Church is "the body of Christ," for it is an expression of Christ in the world. It is, also, "the people of God," for such a phrase describes who Christians are in the world.

In addition to these two expressions (which are basic to understanding what the Church is), Christians use other phrases taken from the New Testament to describe what the Church is. St. Matthew calls it "the kingdom of God' (*Matthew* 21:43), and has Jesus calling it "my Church" and "the kingdom of heaven" (*Matthew* 16:18, 19)— the historical reality in which God's revelation and will are publicly proclaimed and established. St. John calls it a sheepfold of which Christ is the Good Shepherd (*John* 10:1–11), and a vineyard in which Christ is the true, or parent, vine (*John* 15:1–5; see also *Matthew* 21:33–43). St. Paul calls the Church "God's building" (*1 Corinthians* 3:9), "God's family" (*1 Timothy* 3:15), and the "bride of Christ" (*Ephesians* 5:22–32), wherein the seed of Christ is planted and the Christian is nurtured (*Galatians* 4:26).

While each of these says something about the Church, perhaps the best description of the Church which combines the idea of the body of Christ, the people of God, and a social institution is the one given by St. Paul in his second letter to the Corinthians, in which he describes the Church as a pilgrim "exiled from the Lord, going as we do by faith and not by sight."

For we know that when this tent we live in—our body here on earth—is torn down, God will have a house in heaven for us to live in, a home he himself made, which will last for ever. And now we sigh, so great is our desire to have our home which is in heaven put on over us; for by being clothed with it we shall not be found without a body. While we live in this earthly tent we groan with a feeling of oppression; it is not that we want to get rid of our earthly body, but that we want to have the heavenly one put on over us, so that what is mortal will be swallowed up by life. God is the one who has prepared us for this change, and he gave us his Spirit as the guarantee of all that he has for us.

So we are always full of courage. We know that as long as we are at home in this body we are away from the Lord's home. For our life is a matter of faith, not of sight. We are full of courage, and would much prefer to leave our home in this body and be at home with the Lord. More than anything else, however, we want to please him, whether in our home here or there. For all of us must appear before Christ, to be judged by him, so that each one may receive what he deserves, according to what he has done, good or bad, in his bodily life.

We know what it means to fear the Lord, and so we try to persuade men. God knows us completely, and I hope that in your hearts you know me as well. We are not trying to recommend ourselves to you again; rather, we are trying to give you a good reason to be proud of us, so that you will be able to answer those who boast about a man's appearance, and not about his character. Are we really insane? It is for God's sake. Or are we sane? It is for your sake. For we are ruled by Christ's love for us, now that we recognize that one man died for all men, which means that all men take part in his death. He died for all men so that those who live should no longer live for themselves, but only for him who died and was raised to life for their sake.

No longer, then, do we judge anyone by human standards. Even if at one time we judged Christ according to human standards, we no longer do so. When anyone is joined to Christ he is a new being: the old is gone, the new has come. All this is done by God, who through Christ changed us from enemies into his friends, and gave us the task of making others his friends also. Our message is that God was making friends of all men through Christ. God did not keep an account of their sins against them, and he has given us the message of how he makes them his friends.

Here we are, then, speaking for Christ, as though God himself were appealing to you through us: on Christ's behalf, we beg you, let God change you from enemies into friends! Christ was without sin, but God made him share our sin in order that we, in union with him, might share the righteousness of God.

In our work together with God, then, we beg of you: you have received God's grace, and you must not let it be wasted. Hear what God says:

"I heard you in the hour of my favor,
I helped you in the day of salvation."

Listen! This is the hour to receive God's favor, today is the day to be saved!

We do not want anyone to find fault with our work, so we try not to put obstacles in anyone's way. Instead, in everything we do we show that we are God's servants, by enduring troubles, hardships, and difficulties with great patience. We have been beaten, jailed, and mobbed; we have been overworked and have gone without sleep or food. By our purity, knowledge, patience, and kindness we have shown ourselves to be God's servants; by the Holy Spirit, by our true love, by our message of truth, and by the power of God. We have righteousness as our weapon, both to attack and to defend ourselves. We are honored and disgraced; we are insulted and praised. We are treated as liars, yet we speak the truth; as unknown, yet we are known by all; as though we were dead, but, as you see, we live on. Although punished, we are not killed; although saddened, we are always glad; we seem poor, but we make many people rich; we seem to have nothing, yet we really possess everything.

Dear friends in Corinth! We have spoken frankly to you, we have opened wide our hearts. We have not closed our hearts to you; it is you who have closed your hearts to us. I speak now as though you were my children: show us the same feelings that we have for you. Open wide your hearts!

Do not try to work together as equals with unbelievers, for it cannot be done. How can right and wrong be partners? How can light and darkness live together? How can Christ and the Devil agree? What does a believer have in common with an unbeliever? How can God's temple come to terms with pagan idols? For we are the temple of the living God! As God himself has said:

"I will make my home with them and live among them,
I will be their God, and they shall be my people."

And so the Lord says:

"You must leave them, and separate yourselves from them.
Have nothing to do with what is unclean,
And I will accept you.
I will be your father,
And you shall be my sons and daughters,
Says the Lord Almighty."

All these promises are made to us, my dear friends! Let us, therefore, purify ourselves from everything that makes body or soul unclean, and let us seek to be completely holy, by living in the fear of God.

2 Corinthians 5; 6; 7:1

How Is the Church Pilgrim?

God is revealing many things through St. Paul in this selection, but what He seems to be saying is this: although we are in exile from the Lord (that is, away from our true homeland where we shall more fully share the life of God in our risen dimension of existence), we have many things to do here on earth. Our principal mission as Christians is to establish the kingdom of God among people. To do this, we must attempt to reform the world in the image of Christ. This is what the Church has been attempting to do throughout its long history. The process has been slow, and there have been many peaks and valleys, but it has gone on inexorably, in spite of the challenges of time and place, of history and culture, and of human weakness and deliberate sin.

As a pilgrim Church, Christians are sent into the world to bear witness to the saving actions of Jesus, to celebrate the ultimate, or eternal, values, to shape Christian communities into the image of Christ, and, in so doing, to reform society. As we have said, this is the missionary imperative of the Church; it is the cause of and the reason for its movement into the non-Christian world.

In carrying out this imperative, the Church has formed communities, or enclaves, of Christians wherever and whenever it has been possible. It is these communities, united with the universal church, that form the Christian Church, and it is these communities, called dioceses and parishes, that have the responsibility for reforming the earth.

The Church

This is why Christians themselves must *be* Christ to the world. This is the reason that Jesus, according to Matthew, said to his loyal followers: "Go, therefore, make disciples of all nations; baptize them in the name of the Father and of the Son and of the Holy Spirit, and teach them to observe all the commands I gave you." (*Matthew* 28:19, 20)

Jesus' idea was that Christians had to reform themselves—make themselves different from the sinful world around them—so that they could reform those with whom they came in contact. They were to have different motives, different values, and different habits of living from those among whom they lived. This is what St. Paul wrote:

In particular, I want to urge you in the name of the Lord, not to go on living the aimless kind of life that pagans live. Intellectually they are in the dark, and they are estranged from the life of God, without knowledge because they have shut their hearts to it. Their sense of right and wrong once dulled, they have abandoned themselves to sexuality and eagerly pursue a career of indecency of every kind. Now that is hardly the way you have learned from Christ, unless you failed to hear him properly when you were taught what the truth is in Jesus. You must give up your old way of life; you must put aside your old self, which gets corrupted by following illusory desires. Your mind must be renewed by a spiritual revolution so that you can put on the new self that has been created in God's way, in the goodness and holiness of the truth.

So from now on, there must be no more lies: *You must speak the truth to one another,* since we are all parts of one another. *Even if you are angry, you must not sin:* never let the sun set on your anger or else you will give

MARYKNOLL

self-righteousness, but by love—the love that Christians had for each other which brought peace and joy to the Christian community, where all were equal, all were holy, all worshipped God and led "Christ-like" lives. Their love for each other was not sentimentality. It was practical, affecting all aspects of community living. And it was religious: it was based on the Christian belief in a loving, saving God who is Father of all people.

How rich are the depths of God—how deep his wisdom and knowledge—and how impossible to penetrate his motives or understand his methods! *Who could ever know the mind of the Lord? Who could ever be his counsellor? Who could ever give him anything or lend him anything?* All that exists comes from him; all is by him and for him. To him be glory for ever! Amen.

Think of God's mercy, my brothers, and worship him, I beg you, in a way that is worthy of thinking be-

the devil a foothold. Anyone who was a thief must stop stealing; he should try to find some useful manual work instead, and be able to do some good by helping others that are in need. Guard against foul talk; let your words be for the improvement of others, as occasion offers, and do good to your listeners, otherwise you will only be grieving the Holy Spirit of God who has marked you with his seal for you to be set free when the day comes. Never have grudges against others, or lose your temper, or raise your voice to anybody, or call each other names, or allow any sort of spitefulness. Be friends with one another, and kind, forgiving each other as readily as God forgave you in Christ.

Ephesians 4:17–32

How was the transformation of the world from "pagan"* to Christian to be accomplished? By the influence Christians were to have on people through the kinds of lives they lead.

People were to be transformed, not by force, not by obnoxious proselytizing, not by fanatical actions, pietism, nor by prideful

---

* St. Paul uses the term "pagan" here to signify not simply persons who do not worship the One, True God, but more especially persons who are hedonistic and irreligious.

ings, by offering your living bodies as a holy sacrifice, truly pleasing to God. Do not model yourselves on the behavior of the world around you, but let your behavior change, modeled by your new mind. This is the only way to discover the will of God and know what is good, what it is that God wants, what is the perfect thing to do.

In the light of the grace I have received I want to urge each one of you not to exaggerate his real importance. Each of you must judge himself soberly by the standard of the faith God has given him. Just as each of our bodies has several parts and each part has a separate function, so all of us, in union with Christ, form one body, and as parts of it we belong to each other. Our gifts differ according to the grace given us. If your gift is prophecy, then use it as your faith suggests; if administration, then use it for administration; if teaching, then use it for teaching. Let the preachers deliver sermons, the almsgivers give freely, the officials be diligent, and those who do works of mercy do them cheerfully.

Do not let your love be a pretense, but sincerely prefer good to evil. Love each other as much as brothers should, and have a profound respect for each other. Work for the Lord with untiring effort and with great earnestness of spirit. If you have hope, this will make you cheerful. Do not give up if trials come; and keep on praying. If any of the saints are in need you must share with them; and you should make hospitality your special care.

Bless those who persecute you: never curse them, bless them. Rejoice with those who rejoice and be sad with those in sorrow. Treat everyone with equal kindness; never be condescending but make real friends with the poor. Do not allow yourself to become self-satisfied. Never repay evil with evil but let everyone see that you are interested only in the highest ideals. Do all you can to live at peace with everyone. Never try to get revenge; leave that, my friends, to God's anger. As scripture says: *Vengeance is mine—I will pay them back,* the Lord promises. But there is more: *If your enemy is hungry, you should give him food, and if he is thirsty, let him drink. Thus you heap red-hot coals on his head.* Resist evil and conquer it with good.

You must all obey the governing authorities. Since all government comes from God, the civil authorities were appointed by God, and so anyone who resists authority is rebelling against God's decision, and such an act is bound to be punished. Good behavior is not afraid of magistrates; only criminals have anything to fear. If you want to live without being afraid of authority, you must live honestly and authority may even honor you. The state is there to serve God for your benefit. If you break the law, however, you may well have fear: the bearing of the sword has its significance. The authorities are there to serve God: they carry out God's revenge by punishing wrongdoers. You must obey, therefore, not only because you are afraid of being punished, but also for conscience' sake. This is also the reason why you must pay taxes, since all government officials are God's officers. They serve God by collecting taxes. Pay every government official what he has a right to ask—whether it be direct tax or indirect, fear or honor.

Avoid getting into debt, except the debt of mutual love. If you love your fellow men you have carried out your obligations. All the commandments: *You shall not commit adultery, you shall not kill, you shall not steal, you shall not covet,* and so on, are summed up in this single command: *You must love your neighbor as yourself.* Love is the one thing that cannot hurt your neighbor; that is why it is the answer to every one of the commandments.

Romans 11:33–13:10

What St. Paul is saying is that if Christians truly love one another they will attract "outsiders" to their community. In so doing, they will transform (reform) the world.

The history of the Church is the story of how this was done. One Christian community after another was formed, and these, in turn, formed other Christian communities, shaping them in the image of Christ insofar as this was possible. They were, in effect, pilgrims, visiting as it were a foreign land, bringing to those who did not know Christ the good news of his coming and of his mes-

sage of salvation. They were shaping and molding the world, making it ready for the Second Coming of Christ when he will present the world to the Father, reformed and reshaped in his image.

Like the pilgrims who came to America, the Church moves into new lands, always searching, always seeking for ways to transform that world. Keeping its ideal and purpose in mind, the Church adapts to situations it meets, making human judgments on the best ways to transform the world.* Most of the time its judgments are right; sometimes except in matters of faith and morals they are embarrassingly wrong; but always they are made to bring the meaning of Jesus to people who do not know him.

This movement of the Church into communities of nonbelievers accounts for the wide divergence of Christian expressions, and for the growth and emergence of the Church as a force shaping the values of the world. Age after age, period of time after period of time, the Church has brought the message of Christ to people in terms which the people of the time could understand, assimilate, and practice.** Through all of its history, in each of its communities, there has been, as St. Paul said, "one Lord, one faith,

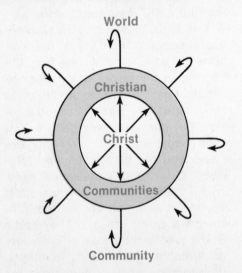

World

Christian

Christ

Communities

Community

---

* At times, it is true, the movement of some Christians into other communities has been misguided, over zealous, or even selfish. But the predominant thrust of Christian missionary effort has been to bring Christ to the world that does not know him.

** It is important in studying any history not to expect from a previous age the sophistication in understanding and practice of a later age. Each historical period builds on previous periods, accepting what is central, omitting what is no longer useful, and adding that which makes the forming idea more understandable and more practice-able for the people of a particular time. It must always be remembered that only the possible is achievable given the limitations inherent in the human condition.

one baptism, and one God who is Father of all, over all, and within all."

I urge you, then—I who am a prisoner because I serve the Lord: live a life that measures up to the standard God set when he called you. Be humble, gentle, and patient always. Show your love by being helpful to one another. Do your best to preserve the unity which the Spirit gives, by the peace that binds you together. There is one body and one Spirit, just as there is one hope to which God has called you. There is one Lord, one faith, one baptism; there is one God and Father of all men, who is Lord of all, works through all, and is in all.

Each one of us has been given a special gift, in proportion to what Christ has given. As the scripture says,

"When he went up to the very heights

He took many captives with him;
He gave gifts to men."
Now, what does "he went up" mean? It means that first he came down— that is, down to the lower depths of the earth. So he who came down is the same one who went up, above and beyond the heavens, to fill the whole universe with his presence. It was he who "gave gifts to men"; he appointed some to be apostles, others to be prophets, others to be evangelists, others to be pastors and teachers. He did this to prepare all God's people for the work of Christian service, to build up the body of Christ. And so we shall all come together to that oneness in our faith and in our knowledge of the Son of God; we shall become mature men, reaching to the very height of Christ's full stature. Then we shall no longer be children, carried by the waves, and blown about by every shifting wind of the teaching of deceitful men, who lead others to error by the tricks they invent. Instead, by speaking the truth in a spirit of love, we must grow up in every way to Christ, who is the head. Under his control all the different parts of the body fit together, and the whole body is held together by every joint with which it is provided. So when each separate part works as it should, the whole body grows and builds itself up through love.

Ephesians 4:1–16

The pilgrim Church is moving through the historical world to bring creation to its completion—the completion God had in mind when He created the world. It is through the Church that God is affecting the world, however slowly, for it is through people that God affects people.

Who Needs
the Church?

5

As we have said, Christians believe that God created the world for a purpose. They believe that He created so that He might share His Divine Life with His creation— with something capable of sharing that Life, something made in His image. (*Genesis* 1: 26) They believe that He created the universe, and by implanting in it the dynamics of growth brought it to the point where it could begin to reflect His image. They believe this point was reached when people appeared on earth.

In keeping with the slow process of development to higher things, people, too, developed over, perhaps, two million years, to a stage at which they could begin to comprehend the purpose of creation. When this level of sophistication was reached, God, Christians believe, began to reveal His plan and purpose in creation by selecting the Jewish people to make His plan and purpose known.

Christians also believe that God prepared the Jewish people for the final revelation of His plan and purpose through a slow but steady process of revelation of Himself as a saving God. Then, when the world was ready, Christians believe, God revealed His plan and purpose by Himself becoming a man in the person of Jesus. In so doing,

EPA NEWSPHOTO

Christians believe, God saved the world from a nondivine existence by taking His creation unto Himself and giving it His own life.

Through his life, his words, and his work in the world, but especially through his resurrection, Christians believe that Jesus revealed God's plan and purpose in creating in its entirety. The fullness of this plan and purpose was made clear when the Holy Spirit came to the apostles and enlightened them about the meaning of Jesus for people.

So, having established that Jesus came to save the world from a nondivine existence and to reveal to people that they were to share God's life forever in a risen dimension of existence, the question arises, "Who needs the Church?" The answer, for Christians, is: the world needs the Church.

The world needs the Church because, by God's design, the Church is Christ to the world. In other words, the Church prolongs the Incarnation in time. It makes Christ present to the world, and brings his message of salvation to all people. The world needs the Church because it is through the Church that the Holy Spirit acts in the world through people doing the work of the Holy Spirit in the Church.

The Church is the conscience of the world, calling people from their sinful ways to the worship of the Father. It is the means whereby the kingdom of God is, and can be, realized on earth. It is God's people called to transform the world through the transformation of their lives into the image of Christ who, St. Paul reveals, is the "first-born of many brothers." (*Romans* 8:29)

The world needs the Church because, if creation needed Christ to bring it to its potential (its reason for being), the world needs the Church to bring it to its potential: peace among men through love and shared life with God forever. The world needs the Church because it is through the Church that Jesus is preparing the world for ultimate and complete union with God.

But the Church is you, here and now. It is not some faceless "thing," a ghostly something that has no true reality. It is you, and people like you, who have accepted the witness that Christ is the Son of God come to save the world, living the Christian life. It is you who must be Christ to your world because it is in you that Christ chooses to live and through you to make himself visible to the world. It is you who must be the pilgrim, moving into the sinful world in which you live, and by your own life transforming that world. It is you who must be the social expression of Christ in your world. That is why he called you to be a Christian—so that he could show himself to the world through you. It is you, living as Christ commanded, who will draw others to your way of life, and in so doing will change the world from its sinful ways.

The world needs you to be its Christ. The world needs you to transform it, to bring it to peace, to make it grow and prosper, to save it from the spiritual, moral, physical, intellectual, ecological, and economic exploitation visited on it by selfish people. Like Christ, you are sent into the world by God so that the world may have life.

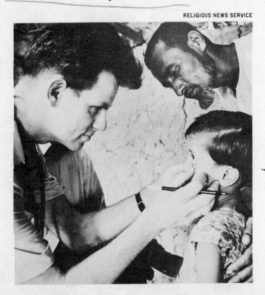

RELIGIOUS NEWS SERVICE

And Christians need the Church. They need the support of their fellow Christians and the means of special grace afforded them through the Church. They need its doctrines to guide them to keep the gospel message free from ignorance. They need its laws to help them live the Christian life in their moments of weakness. They need its liturgy so that with their fellow Christians they can celebrate the Christ-event in creation. They need the Church to keep fresh in their minds that

Christ is the visible likeness of the invisible God. He is the first-born Son, superior to all created things. For by him God created everything in heaven and on earth, the seen and the unseen things, including spiritual powers, lords, rulers, and authorities. God created the whole universe through him and for him. He existed before all things, and in union with him all things have their proper place. He is the head of his body, the church; he is the source of the body's life; he is the first-born Son who was raised from death, in order that he alone might have the first place in all things. For it was by God's own decision that the Son has in himself the full nature of God. Through the Son, then, God decided to bring the whole universe back to himself. God made peace through his Son's death on the cross, and so brought back to himself all things, both on earth and in heaven.

Colossians 1:15–20

Finally, God needs the Church to make it possible for Him to carry out the mission of His Christ in people until the end of time, and Jesus needs the Church to express himself in the world and so to prepare people for ultimate union with the Father at the end of earth-time.

The Meaning of Jesus for Christians

Christians believe that creation is an expression of God's Love and that things were created to receive God's Love. They believe that this was made possible through His coming into creation in the person of Jesus. For Christians, Jesus is the epicenter of creation: before his coming all things were prepared for his presence; after he lived, died, and rose again, all things flow from his presence in creation.

Creation
God prepares the world for His Christ

1 The earth is formed—4.5 billion years B.C.

2 Life appears on earth—2 billion years B.C.

3 Animals appear on earth—250 million years B.C.

4 First man-like species appears on earth—14 million years B.C.

5 First true people emerge—2 million years B.C.

6 Religious shrines become common—200,000 years B.C.

7 National religions develop—5000 years B.C.

8 Abraham moves from Ur to Canaan—1900 years B.C.

9 Moses and the Jewish People make a covenant with God—1300 years B.C.

10 Jesus comes to earth.

☧
Jesus prepares the world for union with his Father

1 The Holy Spirit comes—33 A.D.

2 Jewish-Christian communities formed—33 to 70+ A.D.

3 Christian communities formed in Greek and Roman spheres of influence—50 to 500 A.D.

4 Christian communities rebuild civilization during the Dark Ages—500 to 1000 A.D.

5 Christian communities form a new culture—1000 to 1500 A.D.

6 Christianity faces new challenges.

7 The Church meets the needs of new world horizons—1500 to 1960 A.D.

8 Christians of various cultures express their Christianity in a democratic society—1492 A.D. to present.

9 The Church faces the needs of a global society—1960 A.D.

10 The Church of the future.

* The dates given in this chart are approximations. One period of development flows into the next and itself continues for an undetermined length of time.

End Time

The Church as the Social Expression of Christ in History

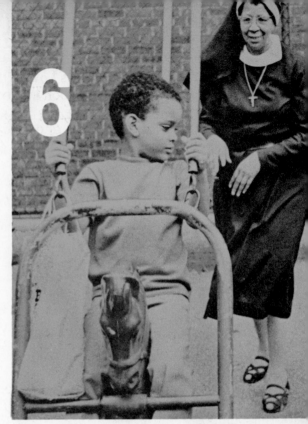

6

RELIGIOUS NEWS SERVICE

Because the Church is people, it can express itself only in the realities of people's lives. It can only be what the people who are the Church make it at any given time in any given place. The more closely the people of a particular Church-community resemble the model given by Christ, the more are they Christ to the world. In other words, the level of response of individual Christians to the call of God to be His Christ to the world is the measure of the effectiveness of the Church as the body of Christ. It cannot be any better than the people who are the Church; it can only be what it is possible to be at any given moment in history.

The level of response is both individual and general. As we have said, levels of response vary with each individual; but the sum total of responses in any given community of Christians makes up the level of response within that community, and the sum total of responses of all the Christian communities which make up the Church at any given time, makes up the level of response of the total Church.

But the level of response in the individual, in the small community, and in the total Church ebbs and flows (as it does in any human situation), depending on many factors. It depends, of course, on the grace of God and the response to that grace in a particular case. It depends on the freedom of the individual or the small community to express its faith; on the political, cultural, environmental, spiritual, and moral influences at work at a particular time and in a particular place; on the level of real understanding of the meaning of Jesus in a person's life; on the participation by individuals in the liturgical and social life of the Christian community; and on the leadership provided by the charismatic Christians within the community. How these things have affected the Church as the social expression of Christ in history is the subject matter of Part Two of *The Emerging Church*.

As a person looks at the history of the Church, he can hardly but be struck by the miracle of growth and influence of the Church. From the vision of one Man (not excepting the grace of God, of course) and the convictions of a small group who believed in him, Christianity has had a profound effect on the political, social, moral, spiritual, and religious outlook of people. In spite of the human limitations of its members, the opposition of its opponents, the sinfulness of people, the influence of counter forces, and the pride and prejudice and misuse of power within its own ranks, the Church has brought the message of Christ to the world for over 1,900 years. It has overcome nearly insurmountable odds, periods of depression and persecution, and the force of history, and remained, in the main, true to what it is.

And when a person considers the odds against it, he can only be amazed at the continuity of the faith (and the growth in understanding of that faith) that has characterized the Church. The faith of Peter and Paul, of Augustine and Aquinas and Chardin, of Mary and Catherine of Siena and Teresa of Avila, of Francis of Assisi and Tom Dooley, of Pope Linus and Pope Paul VI, of American Catholics and Italian Catholics, of peas-

RELIGIOUS NEWS SERVICE

ants in Korea and South America, of people in California and Connecticut, of the rich and the poor, of the learned and the not-so-well educated is the same. It may be understood differently and expressed in a variety of ways, but it is always the same faith—faith in Jesus, the Son of God, as savior of people.

Finally, when a person considers the history of the Church, he can only be astonished at the number of persons God has sent as his prophets to his Church (we call them saints), who through their personal lives, their leadership, their activities, and their dedication to their mission have led the Church through good years and bad and made it possible for others to express their faith in keeping with the gospel message. Through their influence they have moved the world closer to its salvational potential and helped prepare it for its ultimate union with God. The content of *The Emerging Church* is the story of this preparation. It presents how the Church developed, why it developed as it did, and what this development has meant. It deals primarily, but not exclusively, with the Roman Catholic Church, because it is the faith-community of most of those who will use this book to help them understand how their faith-community accepted the challenge of Christ to be his witnesses in the world.

1. What does your book mean by "God's plan for the salvation of people"?

2. What is the meaning of the expressions, "grace of God," "God operates in His creation naturally," and "God directs things to their natural end"?

3. According to your book, what do Christians believe is the natural end for which people have been created?

4. In what sense is the Church the body of Christ? How is this so? Is it presumptuous of the Church to think it is? Why? Why not?

5. What is the meaning of "The Church as the people of God"?

6. Discuss the meaning of the quotation from Hans Küng's *The Church.* (pp. 10–11)

7. A writer once said, "When Jesus said 'Come follow me,' he did not say how close." Discuss this in light of the material presented in "The Church as the People of God."

8. What is the meaning of the terms "transhistorical" and "transcultural"? How and why are they especially applicable to the Church? Can you give examples of things which are historical or cultural only?

9. Discuss the meaning of the phrase "the interaction between what the Church is and how it expresses itself historically and culturally."

10. Why and in what way is the Church a social institution?

11. What seems to have been the chief social action of the first Christians? How did they attract others to their community? Does this action have a place in the Church today? How?

12. What is the role of the bishops in the Church? Are the bishops "more Christian" than others in the Church? Is the pope? Are priests?

13. What do you understand by "The Church as Pilgrim"?

14. How do Christians best affect the world in which they live? Is it difficult to be a good Christian? Why? Why not? Is it necessary to be a good Christian? Is it effective? Why? How? Why must the Church be essentially, a "mission church"?

15. What do you understand by the term "saint"? In what sense are all Christians "saints"? What expression in the Creed affirms the Christian belief in the common unity of all Christians? Can you name some saints who have had a great effect on the history of the world? Who is your patron saint? Why do Christians often name their children after saints? Do you think this is a good idea? Why? Why not?

16. Someone has called the saints the "Catholic Hall of Famers." What do you suppose he meant?

17. Who, according to your book, needs the Church? Do you think you need the Church? Why? Why not? Does the world need you as a Christian? Why? Why not?

18. What does your book mean by "Jesus prepares the world for union with his Father"? (Refer to the chart, page 29).

19. Write a brief paragraph describing what you understand by "the Church."

20. In an intraclass dialogue discuss the meaning of the expression, "The Jesus of history, the Christ of faith."

21. You have heard the expression "The Four Horsemen of the Apocalypse." Read *Revelation* 6:1–8, then look up the meaning of the expression in any good dictionary or encyclopedia to find out what the expression means. Are the "four horsemen" still stalking the earth? Give examples. What can Christians do about them? Should they? Why? Why not?

22. Look up the following selections from the New Testament. Tell what each is about and how each relates to the selections given on pages 21–24.

> *Ephesians* 1:3–14
> *Colossians* 2:6–8
> *Thessalonians* 4
> *Ephesians* 4:17–32
> *Philippians* 1:27–30
> *James* 1:19–27

23. Be prepared to give a brief report on the substance of each of the religions mentioned in the chart on page 2.

24. Your book often uses the expression, "The meaning of Jesus for people." Write a paragraph describing what you understand by this phrase.

25. What is the meaning of the title of your book: *The **Emerging** Church?*

PART TWO

The Church Expresses Itself in History

"Go back and tell John what you have seen and heard: the blind see again, the lame walk, lepers are cleansed and the deaf hear, the dead are raised to life, the Good News is proclaimed to the poor, and happy is the man who does not lose faith in me."

Luke 7:22–23

The joys and hopes, the griefs and the anxieties of men of this age, especially those who are poor or in any way afflicted, these are the joys and hopes, the griefs and anxieties of the followers of Christ. Indeed, nothing genuinely human fails to raise an echo in their hearts. For theirs is a community of men. United in Christ, they are led by the Holy Spirit in their journey to the Kingdom of their Father and they have welcomed the news of salvation which is meant for every man. That is why this community [the Church] realizes that it is truly linked with mankind and its history by the deepest of bonds.

"Constitution on the Church in the Modern World" (Westminster, Maryland: Newman Press, 1966).

The Principles of Historical Development

History is the story of how people live. It can be told from many angles depending upon the storyteller's intent and purpose. It can be a general survey or it can be the story of a particular people. It can be an economic, a political, or a cultural story—or it can be a combination of all three. It can dwell on the economics, the politics, the culture, the rulers, the people, the wars, the explorations, the inventions, and so forth. It can be optimistic or pessimistic. In any case, history, as it is recorded (as distinct from how it is lived) is subject to the choices of the writer, depending upon what he is trying to do.

In this part of *The Emerging Church*, we will develop the thought begun in Part One. There we attempted to show what the Church is. In this part, we shall see how it expressed itself in the lives of those who call themselves Christians. We shall see that the history of the Church is an ongoing process; it is never static, and never reaches its ideal. We will trace its roots in Judaism, its expression in the Greco-Roman society of the first four centuries, and see it rebuild civilization during the Dark Ages. We will see how it forged a Christian culture and faced the challenges of world expansion. Finally, we shall see the Church as it is in our technological world, and how it expresses itself in a democratic society in America. During the course of our survey, we shall see that the developing understanding of the meaning of Jesus in the Catholic Christian Church is expressed culturally, and in every case is limited in this expression to the real possibilities of the people who live at a particular time in history.

We have selected those items in history which contribute essentially to the development of what we are trying to demonstrate.

The history in this book is written with a particular faith-orientation: that the man Jesus is God acting in history to bring people, and through them the creation begun billions of years ago, to the Ultimate Divine Life. Because of this orientation the materials selected concentrate on the Christian effect upon the culture where Christianity existed, and the effect of the culture upon the expression of Christianity.

For this reason, the history in this volume is, for the most part, the history of Western Europe, because that is where the expression of Christianity we profess was found. It is in this history that we are interested for the purposes of our discussion.

No one knows what the history of civilization would be had the Christ-event been first preached, say, in China, or Africa, or the Pacific Islands, rather than in Western Europe. About all we can say is that the culture of China or India or Africa would have been Christian and that this Christianity would have had the cultural tones of the country in which it was preached. The fact is, Christianity moved westward, for the most part, and has the cultural overtones of Western Civilization. And Western Civilization has the cultural overtones of Christianity.

But this part of *The Emerging Church* is not intended as a glorification of Western Civilization. It is intended to present the developing understanding of the meaning of Christ from the beginnings of Christianity to the present time. Its purpose is to help the reader understand how Christianity as expressed in Roman Catholicism came to its expression at the present stage of human history. *We are what we are because of what our ancestors have been.* By understanding what Christianity meant and how

it was expressed within the limitations of the human conditions of the past, Christians of the present can appreciate their own Christian understanding and pass on to future generations their own vision of the meaning of Christ for them.

When Christians of this generation understand that the Mystery of Christ lives in them and that they have a prophetic mission in the world, their Christianity will come alive, will not be an appendage to their "real" lives but will enable them to live more intensely—

to be for their own generation what Christ was for his: the witness to God acting in the world.

In addition to seeing how Catholic Christianity is always expressed culturally and within the possibilities open to people at any given time in their history, we shall see that in the historical development of people, there are two human factors which affect that history. One is the law or principle of continuity; the other is the law or principle of change.

The first emphasizes the fact that people seem to resist change. They prefer to cling to old ideas and ways of doing things, to stick with methods and concepts that worked for their ancestors. Human beings seem to feel most comfortable and secure when following the tried and true wisdom of the past. Much of people's daily activity is regulated by their physical environment, and, except for the turning of the seasons, this environment seldom varies much. The same jobs have to be done with the same tools most of the time. Without external pressures, people's lives would change very little from age to age. Some people go so far as to glorify the past; they think that the only way life should be lived is the way it was in "the good old days."

On the other hand, there is always something new coming along to disturb the status quo. New ideas appear constantly. Imaginative thinkers challenge the inherited ideas of the past and suggest new ways of living. New wisdom is always being accumulated on top of the old. There are always some nonconformists in every society who like to do things differently just to be different, and these individuals are often the pioneers of progress. Imperceptibly, inventions and discoveries open up unknown lands or techniques, even though relatively few people migrate to them or at once cease using the old methods. Individual people can seldom realize it because a single life span is short, but *the world and people are nevertheless always evolving, always undergoing transformation*. This is the principle of change.

Human history is the story of how these two impulses affect people, pulling them this way and that, sometimes slowly, sometimes rapidly. Just as Nancy at age forty is the same person as Nancy at the age of ten, but also in many ways she is not the same, so do people grow and develop, always becoming something new but somehow remaining the same.

This constant interaction between the forces of change and the forces of continuity is especially important in the history of Christianity. It explains the fact that the Church has somehow remained the same, yet has changed as it encountered the various cultures in which it was preached and the various historical developments which make up the history of the world. The history of the Church, as we have said, is a history of faith. The business of the Church is to recall to people the faith-dimension which is its heritage.

Yet religious beliefs are only one of the many factors that shape human life. People also need economic and political organization, ways to earn a living and stay alive. They have to live with their fellow men, learn how to use material creation to their own advantage and to control it for their own health and welfare, and to devise languages in order to communicate. And so *the unchangeable Christian message must be constantly adjusted to the varying factors in the human environment*. There is in Christian history a constant interaction between this special kind of continuity principle and the perennial law of change. You will notice this interaction at work in the materials presented in this second part of *The Emerging Church*.

7 Jewish Christianity

St. Pg. 50

Painting attributed to St. Luke
RELIGIOUS NEWS SERVICE

Christian Communities Formed in Israel

Although we now experience Christianity as a worldwide religion, the apostles and first followers of Jesus were not concerned about the global impact of Christianity. Their first preoccupation was how to convince those of Jesus' countrymen who had seen him that he really was the Jewish Messiah. The first Christians were a distinct minority within the Jewish population and were only one of at least twenty-four groups in the country at that time proclaiming that a Messiah was about to deliver them from the evil of Roman domination and restore Israel to its former place in the political world.*

To refer to the post-Easter fellowship of the disciples of Jesus as the eschatological community of salvation, as the ekklesia of God, as the congregation, community or Church of God—are not these descriptions somewhat exaggerated? We may ask whether the reality of this "Church" did not look very different, and whether, as far as its external appearance and its

---

* See page 3 where two such Messiahs are mentioned.

39

NC PHOTO

everyday practical actions were concerned, this "Church" was really more than a sect of Jews who believed in the Messiah and had a particular creed. How much more were they than the Zealots, who called for political revolution, or the Pharisees, who called for moral reform according to the law, or the Essenes, who withdrew, regarding themselves as the elect community, into the desert? Were they more than people with a particular religious slant, with a particular conception of religion in theory and practice, but retaining otherwise their links with Judaism?

Even the *Acts of the Apostles* . . . clearly reveal that the fellowship of Jesus' disciples even after Pentecost appeared to be no more than a religious party within the Jewish nation: "the sect of the Nazarenes" (*Acts* 24:5, cf. 24:14, 28:22). They were a kind of separate synagogue, of which there were several at the time, or a group of disciples with their own master.

A number of points seem to support this view. The disciples of Christ did not withdraw from life as much as, for example, the Essenes. They met in the temple (*Acts* 2:46), apparently approved Jewish sacrificial customs (cf. *Mt.* 5:23 f.) and the paying of the temple tax (cf. *Mt.* 17:24–27) and apparently submitted themselves to the judgment of the synagogues (cf. *Mk.* 13:9; *Mt.* 10:17). Despite their Master's critical attitude and his relative freedom *vis-à-vis* the cultic and ritual dictates of the law, they seem to have complied fully with the Old Testament law (cf. *Mt.* 5:17–19); observation of the law seems to have been enjoined on all members of the community as a basic condition of their sharing in salvation. How far indeed could the disciples of Jesus claim to be the chosen people of the eschatological age without this observance of the law? Again it is Acts which tells us that at first the disciples definitely did not take up a mission to the Gentiles. . . . Can we not assume that the first disciples of Jesus Christ were fully and entirely members of the people of Israel, whose religious and legal practice marks a continuation of their life as part of the Jewish nation?

The disciples of Jesus saw themselves as the *true* Israel. But this was equally true of the Pharisees, the Sadducees, the Zealots, and the Essenes. Clearly it took time and various historical experiences before the disciples saw themselves clearly as not only the true, but the *new* Israel. The foundations for this view had already been laid: the faith, rooted in their personal encounter with the risen Christ, that with the death and resurrection of Jesus the crucial and decisive eschatological saving event had occurred. In contrast to all other "parties" the fellowship of those who believed in Christ could look back to this decisive event; for them the Old Testament promises had been fulfilled, the eschatological spirit had been bestowed on them, they had been given hope, based on the fact that the Messiah had really come, of the coming consummation of the reign of God. They *were* already the new Israel, even if externally little different from the old. In the light of this saving event which had already occurred they could remain members of the people of Israel, share in its cult, keep its laws, affirm its history and its expectation—and yet see all these things in a fundamentally new way because of Jesus Christ. They could retain Jewish forms and yet give them an entirely new content, because of Jesus Christ; and this new content was bound, sooner or later, to burst the bounds of the old forms.*

Why the apostles of Jesus were able to convince many devout Jewish people that Jesus was the promised Messiah and begin a movement that was to have continuous and global impact when others, convinced that "their man" was the true Messiah were unable to do so is a puzzle to historians who do not have a Christian faith orientation. Christians believe that the reason lies in the plan of God for people's salvation. Christians believe that God operates in the world through His Spirit, and they believe that the Spirit acts directly in and through the Christian community. They believe that He acts through the normal channels of creation; that is, chiefly through the conscious activity of chosen human beings. Christians express their belief this way: God expressed Himself *creatively* in the universe He made; He expressed Himself *humanly* in the person of Jesus; He expresses Himself *dynamically* in the activity of the Spirit in the world.

* Hans Küng, *The Church* (New York: Sheed & Ward, 1967), pp. 107–109.

The Beginnings of the Christian Community

This conviction about the Spirit of God acting in the Christian community comes to us from the very first experience of the apostles who were convinced that their success came, not from what they did by themselves, but from what the Spirit of Jesus did through them. That is why, in the *Acts of the Apostles,* written by St. Luke sometime after 70 A.D., in the account of the first days of the apostle's preaching, the stress is on the Spirit of God. This account is an interesting example of biblical theologizing about an event in the life of the People of God interpreted to give evidence of God's action.* What the exact details of those first days were, we do not know. What we do have is an account of the growth in the number of believers and the divine reason for that growth.

> When Pentecost day came around, they had all met in one room, when suddenly they heard what sounded like a powerful wind from heaven, the noise of which filled the entire house in which they were sitting; and something appeared to them that seemed like tongues of fire; these separated and came to rest on the head of each of them. They were all filled with the Holy Spirit, and began to speak foreign languages as the Spirit gave them the gift of speech.
>
> *Acts* 2:1–4

Whatever happened on that day, those present suddenly became aware of the real meaning of Christ, and they attributed this new understanding to the Holy Spirit.

The effect of this new awareness on the followers of Jesus was to move them from discussion of their problems (*Acts* 1) to an action-oriented apostolate. They went out to the people to tell them of their convictions about Jesus. The *Acts of the Apostles* is our record of what happened:

> Now there were devout men living in Jerusalem from every nation under heaven, and at this sound they all assembled, each one bewildered to hear these men speaking his own language. They were amazed and astonished. "Surely," they said, "all these men speaking are Galileans? How does it happen that each of us hears them in his own native language?"
>
> Everyone was amazed and unable to explain it; they asked one another what it all meant. Some, however, laughed it off. "They have been drinking too much new wine," they said.
>
> Then Peter stood up with the Eleven and addressed them in a loud voice: "Men of Judaea, and all you who live in Jerusalem, make no mistake about this, but listen carefully to what I say. These men are not drunk, as you imagine; why, it is only the third hour of the day. On the contrary, this is what the prophet spoke of:
>
>> In the days to come—it is the Lord who speaks—
>> I will pour out my spirit on all mankind.
>> Their sons and daughters shall prophesy,
>> your young men shall see visions.
>> your old men shall dream dreams.

---

* We find a similar example of emphasis in the creative accounts of *Genesis*. The writer of *Genesis* continually stresses God's action to impress upon the Jewish people of his time that the Jewish God was not like the pagan gods, that He was a good God who did good things for people and that He and He alone was the creator of the world.

Even on my slaves, men and
women,
in those days, I will pour out
my spirit....

... "Men of Israel, listen to what I
am going to say: Jesus the Nazarene
was a man commended to you by
God by the miracles and portents and
signs that God worked through him
when he was among you, as you all
know. This man, who was put into
your power by the deliberate intention and foreknowledge of God, you
took and had crucified by men outside the Law. You killed him, but God
raised him to live, freeing him from
the pangs of Hades; for it was impossible for him to be held in its
power....

"For this reason the whole House
of Israel can be certain that God has
made this Jesus whom you crucified
both Lord and Christ."

Hearing this, they were cut to the
heart and said to Peter and the apostles, "What must we do, brothers?"
"You must repent," Peter answered,
"and every one of you must be baptized in the name of Jesus Christ for
the forgiveness of your sins, and you
will receive the gift of the Holy
Spirit...."

They were convinced by his arguments, and they accepted what he
said and were baptized. That very day
about three thousand were added to
their number.

These remained faithful to the
teaching of the apostles, to the
brotherhood, to the breaking of bread
and to the prayers.

Acts 2:5–8, 12–18, 22–24, 36–38, 41–42

Everywhere the apostles went, they, and
those commissioned by them, preached
about Jesus. Little by little, small groups of
Jewish people joined them and lived "faithful to the teaching of the apostles, to the
brotherhood, to the breaking of bread, and
to prayers." (*Acts* 2:42)

How did the apostles and their friends
live? What did these men, most of whom
were from the quiet northern province of
Galilee, do to stay alive? According to the
only record we have (the *Acts of the Apostles*), they went every day to the Temple to
speak to the people who were there, to offer
sacrifice and to pray. They went to private
homes where people gathered to hear them
tell about Jesus. They slept wherever they
could, ate with their friends, visited among
the converts, and "assembled for the breaking of the bread" (The Lord's Supper) at
regular intervals.

They lived a normal Jewish life. Their
habits, customs, language, and religious
practices were devoutly Jewish. They said
Jewish prayers, sang traditional Jewish
songs, celebrated the Jewish holidays, and
observed the Jewish sabbath and the rituals
which were so much a part of the daily life
of every devout Jew. There was nothing to
distinguish them from the ordinary Hebrew
in Jerusalem except that they were constantly talking about the man Jesus.

Gradually they began to have some effect
upon the Jewish community of Jerusalem.
(Some of the apostles, of course, had by this
time moved to other major Jewish communities, but we don't have a record of
them.) Within a relatively short time—perhaps two or three years—there were probably a few hundred Jews in Jerusalem alone
who believed in Jesus, and enough in other
cities to convince the Jewish leaders that
something should be done about it. Among
those given the responsibility of preventing
the Jewish Christians from teaching about
Jesus was a young, zealous, bright Jew
named Saul. It was this Saul who was to become the apostle Paul, even though he was
not one of the "original twelve."

El Greco: *St. Paul*

St. Paul, Prophet of Christ

Paul was about twenty-five years old when Jesus was crucified. Apparently he never saw Jesus while Jesus was preaching in and around Palestine, but he had most likely heard of him. At any rate, Paul was in Jerusalem when the followers of Jesus were spreading the word about Jesus being the Messiah (*Acts* 7), and he didn't like what he heard. In fact, he considered the claims of the followers of Jesus to be blasphemous (*Acts* 26:9–11), and, armed with authority from the chief priests, he took it on himself, as a kind of personal mission, to stamp out what he was convinced was a heretical sect (*Acts* 8:1, 3). He admitted as much in his letter to the Galatian Christians, written some fifteen years after his conversion to Christ.

The fact is, brothers, and I want you to realize this, the Good News I preached is not a human message that I was given by men, it is something I learned only through a revelation of Jesus Christ. You must have heard of my career as a practicing Jew, how merciless I was in persecuting the Church of God, how much damage I did to it, how I stood out among other Jews of my generation, and how enthusiastic I was for the traditions of my ancestors.

Then God, who had specially *chosen* me while I was *still in my mother's womb,* called me through his grace and chose to reveal his Son in me, so that I might preach the Good News about him to the pagans. I did not stop to discuss this with any human being, nor did I go up to Jerusalem to see those who were already apostles before me, but I went off to Arabia at once and later went straight back from there to Damascus. Even when after three years I went up to Jerusalem to visit Cephas and stayed with him for fifteen days, I did not see any of the other apostles; I only saw James, the brother of the Lord, and I swear before God that what I have just written is the literal truth. After that I went to Syria and Cilicia, and was still not known by sight to the churches of Christ in Judaea, who had heard nothing except that their onetime persecutor was now preaching the faith he had previously tried to destroy; and they gave glory to God for me.

Galatians 1:11–24

How did it happen that this young activist (he called himself a fanatic), zealous for the destruction of the Jewish communities that had accepted Jesus as Messiah and

Lord, became the most famous of all Christians?* *The Acts of the Apostles* tells the story, and Paul repeated it many times (See, for example, *Acts* 9:1–22; 26:12–23; *Philippians* 3:4–12; *1 Corinthians* 9:8–11).

Meanwhile Saul was still breathing threats to slaughter the Lord's disciples.

He had gone to the high priest and asked for letters addressed to the synagogues in Damascus, that would authorize him to arrest and take to Jerusalem any followers of the Way, men or women, that he could find.

Suddenly, while he was traveling to Damascus and just before he reached the city, there came a light from heaven all around him. He fell to the ground, and then he heard a voice saying, "Saul, Saul, why are you persecuting me?" "Who are you, Lord?" he asked, and the voice answered, "I am Jesus, and you are persecuting me. Get up now and go into the city, and you will be told what you have to do." The men traveling with Saul stood there speechless, for though they heard the voice they could see no one. Saul got up from the ground, but even with his eyes wide open he could see nothing at all, and they had to lead him into Damascus by the hand. For three days he was without his sight, and took neither food nor drink.

A disciple called Ananias who lived in Damascus had a vision in which he heard the Lord say to him, "Ananias!" When he replied, "Here I am, Lord," the Lord said, "You must go to Straight Street and ask at the house of Judas for someone called Saul, who comes from Tarsus. . . ."

When he heard that, Ananias said, "Lord, several people have told me

Damascus

about this man and all the harm he has been doing to your saints in Jerusalem. He has only come here because he holds a warrant from the chief priests to arrest everybody who invokes your name." The Lord replied, "You must go all the same, because this man is my chosen instrument to bring my name before pagans and pagan kings and before the people of Israel; I myself will show him how much he himself must suffer for my name." Then Ananias went. He entered the house, and at once laid

* For Christians, this is another example of God's acting in history. As in so many other instances in the history of salvation, God acted radically in the life history of Paul to change him from a violent opponent of Christ to a driving apostle.

his hands on Saul and said, "Brother Saul, I have been sent by the Lord Jesus who appeared to you on your way here so that you may recover your sight and be filled with the Holy Spirit." Immediately it was as though scales fell away from Saul's eyes and he could see again. So he was baptized there and then, and after taking some food he regained his strength.

After he had spent only a few days with the disciples in Damascus, he began preaching in the synagogues, "Jesus is the Son of God."

Acts 9:1–11, 13–20

It was after this that Paul's career as an apostle began. For nearly 35 years he traveled throughout the Roman Empire, setting up Christian communities in Rome and nearly every major city in Asia Minor and Greece. He first tried to convince his fellow Jews that Jesus was the Messiah, but later he went to the non-Jewish centers preaching about Jesus to whoever would listen to him. He was the most successful apostle. (See *2 Corinthians* 11:19–32.)

It is not only because Paul established so many Christian centers that the Church is indebted to him, however. *It is also because Paul is the first major Christian theologian.*

ST. PAUL'S JOURNEYS √ The Letters of Paul

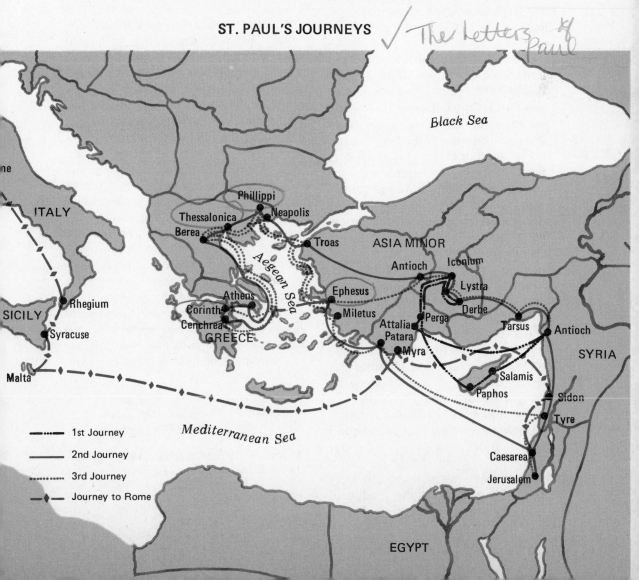

Black Sea

ITALY

Phillippi
Thessalonica   Neapolis
Berea
Troas   ASIA MINOR
Aegean Sea   Antioch   Iconium
Ephesus   Lystra
Athens   Miletus   Derbe
Corinth   Perga
Cenchrea   Attalia   Tarsus   Antioch
GREECE   Patara
Rhegium   Myra   SYRIA
SICILY
Syracuse   Salamis
Paphos   Sidon
Malta   Tyre

Mediterranean Sea   Caesarea
Jerusalem

------ 1st Journey
—— 2nd Journey
······ 3rd Journey
—◆— Journey to Rome

EGYPT

It is from him that Christianity received its "Christology"* and its understanding of the meaning of Christ in the world.**

The importance of St. Paul's role in giving Christianity a theological formulation cannot be over-estimated. It was from his understanding of the meaning of Jesus that the primitive Church was able to understand that it was more than a Jewish sect: It understood that it was destined by divine intervention in history to bring people to salvation in Christ. After Jesus, St. Paul is the outstanding person in Christian history and the most influential.

What was Paul's basic thinking about Christ? It is probably best summed up in his famous letter to the Church at Ephesus.

Blessed be God the Father of our Lord Jesus Christ, who has blessed us with all the spiritual blessings of heaven in Christ. Before the world was made, he chose us, chose us in Christ, to be holy and spotless, and to live through love in his presence, determining that we should become his adopted sons, through Jesus Christ for his own kind purposes, to make us praise the glory of his grace, his free gift to us in the Beloved, in whom, through his blood, we gain our freedom, the forgiveness of our sins.

He has let us know the mystery of his purpose, the hidden plan he so kindly made in Christ from the beginning to act upon when the times had run their course to the end: that he would bring everything together under Christ, as head, everything in the heavens and everything on earth.

Now you too, in him, have heard the message of the truth and the good news of your salvation, and have believed it; and you too have been stamped with the seal of the Holy Spirit of the Promise, the pledge of our inheritance which brings freedom for those whom God has taken for his own, to make his glory praised.

We are God's work of art, created in Christ Jesus to live the good life as from the beginning he had meant us to live it.

Ephesians 1:3–7, 9–10, 13–14; 2:10

Before St. Paul, the first preaching about Jesus, as we saw, concentrated on Jesus as the *Jewish* Messiah. But St. Paul could hardly preach a Jewish Messiah to non-Jews —especially to Roman citizens, many of whom lived in the cities of Asia Minor and Greece where St. Paul preached. What was "Messiah" to them? What was Jesus saving *them* from? What was the role of Jesus in the non-Jewish world? Gradually it came to St. Paul: **Jesus was not simply a Jewish Messiah, he was the savior of the entire world.** St. Paul saw all of creation saved in Christ. He saw Jesus as the focus of history. He became the prophet of Christ.

This theology of St. Paul was not developed overnight. It came from serious thought, growing out of the conviction of Jesus as savior and his own understanding of the meaning of Jesus as it developed in response to challenges to his message as he traveled from place to place and met people from all levels of society in many different cultures. St. Paul realized that Jewish thought forms and Jewish expressions were not the only way to present the meaning of Jesus. From his daring presentation, the Church developed in its own understanding of the meaning of Jesus and of its mission.

---

* Christology is theology which deals directly with Jesus Christ as a Person. Thus, Christology might be called the science of the study of Jesus.

** It might be said that the original apostles preached the *Person* of Jesus in biographical form; but Paul preached the *meaning* of Christ in theological form.

Jerusalem's Old City and Wailing Wall

St. Paul and the Development of Doctrine

The acceptance of the idea of Jesus as savior of all creation created a special problem for the Church as it moved into non-Jewish cultures. This was the problem of the relationship of non-Jewish converts to Christianity and to the Jewish way of life.

As soon as St. Paul began to convert non-Jews in any great number, the inevitable question arose: did they have to observe the Jewish Torah and its traditions?* This question forced the leaders of the Church (the apostles) to answer a basic question which really hadn't come up when all converts to Jesus were Jews: What was the relationship of Christianity to Judaism? Their answer brought about an even clearer understanding of the worldwide meaning of Jesus.

The answer to both of these questions came relatively early in the life of the Christian community. The first question became a prime issue within a few years and was settled for all time within the first twenty years of the Christian community, at the Council of Jerusalem in 49 A.D.**

* This is the entire way of life of the Jewish people including the regulations governing the most minute details of daily living, the customs and practices "handed down from the ancestors," and the interpretations by the scholars and teachers.

** This "first Council" established the general pattern for most subsequent Councils including Vatican II. In every Council the following features appear: 1) a general problem, 2) a meeting of the leaders (bishops), 3) open discussion of all sides of the problem, 4) a decision by the chief bishop, 5) an announcement of the conclusions. It is from this first meeting of the apostles to decide a major issue that we get our concept of "collegiality" (the sharing of authority among the leaders) and of papal "primacy" (the necessity of having a "president" of the assembly who speaks in the name of the group).

Paul, the Greatest Apostle

Paul, the prophet of Christ, was born in Tarsus, an important Roman city in the province of Cilicia located on the northeastern shore of the Mediterranean, about 400 miles north of Jerusalem.

Because he was born in a Roman city, Paul was a Roman citizen, but he was born a Jew, of the tribe of Benjamin. He was educated at home in his early years in the Jewish tradition of the Pharisees. He was sent to Hebrew schools to learn the Scriptures and the traditions of the Fathers (he had to memorize the Scriptures and be able to recite from memory the principal thoughts of the famous rabbis of Jewish history), then he was sent to Jerusalem to study under famous rabbis of the Pharisaic school of interpretation. He became a dedicated, zealous Jew, proud of his heritage. During most of his life, of course, he had lived in and among Greeks and Romans; hence he spoke Latin and Greek, learned much from the art, culture, and philosophy of the Greeks and Romans, and familiarized himself with their current religious beliefs and practices.

Paul was short in stature, we are told, and extremely bright. He had almost unlimited energy, a volatile temperament, and great dedication to what he believed was right. He was a forceful, persuasive speaker, a brilliant writer, a master logician, and a man of great courage. He was, many believe, one of the four or five great religious geniuses the world has ever known.

After he was converted to Christ, he became, perhaps, the greatest missionary the Church has had. He traveled tirelessly throughout the Roman empire, setting up Christian communities in almost every town he visited (staying, often, for long periods of time until his converts learned "the Christian way"). He was a man of great spirit, total generosity, broad knowledge, and penetrating mind. His adventures on land and sea have all the interest and color of romantic novels: he was beaten, stoned, scourged, imprisoned, shipwrecked, and finally beheaded. After thirty-five years as "The Apostle of the Gentiles," Paul was put to death in Rome about 67 A.D. He had been, truly, the prophet of Christ.

"It is in the Apostle of Tarsus," says George T. Montague, S.M., one of the world's foremost authorities on St. Paul, "that we get a real introduction to theology, for we see how Paul, penetrating the Roman Empire with the message of Christ, is faced with questions of doctrine and moral from Jew and Gentile, from persecutor and magistrate and convert. In answer, he not only recalls the basic truths of the kerygma*, but deepens his own understanding of them and finds in them ever new depths. For Paul, above all, Christ is the living, risen Lord coming at the end of time but likewise present and active in the Church, transforming and giving meaning to all its experiences."**

---

* The preaching of the Gospel of Christ.
** George T. Montague, S.M., *The Living Thought of St. Paul* (Beverly Hills: Benziger, Bruce and Glencoe, 1966), Introduction.

Below is the scriptural record which summarizes the state of the question, the debates, and the conclusion of the Council. It is taken from the *Acts of the Apostles*.

Then some men came down from Judaea and taught the brothers, "Unless you have yourselves circumcised in the tradition of Moses you cannot be saved." This led to disagreement, and after Paul and Barnabas had had a long argument with these men it was arranged that Paul and Barnabas and others of the church should go up to Jerusalem and discuss the problem with the apostles and elders.

All the members of the church saw them off, and as they passed through Phoenicia and Samaria they told how the pagans had been converted and this news was received with the greatest satisfaction by the brothers. When they arrived in Jerusalem they were welcomed by the church and by the apostles and elders, and gave an account of all that God had done with them.

But certain members of the Pharisees' party who had become believers objected, insisting that the pagans should be circumcised and instructed to keep the Law of Moses. The apostles and elders met to look into the matter, and after the discussion had gone on a long time, Peter stood up and addressed them.

"My brothers," he said, "you know perfectly well that in the early days God made his choice among you: the pagans were to learn the Good News from me and so become believers. In fact God, who can read everyone's heart, showed his approval of them by giving the Holy Spirit to them just as he had to us. God made no distinction between them and us, since he purified their hearts by faith. It would only provoke God's anger now, surely, if you imposed on the disciples the very burden that neither we nor our ancestors were strong enough to support? Remember, we believe that we are saved in the same way as they are: through the grace of the Lord Jesus."

This silenced the entire assembly, and they listened to Barnabas and Paul describing all the signs and wonders God had worked through them among the pagans.

When they had finished it was James who spoke. "My brothers," he said, "listen to me. Simeon has described how God first arranged to enlist a people for his name out of the pagans. This is entirely in harmony with the words of the prophets, since the scriptures say:

After that I shall return
and rebuild the fallen House of
    David;
I shall rebuild it from its ruins
and restore it.
Then the rest of mankind,
all the pagans who are conse-
    crated to my name,
will look for the Lord, . . ."

"I rule, then, that instead of making things more difficult for pagans who turn to God, we send them a letter telling them merely to abstain from anything polluted by idols, from fornication, from the meat of strangled animals and from blood. For Moses has always had his preachers in every town, and is read aloud in the synagogues every sabbath."

Then the apostles and elders decided to choose delegates to send to

Antioch with Paul and Barnabas; the whole church concurred with this. They chose Judas known as Barsabbas and Silas, both leading men in the brotherhood, and gave them this letter to take with them:

"The apostles and elders, your brothers, send greetings to the brothers of pagan birth in Antioch, Syria and Cilicia. We hear that some of our members have disturbed you with their demands and have unsettled your minds. They acted without any authority from us, and so we have decided unanimously to elect delegates and to send them to you with Barnabas and Paul, men we highly respect who have dedicated their lives to the name of our Lord Jesus Christ. Accordingly we are sending you Judas and Silas, who will confirm by word of mouth what we have written in this letter. It has been decided by the Holy Spirit and by ourselves not to saddle you with any burden beyond these essentials: you are to abstain from food sacrificed to idols, from blood, from the meat of strangled animals and from fornication. Avoid these, and you will do what is right. Farewell."

The party left and went down to Antioch, where they summoned the whole community and delivered the letter. The community read it and were delighted with the encouragement it gave them.

Acts 15:1–17; 19–31

The Council did not settle all the problems facing the Christian community, of course, nor was everyone happy with the decision. However, the first hurdle in self-understanding was cleared, due to the insight and the persuasiveness of St. Paul and his companion, St. Barnabas.

What was now clear, of course, was that followers of Christ were not necessarily Jews and therefore they were not bound by the Jewish Torah.

This does not mean to say that Christians no longer observed any laws or that they made up laws to suit themselves individually. It means that mere observance of law as set down in the Torah, for them, was not the guarantee of salvation. Their faith was in the Person of Christ, not in the observance of the laws of the Jewish Torah–tradition, as good as they might be.

The Distinguishing Features of Christianity

As time went on, more and more Jewish people and many non-Jews became followers of Christ. At first, of course, they could hardly be distinguished from other Jews, but, as their numbers grew, they became more and more noticeable.

What distinguished the Jewish (and non-Jewish) Christians from their Jewish and pagan neighbors? First, of course, was their faith in Jesus as savior and their consciousness that they were, in Christ, the "new" people of God. Second was their baptism in Christ. Third was their community prayer service. Fourth was their expression of brotherhood. Fifth was their leadership. The sixth thing that made the followers of Christ different from others was their view of death and their conviction that they would be joined with Christ "at the right hand of the Father." Finally, there was the Christian celebration of "The Lord's Supper."

The "Lord's Supper," of course, is a reference to the Eucharist, to the Mass, as Catholic Christians now call it. *It is the most ancient and most distinguishable feature of the Catholic liturgy.* The first Christians came together to celebrate Christ among

them, as he had asked them to do, by doing as he had done. Their celebration of the Eucharist was their way of participating in the sacrificial death of Jesus.

The earliest record we have of this Christian celebration is in St. Paul's first letter to the Corinthian Christians which he wrote, interestingly enough, to correct some abuses which had cropped up:

> The point is, when you hold these meetings, it is not the Lord's Supper that you are eating, since when the time comes to eat, everyone is in such a hurry to start his own supper that one person goes hungry while another is getting drunk. Surely you have homes for eating and drinking in? Surely you have enough respect for the community of God not to make poor people embarrassed? What am I to say to you? Congratulate you? I cannot congratulate you on this.
>
> For this is what I received from the Lord, and in turn passed on to you: that on the same night that he was betrayed, the Lord Jesus took some bread, and thanked God for it and broke it, and he said, "This is my body, which is for you; do this as a memorial to me." In the same way he took the cup after supper, and said, "This cup is the new covenant in my blood. Whenever you drink it, do this as a memorial of me." Until the Lord comes, therefore, every time you eat this bread and drink this cup, you are proclaiming his death, ...
>
> *1 Corinthians* 11:20–26

This "coming together in the Lord," as St. Paul points out (Catholic Christians call it "going to Mass"), was to recall the sacrificial death of Christ and to celebrate his resurrection. It came, as you know, from the so-called Last Supper in which Jesus, in the setting of the Jewish Paschal Meal (the yearly celebration of the Jewish deliverance from Egypt), took the unleavened bread which was customarily distributed and, in addition to the usual prayers of thanksgiving, said, "This is my Body which will be given for you. Do this as a memorial of me." (See *Luke* 22:19.) Then at the end of the meal, using the traditional cup of wine offered in thanksgiving, Jesus passed it among his apostles and said, "Drink all of you from this; for this is my Blood, the Blood of the Covenant, which is to be poured out for many for forgiveness of sins." (See *Matthew* 26:27, 28.)

Christians' consciousness of their being a "new" people of God in Christ and of their being baptized in Christ gave them a strong sense of community—of a special fellowship with each other in Christ. This brotherhood brought them together as a community, or in small groups in private homes, for special services of prayer, for recalling the words and actions of Christ, for reciting together "their prayer"—the Lord's Prayer—and for worship of Jesus as "The Lord." This last, of course, gradually drew Christians away from the Law as their way to God and brought the Person of Jesus to the forefront as "the Way, the Truth, and the Life," as he had said he was. (*John* 14:6)

Christians, of course, looked to the apostles as their leaders because they had been with the Lord and had been appointed by him to establish his kingdom. As the community of Christians grew and extended beyond the geographical limits of Palestine, they still looked to the apostles, with Peter as their head, as the ultimate authorities on the Christian way. As time went on and the communities became too widespread for the apostles to oversee each community, leadership was vested in those who had been with the apostles or who had been appointed by them. Thus, even though the apostles were not present, their leadership was felt and

continued, and the "apostolic tradition," as it came to be known, was found in the ones who succeeded the apostles in their mission of leadership. It was this special type of leadership which later gave rise to the hierarchy of the Church composed of bishops, consecrated as successors of the apostles, and headed by the successor of Peter, the bishop of Rome, the Pope.

It is interesting to note that the Christian moral way of life was not too distinguishable from the Jewish, except perhaps in its motivation. The Torah commanded that Jews love God and their neighbor. The many details concerning the smallest aspects of Jewish life had as their base respect for all created things. The Jewish Law was deeply concerned about justice (The "eye for an eye" concept was not intended as a cruel thing, but as a warning to God's people that no punishment should be harsher than the offense.) and about the reason for the Jewish Law: God commanded the Jewish way of life to keep the Jewish people from falling into the habits of their pagan neighbors. It prohibited especially idolatry, magical practices, disrespect for one's parents, and taking advantage of one's neighbor because of power, wealth, or ambition. The problem for many people in Jesus' time was that they believed the Law had lost its purpose, as may happen when law becomes so picky, and tended to be observed simply because it was the Law. The prevailing interpretation was that the Law by itself saved the Jews.

Jesus, in repeating the "two commandments" deemphasized the law-for-the-sake-of-law idea, and restressed the original Jewish notion of the personal worth of each individual within the Law.* Jesus knew the intent of the law. He was well aware of the fact that Jewish law, in contrast to the laws many neighboring nations, was intended preserve the Jewish way of life and to protect the dignity and worth of each individual. In recalling this basic aspect of the law, Jesus was attempting to correct what he considered an abuse in the current interpretation of the law. Apparently he felt that the framework of the law and its present application prevented a devout Jew from showing real concern for his neighbor.

In this way Jesus taught his followers that, wherever the framework of the law really interfered with this concern, the law had to give way. The conflict between Jesus' idea and the mainstream of Jewish thought apparently rested on the difference between the need for meeting the existential situation (Jesus' way) and the need for observing the law until it was changed (the Jewish leaders' concept).

The problem, a constant challenge for all persons concerned with lawful society, boils down to the question of whether or not an individual can ever dispense with the law. Jesus felt that a person could under one condition: that the intent was based upon solid religious concern for the good of another. Jesus did not in any sense do away with the need for law. He knew that society depends on law, but he knew also that law applied without concern for the dignity of each in-

---

* See, for example, *Luke* 10:25–37.

dividual could be oppressive. Ultimately, Jesus' vision of life showed him that people's freedom of conscience sometimes demands that they dispense with the law for the moment so that community good will be achieved.

Jesus' own personal self-integration (his own inner freedom) enabled him to preach an ethical ideal that impelled his followers to greater goodness. They could no longer simply keep the external law of social necessity; they had to respond to the inner necessity to be a real person. Jesus did not give laws to be observed as ends in themselves or as measures of how "good" each one was; he gave them as guidelines toward the ideals to be striven for.

St. Paul expressed this mind of Christ as follows:

> Avoid getting into debt, except the debt of mutual love. If you love your fellow men you have carried out your obligations. All the commandments: *You shall not commit adultery, you shall not kill, you shall not steal, you shall not covet,* and so on, are summed up in this single command: *You must love your neighbor as your-*

self. Love is the one thing that cannot hurt your neighbor; that is why it is the answer to every one of the commandments.

Romans 13:8–10

Leading the non-Jewish Christian converts from paganism to the Christian ideal of deep concern for their neighbors was something else again. These converts did not have the ethical background of the Jewish converts, so St. Paul and the other Christian leaders got down to brass tacks about certain things. They reminded their Gentile converts that Jesus' ethical teaching was not some vague "love-in," but dealt with the nitty-gritty of everyday relationships with people. They reminded them that there were certain things which Christians did not do. For example, in his first letter to the Christians of Corinth,* St. Paul wrote:

> You know perfectly well that people who do wrong will not inherit the king-

---

* A city in Greece so notorious for its depravity that the term "corinthian" was a synonym for evil.

Catacomb painting

dom of God: people of immoral lives, idolaters, adulterers, catamites, sodomites, thieves, usurers, drunkards, slanderers and swindlers will never inherit the kingdom of God. These are the sort of people some of you were once, but now you have been washed clean, and sanctified, and justified through the name of the Lord Jesus Christ and through the Spirit of our God.

"For me there are no forbidden things"; maybe, but not everything does good. I agree there are no forbidden things for me, but I am not going to let anything dominate me. Food is only meant for the stomach, and the stomach for food; yes, and God is going to do away with both of them. But the body—this is not meant for fornication; it is for the Lord, and the Lord for the body. God who raised the Lord from the dead, will by his power raise us up too.

You know, surely, that your bodies are members making up the body of Christ; do you think I can take parts of Christ's body and join them to the body of a prostitute? Never! As you know, a man who goes with a prostitute is one body with her, since *the two,* as it is said, *become one flesh.* But anyone who is joined to the Lord is one spirit with him.

Keep away from fornication. All the other sins are committed outside the body; but to fornicate is to sin against your own body. Your body, you know, is the temple of the Holy Spirit, who is in you since you received him from God. You are not your own property; You have been bought and paid for. This is why you should use your body for the glory of God.

1 Corinthians 6:9–20

In his letter to the Christians of Galatia—a Roman province in Asia Minor—St. Paul clarifies for his converts the difference between Christian liberty and moral irresponsibility. He stresses that *actions* are the test of a person's concern for the real welfare of one's neighbor—actions that are motivated by the Spirit of Christ.

My brothers! What good is it for someone to say, "I have faith," if his actions do not prove it? Can that faith save him? Suppose there are brothers or sisters who need clothes and don't have enough to eat. What good is there in your saying to them, "God bless you! Keep warm and eat well!" —if you don't give them the necessities of life? So it is with faith: if it is alone and has no actions with it, then it is dead.

James 2:14–17

Let me put it like this: if you are guided by the Spirit you will be in no danger of yielding to self-indulgence, since self-indulgence is the opposite of the Spirit, the Spirit is totally against such a thing, and it is precisely because the two are so opposed that you do not always carry out your good intentions. If you are led by the Spirit, no law can touch you. When self-indulgence is at work the results are obvious: fornication, gross indecency and sexual irresponsibility; idolatry and sorcery; feuds and wrangling, jealousy, bad temper and quarrels; disagreements, factions, envy; drunkenness, orgies and similar things. I warn you now, as I warned you before: those who behave like this will not inherit the kingdom of God. What the Spirit brings is very different: love, joy, peace, patience, kindness, goodness, trustfulness, gentleness and self-control. There can be no law against things like that, of course. You cannot belong to Christ Jesus unless you crucify all self-indulgent passions and desires.

Since the Spirit is our life, let us be directed by the Spirit.

Galatians 5:13–25

As we noted much earlier, the Christian Church is not made up of an elite group, and it is not for some special group of the favored. It is for all people. Paul's epistles (and those we have from James, Peter, Jude, and John as well) reflect this awareness. As Paul says, "all are called," no matter what their station in life or their past, to be followers of Christ. Taking this for granted, Paul and the others take into consideration the realities of life, each person's past and his habits of living, and the forces of culture and environment which shape each person's response, and call on every Christian to abandon his past and to press on with courage to the practice of the Christian way. They call on all Christians to practice virtue, to be good people, to act in love, and to "walk where the Spirit leads." It was because of this that, in time, Christians did make a difference in the world in which they lived and moved the world from its past into its future.

Gradual Cultural Changes in Christian Expression

For forty years the Judaism of Jerusalem was the strongest single cultural influence upon Christianity. Definite differences in doctrine and a particular memorial celebration distinguished the Jewish Christians from other Jews, but by and large early Christianity was Jewish in its cultural expression. Although the Jewish influence was to remain strong for perhaps another fifty years, its pressure upon Christianity was slowly waning and by the end of the first century it was evident that Christians were more distinctively Christian than they were Jewish.

There were three reasons for the lessening influence of Palestinian Judaism in Christian circles. The first was the increasing number of Gentile converts who had no Jewish cultural background. The second was the total destruction of Jerusalem about 70 A.D. by the Romans, who were fed up with the nearly constant guerilla warfare of certain Jewish patriots.* The third was the growing formalization of what constituted the Jewish way of life which was defined by the Jewish leaders after the destruction of Jerusalem in order to preserve the heritage once symbolized by the Temple. It was this form of Judaism which the later gospel writers wrote about and against. Between the two (Jewish Christianity and rabbinical Judaism) there was continuous and open disagreement. It was this fact, together with the Pauline doctrine of salvation in Christ and not in the Torah and the admittance of Gentiles to the company of Christians, which led to a complete split and the formation of a separate Christian Church, whose leaders were not Jews in the strict sense, but Christians.

Jewish ceremonial dishes   EDITORIAL PHOTOCOLOR ARCHIVES

* For an interesting and rather detailed account of the long struggle, see Max I. Dimont's *Jews, God and History* (New York: Signet, 1964), p. 101f.

After the destruction of Jerusalem, Christian leadership came more and more from places like Antioch in Syria, a Roman town about 300 miles north of Jerusalem, Alexandria in Egypt, and the Greek cities where St. Paul had preached. Each of these cultural centers added its own influence to the self-understanding of the Church, and as they were slowly becoming more and more Christian, Christianity was becoming more and more universal. Up to this time Christian thought had been expressed in the thought-forms of the Judaism of Jesus' time; after this, Christian thought began to take on the special characteristics of the languages formed by the cultures of Asia Minor, Egypt, Greece, and North Africa. What effect this was to have on Christianity we shall see at a later date.

As Christianity spread and came into contact with other cultural forms, it encountered a challenge totally different from any it had met before. *This was the challenge of theology.* Although the theological conflict resulted in better understanding of the meaning of Christ and a clearer presentation of Christian belief, it was by far the most serious threat Christianity had encountered. The challenge was in the arena of thought. Here was the real test of Christianity's soundness.

For nearly two hundred years before the coming of Jesus, religions in the Roman empire were becoming less and less distinct from each other. As people began to meet other people through trade and conquest, religions tended to fuse together. This tendency (best illustrated by the inclusion of everal national gods in the famous Mt. lympus* in Greece and the tolerance of me toward all religions) known as *syn-ism*** was a real challenge for primitive tianity because it "stood for" much the hings as Christianity: tolerance, good-d high moral tone—all of the clas-eals of philosophical humanism.

In its most challenging form it appeared under the title of *Gnosticism.* Gnosticism claimed to be a sure way to the knowledge, hence the vision, of God. It claimed that its rites, ceremonies, prescriptions, and its "way" to God were divinely inspired and were transmitted to the elite (the in-group) through a mysterious tradition. It claimed that its magical rites and philosophical formulas offered an infallible means to salvation.

Gnosticism appealed to the educated and sophisticated in the same areas where Christianity began to have an influence. Because the Gnostics could see the good in Christianity, they were convinced that Christianity was just another form of Gnosticism, and they interpreted Christianity as such. For the Gnostics knowledge was the key to the divine secrets. Because they considered matter to be essentially evil and Jesus was a material man, he could not be Messianic, for God would not use evil matter to secure a good end. It was obvious, then, that not Jesus but knowledge—pure thought—was the real savior of people. Their arguments were very profound and very persuasive.

Christianity survived this challenge because Christians relied on the human experience of Jesus as presented in the preaching of the apostles and depicted in the Gospels. For the Christians, faith was in the Person of Jesus, not in knowledge, philosophical speculation, or in magical practices which were supposed to have some secret saving power.

This theological problem faced by the early Christian community highlights a challenge constantly faced by those who propose a particular answer to the mystery of life. The discoveries of each age require a new

---

* See *The Religions of Man,* "The Developing Responses to Mystery."

** The harmonizing of, or union of, conflicting religious beliefs.

understanding of the explanation proposed by any religion. As soon as Christianity moved away from its Jewish surroundings, it came face to face with other thought systems; it therefore faced the challenge of new explanations. To recount all of the challenges faced by the early Christians would require a book of its own. It should be obvious that the Christian Church faces a constant challenge to recast its thought forms for people of new cultures and new times. It must not only face different civilizations and different world views; it must also cope with new languages, new concepts, and new socioeconomic forces. *But always its message and mission are the same: to bring the meaning of Christ as it has received it from the apostles to all people in every age.*

El Greco: *St. Peter*

The End of the First Era

By the close of the first century, Christianity had spread to all the territory of Rome. It had, in reality, become a "universal" church. A phenomenon of the time was the importance all Christian communities placed on the "Roman" Church.

From the time of St. Peter's coming to Rome and St. Paul's imprisonment in Rome, the rest of the Churches looked to Peter, and then to the Roman bishop, the successor to Peter, for guidance in doctrinal matters. The bishop of Rome was often asked for his opinion in ecclesiastical disputes. This was due, not to the fact that Rome at that time was the seat of the Imperial Roman Government, but to the special role St. Peter played

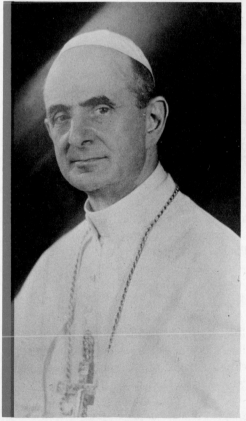

— study of Knowledge —
leading

viewed Judaism, finally, as transitional, for the Messiah had come). They also understood that the commission Jesus gave to his apostles was meant for all people, that Jesus' vision was real and pursuable, and that his future-oriented ideals were meant for this world because the Church is a concrete reality always dealing with the here and now.

Christian theology developed to elaborate the basic conviction that Jesus was divine, that he rose from the dead to bring his new life to all people, and that he was alive and active in his followers through his Spirit. From these beliefs arose the structure of the Church; bishops as successors to the apostles, priests as ministers of God's word and sacrament to assist the bishops, and the entire Church as the New People of God.

The first phase of the Church's thrust in the world developed over some one hundred years. Its second phase—understanding its relationship to the state—was to take place in the next era. Christians were to learn, through persecution, bitter experience, and a large-scale setback that the kingdom of God announced by Jesus was not primarily a political kingdom (even though politics played a large role in its struggle), was not attached to armies, or wealth, or prestige, or power. It was a hard lesson to learn, but it was worth it, for the Church moved steadily forward in its self-understanding and in its role in the world. With amazing swiftness, and in spite of overwhelming odds, it grew from a small group of disciples into a mass of believers spread throughout the Mediterranean basin.

Christians believe that the miraculous spread was due to the Holy Spirit, for it seemingly could not be explained by human means alone. And besides, their belief in a saving God necessitated belief in His action in the world. How else did God work except *through* people whom He guided by the Spirit?

in the formation of the apostles. The other apostles had established Christian centers elsewhere just as Peter had done, but only Peter was considered "first" among equals, whether in Jerusalem, Antioch, or Rome.

As the center of Christianity moved from Jerusalem to Antioch and finally to Rome, its own self-understanding began to emerge. Its struggles for self-identity, its understanding of its mission, its theology, and its structure developed and began to assume patterns which were to remain for centuries.

Christians gradually came to realize that they were not simply a Jewish sect (they

1. Can written history ever be completely objective? Why? Why not? Give examples from your own study of history to support your view.

2. If your answer to the above is negative, do you think that history can ever be true? How? When is history not true?

3. Discuss truth in biblical history. Consult a good encyclopedia or a biblical resource book on truth in the Bible and/or literary forms in the Bible.

4. What is the meaning of "within the possibilities open to people at any given time in their history"? Discuss the tension that always exists between the ideal and the real in any historical situation. Use examples from current American history to illustrate.

5. Distinguish between the principle of continuity and the principle of change. How do they create tensions in society? Give examples to illustrate.

6. Look up the terms "liberal" and "conservative," then discuss whether the terms as currently used in the press are representative of realities in people's lives. Are all who label themselves liberals always truly liberal? Why? Why not? Are those who are conservative always reactionary? Why? Why not?

7. What event triggered the activity of the apostles in the first days of the Church? What effect did it have on the apostles?

8. What is the substance of Peter's pronouncement during his first confrontation with some of the people of Israel?

9. Read *Acts* 3. In what way does Peter's discourse here repeat what he said in his first presentation? Is Peter "anti-Jewish" here or does he say that he understands what happened and why? Support your view with quotations.

10. Read *Acts* 2:42–47 and 4: 32–35. What are these selections about? What do they tell you about the early Church?

11. Consult some reliable resource book like *Daily Life in the Time of Jesus* by Henri Daniel-Rops and prepare a report on how people lived in the first century A.D.

12. Try to find out when the designation "A.D." began to be used to note historical dates. What do the letters stand for?

13. Did the apostles aim to start a whole new Church? Why? Why not?

14. What was the basic difference between the apostles' idea of salvation and the Jewish teaching about salvation?

15. Why was St. Paul so opposed to Jewish Christians? What event changed his attitude and actions?

16. Why is St. Paul considered the most famous missionary in the history of the Church?

17. Why is St. Paul considered the first important theologian in the history of the Church? What fundamental concept did he contribute to the Church's understanding of its mission?

18. Reread the selection from Ephesians on page 48. Then, with the footnotes on page 48 in mind, write a paragraph on what Paul is saying about Christ.

19. Why does your book call St. Paul "The prophet of Christ"?

20. Be prepared to give a description of St. Paul. If you can, consult a life of Paul or an encyclopedia for details on his life.

21. Why was the Council of Jerusalem important to the history of the Church? What does the debate described in *Acts* 15 tell you about the development of doctrine in the Church?

22. Pace through the first fifteen chapters of *The Acts of the Apostles*. Who seems to be the acknowledged leader of the apostles? Give examples from your research. Look up a definition or description of what *The Acts of the Apostles* is.

23. In what ways did Jewish Christians seem to differ from Jewish non-Christians? Be prepared to explain each.

24. When Jesus (and the apostles) stressed love over law in Christian living, were they saying that law is not needed? Why? Why not? Does law make love possible? How did Jesus' idea of observance of The Law differ from the views of his Jewish contemporaries?

25. How did Paul's approach to the moral life of converts from paganism differ from the approach to the moral life of Jewish Christians? Why was a change in approach needed?

26. What was the strongest cultural influence on the development of early Christianity? Why was this so? Why did it change?

27. What was the role of the bishops in the early Church? Who was the "chief bishop"? What was the special relationship that the bishops had to the apostles? Could anyone be called a bishop?

28. What is "Syncretism"? Why was it a kind of threat to early Christianity? Do you think there is a tendency toward syncretism today? What was "Gnosticism"? What is the fundamental difference between Gnosticism and Christianity?

29. How do Christians explain the miraculous spread of Christianity? Are there "human" reasons for its spread? What are some of them?

30. Prepare a discussion on the four gospels. Find out how they were written, why they were written and for whom, how they came to us, how these and not others are "the gospels," and how they differ from the epistles.

31. Prepare a paper on the destruction of Jerusalem about 70 A.D.

Capital Punishment
Moral Dilema

Christianity Established

8

pro's + con's of
capital punishment

pro - crime rate
would decrease.

cons - 1. you may be
killing an innocent
man.
2. you yourself
have no right to
kill anybody.

Christian Communities Formed in Greek and Roman Spheres of Influence

Christianity appeared on the world scene at a very opportune time, for the initial growth of Christianity was directly related to the political fortunes of the Roman Empire.

By the time Jesus was born (during the reign of the great Augustus, 27 B.C.–14 A.D.) peace had reigned for twenty-five years in the territory controlled by Rome. There had been uprisings in various sections of the Empire, but, by and large, the entire Mediterranean basin was a rather nice place to live. Crime was at an all-time low, pirates were swept from the seas, and bandits led a precarious existence. Two important features of the Roman civilization which helped the spread of Christianity were the Roman roads and the Greek language. The one was a central factor in the economic prosperity of the empire; the other gave the advantage of a common language.

Christians interpreted the times as providential. If the Roman civilization had not been so advanced, it is probable that Christianity would have had a harder time spreading. In Christian eyes the times *were* providential; they contributed to the growth of Christianity, but also provided a new challenge: *What was the relationship of Christianity to world politics and world culture?* The response to this challenge gave Chris-

BROWN BROTHERS

tianity a partial answer in its continued quest for self-understanding.

The growth of the Christian Church was closely associated with the political and cultural conditions of the time. The effect of this association shaped the doctrinal, liturgical, and moral stance of the Church down to the present day.

People affect the Church
People reacting to the 10 Commandments

The Roman World

What was this "Roman World" which affected the Christian Church so fundamentally that its basic forms and expressions remained well into the twentieth century?

It is simplest to say that it had two predominant strains. *The one, Roman, was political; the other, Greek, was cultural.* Rome was the predominant political power and ruled the Mediterranean world. Greece was the center of culture and had been so for over six hundred years, even though its territories had been conquered before by the Romans one hundred fifty years before Christ.

Greek culture has been the principal inspiration of Western civilization and one of the great forces in the development of people the world has ever seen. In practically every aspect of human life the Greeks of this period led the way or at least laid the foundation for the achievements of Western culture. The Greeks (from the seventh century before Christ through the fourth century after Christ) were leaders in the fields of art and architecture, poetry and history, statesmanship and law, literature and rhetoric, science, and philosophy.

Perhaps the greatest legacy of the Greeks, however—and surely the inspiration for all their great achievements—was their belief that every human being must be respected for his own sake as a free creature. "The world is full of wonderful things," wrote the Greek dramatist Sophocles (496–406 B.C.), "but nothing is more wonderful than man." This concept was the basis for their philosophy, their system of government, their art and architecture, and even for their representations of their gods.

The most important influence the Greeks have exerted over the centuries is in the field of thought. Because they had good respect for human nature, they paid greatest atten-

BROWN BROTHERS

tion to those things which would enable every person to lead what they considered the good life; hence, their constant attention to all fields of learning. They had good schools and good teachers and encouraged all their bright young men to search for truth wherever it led. It is amazing how profound they were—and how basic—in spite of the limited resources at hand. In the field of thought they are most noted for their philosophy (the search for wisdom), as represented by their two great philosophers Plato (429–347 B.C.) and Aristotle (384–322 B.C.), who have had a greater influence on Western minds than any other thinkers. **Both had a great effect upon Christianity because their thought systems were the medium used to express Christianity in the crucial period after the first hundred years.**

The Greek way of life was admired by every culture in the Mediterranean world and affected every culture to a greater or lesser degree depending on their sphere of influence.* None admired the Greeks more —or envied them more—than the Romans.

The Roman armies brought Greece under the rule of Roman government about 200 B.C. By comparison with the Greeks, the Romans were a barbarous, uncivilized people; in fact, the Greeks despised their Roman conquerors, and their cool, detached attitude toward the Romans not only humiliated the Romans, but infuriated them. In an effort to imitate the Greeks and to learn from them, the Romans brought many Greeks to Rome as slaves to be their teachers. The program was successful, for Roman art, literature, and philosophy flourished only after Rome had conquered the Greeks. Roman achievements in these fields are almost a direct copy of the prevailing Greek modes. It was thus the influence of Greek culture upon Roman civilization that made Rome what it was except for one uniquely Roman contribution: the highly organized

ARISTOTELE

and efficient Roman system of government. By it the Romans controlled the entire Mediterranean world—the area including present Portugal, Spain, France, Southern England, Southeastern Germany, and all of the lands bordering on the Mediterranean in Europe, Africa, and the Near East. (See the map, page 69.)

It was in this world that most Christians lived once they had moved out of the Jerusalem area. As early as St. Paul's journeys in the first years after the death of Jesus, Christianity had begun to move into the Roman world; and as more and more non-Jews became Christians, the influence of Greek thought upon the Christian message became greater and gradually modified Jewish-Christian modes of thought.

In the previous chapter we saw one effect of non-Jewish culture upon Christianity in the decisions made at the First Council in

---

* Alexander the Great (356–323 B.C.) had brought Greek culture to every major country in the Middle East. This is the territory we refer to as "the Greek world."

Jerusalem. We shall now explore further influences of non-Jewish culture on Christianity in its next two hundred years.

Christianity did not move into the Greco-Roman world in a vacuum. Some people of Greece and Rome were familiar with the Hebrew way of life and the Hebrew Scriptures,* and admired the Hebrew religious orientation and ethicial life. Many Greeks and Romans had become Jews, and almost every major city employed some Jews in high positions of government because of their intelligence and attention to work.

When the first Jewish Christians came to preach Jesus in the great cities of the Roman Empire, they found Jewish communities well established and flourishing. The message was preached first to the Jews, it was to them that Paul went first, but many pagans were attracted as well. As more and more non-Jews became Christians, the Christian preaching began to reflect the Greek modes of thought. *It was not long before Greek thought replaced Jewish thought as the standard way of expressing the meaning of Jesus.*

The Greeks were highly speculative people. Their philosophical traditions had trained them to look into the nature of things, to analyze, to ask why, to go to the center of the thought. This created a major shift in the Christian doctrinal presentation. *In the Jewish phase of Christianity the emphasis had been upon the experience the apostles had had of Jesus. In this Greek phase, the emphasis was upon the philosophical and theological meaning of Jesus.* It is because of this shift that we see, in this second phase of Christianity, the rise of Christian theology and the beginnings of those doctrinal debates which were to give the Church profound new insights into the meaning of Jesus. These discussions, chiefly centering around the nature of Jesus as the Son of God, caused Christianity to begin to develop its dogmatic style of crystallizing its beliefs in precise creeds with a technical vocabulary.

Why were so many Greeks, and later Romans, converted to Christianity? There were four principal reasons. The first was because the Greeks were highly speculative people. Those who were educated had all but aban-

---

* The Hebrew Scriptures had been translated into Greek nearly *two hundred years* before Christ.

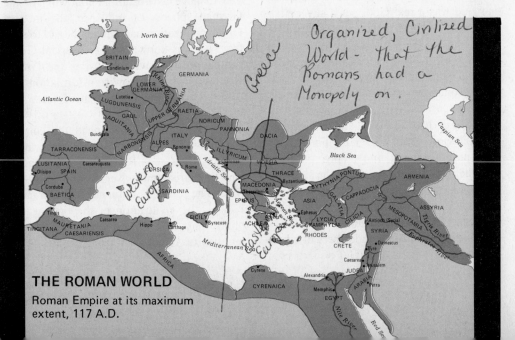

THE ROMAN WORLD
Roman Empire at its maximum extent, 117 A.D.

doned traditional Greek religions. For them, religion was all form; it had no faith. Because they thought through to the heart of things, they could see that the Greek "gods" were all too human; they had nothing of the Divine in them. For most educated Greeks, philosophy was substituted for faith: its lofty ideals moved them toward the goal they sought, the "perfection" of the human person. When Christianity came, it met the Greek mind where it was—on a philosophical level. (See *Acts* 17 for an example of Paul's preaching to Greek philosophers.) For the thoughtful Greeks, Christianity had substance. It challenged their minds.

A second reason Christianity appealed to the Greeks was that their religions, and others like them, were *practical* religions; Christianity was not. In their own religions, bargains were made with the gods, each of whom had a practical function: the securing of some favor for the petitioner, who said, in effect, "You do this, and I'll do that. Otherwise, no deal." Christianity preached a unique God who could not be bribed or bargained with. It preached a saving, suffering, compassionate God; not a vengeful, hedonistic god. It preached the loftiest of ideals and a God who embodied the deepest desires of people. For the Greeks, the Christian God was a real God, not a super man.

A third reason for the success of Christianity among the Greeks was the essential goodness of the lives of the Christians. They saw that Christians led lives of virtue, not to secure some personal, selfish end, but for religious reasons. They did things that were right out of love for God and His people. Christians were, in the main, honest, upright, pure, forgiving, and deeply concerned with the sufferings of the poor, the sick, and the abandoned. They came closest to exemplifying the Greek ideal. This thoughtful Greeks could understand and admire.

Finally, the Greeks, and others of educa-tion in the Mediterranean world were attracted to Christianity because of the inner beauty and obvious peace of the lives of the Christians. These people saw the Christians possessing what they most sought after. It was this which attracted them first, and led them to experience the goodness of the lives of the Christians, which in turn introduced them to the Christian God, leading them finally to an understanding of and an appreciation for the nature of religion as Christians understood it.

The conversion of the Greeks and others in the Roman Empire was not swift or easy. It required hard work, complete dedication, and the living of the Christian life in the face of ridicule, at first, of a rather decadent society, and, eventually, persecution. In the end, however, the religion that had arisen in an insignificant Middle Eastern culture, spread to every corner of the Roman Empire, and within two hundred years had changed it from paganism to Christianity.

The Christian Greek Influence

It is important to remember that Christianity did not *replace* Greek culture—it *Christianized* it. By the time Christians began to have a substantial following in the Grecian spheres of influence, the face of Greek civilization had already begun to shift from what is known as the Classical Greek Period, to what we refer to as the Greco-Roman Period—a slow transformation that resulted from the interaction of these two major cultures.

Greek Christians continued the cultural traditions into which they were born, transforming the Greco-Roman life from paganism to Christianity over a long period of time. The principal influence that Christians had on the civilization of the time was in philosophy and ethical conduct. A great number of Greek scholars became Chris-

tians and brought their Greek learning to bear on the Christian message.

The great teachers, preachers, and scholars who became Christians, and by their influence Christianized Greek culture, are called the Greek Fathers of the Church. Those men, whose lives span the 300 years from about 150 A.D. to 450 A.D., combined holiness and learning to such an extent that their contributions to civilization remain unique in the history of culture.

During this period, sometimes referred to as the period of Christian intellectualism, there was an astonishing development of Christian thought. The Greek Fathers (called "Greek" because they taught and wrote in Greek, the language of the Eastern Church) trained to be scientifically scrupulous in their pursuit of any topic, began a systematic explanation of the mysteries of Christianity. The result was an explosion of Christian knowledge, a better understanding of the Mystery of Christ, and an almost complete change in culture from paganism to Christianity in the Eastern Roman Empire.

Typical of these great men, and one of the first, was Origen (185–254 A.D.).* Origen lived in Alexandria in Egypt at a time when strong religious and philosophical ideals were wrestling for first place among the intellectuals of the city. Sophisticated Greeks, learned Jews, and clever Gnostics laughed at Christians for having "an unreasoned and vulgar faith." Although it is true that there had been learned Christian teachers before Origen, none had really come to grips systematically with the problems that Christianity posed for highly educated people. Origen began the long tradition in the Christian Church which treats theology as a religious

---

* The most famous Greek Fathers—or Fathers of the Eastern Church—are Sts. Athanasius (died in 373), Basil (379), Cyril of Jerusalem (387), Gregory Nazienzen (390), Gregory of Nyssa (395), John Chrysostom (407), Cyril of Alexandria (444), and John Damascene (749). Origen, who fell into some disfavor because of some of his later ideas, is presented in the text because he began the long tradition of intense scholarship and writing for which the Eastern Church is famous.

Three Fathers of the Eastern Church

All 3 were saints.

St. Athanasius (293–373 A.D.), bishop of Alexandria, Egypt, from 328 to 373, dominated both secular and church history during his lifetime and for many centuries after. He was a dynamic, forceful, energetic bishop, a scholar, and an eloquent speaker. Although he was a great scholar and a superb writer, his approach to teaching his people was very simple. "Christ came to save us," he was fond of saying, "He came in order that we might become 'like God.' How could he make us divine if he himself were not God? He who possesses something only as a reflection or on loan cannot give it to others." Because of his work in the various Church Councils and his debates against the Gnostics and Arians, as well as his speaking and writing, he became known as the defender of the divinity of Christ. His life and work portrayed what the people of Alexandria said of him when he was consecrated bishop: "He is a trustworthy man, a good man, a true Christian, an ascetic, a real bishop!" Before he died, he was recognized as the outstanding theological authority in the whole Church.

1. Dominated the secular and church History. Head Honcho

St. Basil (330–379 A.D.), who a Byzantine writer of the twelfth century called "the greatest of the Fathers, the master of the ascetic universe," was a monk of Cappadocia, a small country on the Asian shores of the Black Sea. He was a scholar, a deeply spiritual man, a prolific writer, and "the Father of Eastern Liturgy" which

1. Known for his ability as a writer. Known for organizing Monestaries.

is still used in the Eastern Catholic churches and the Orthodox Churches. His influence on monastic life, on spirituality, on liturgy, and on prayer were so great that he is considered as having no peer in these areas. His monastic ideas and organization were the basis for monasticism in the Western Church, which was the greatest influence in the forging of a new civilization in the West after the decline of Roman civilization.

St. John Chrysostom (344–407 A.D.) was the bishop of Constantinople, one of the most important cities in the Eastern Empire. He was an outstanding scholar, writer, and speaker. He is most famous as an orator (he is known by his nickname, "Chrysostom" which means "golden mouthed"), attracting, we are told, thousands to his sermons and speeches. He was an eloquent and courageous champion of the faith, and a fearless defender of his people against the barbaric chiefs of the Goths who had invaded Constantinople. He was called the conscience and the spiritual leader of the Eastern Church, constantly reminding people of their Christian commitment and that "God has made you His friend." He was the leading moralist of his time, but his single-mindedness in moral things was always tempered by his compassion for people. He is known as the founder and best example of pulpit oratory— his materials and style are still used in Church and secular circles as models for public speaking.

1. Noted for his ability as a speaker. Very impt in the Church

Pulpit. very talented in presenting sermons in th

72

t. Athanasius

. John Chrysostom

science, founded, of course, upon the Faith as presented in the Scriptures, but subjecting its meaning to the rigors of intellectual examination.

Origen was particularly suited for this job. He was extremely bright, enthusiastic and gifted with exceptional judgment and quick insight. By the time he was eighteen, Origen was the head of a school (he was forced to go to work because the family needed support when his father was martyred). Within a few years the Christian school Origen headed was as famous as any of the Greek, Jewish, or Gnostic schools in Alexandria, and Origen was considered the leading intellectual in the East. He was a prodigious worker and turned his sharp mind to theology, philosophy, Scripture, morals, law, and poetry. It was to Origen that the phrase "he lived like a Christian but thought like a Greek" best applied, for he was an intense and holy Christian completely dedicated to Christian scholarship. From his time, Christian theology and philosophy ranked with the theology and philosophy of the non-Christians, and in his followers it surpassed all of them.

The average Greek, Egyptian, Syrian, or North African Christian, of course, was not directly involved in the theological developments of the era. He was living by faith—faith in Jesus as savior. He accepted the gospel message and expressed his faith in the way he lived and the way he worshipped. He lived according to the demands of the gospel, worshipped with his community in the liturgies of the Eastern Church, and developed a piety and a prayer life that had a profound effect on the development of civilization in the Eastern Mediterranean. He was intensely loyal to the Church, to his own faith-community, to his bishop, and to the Person of Jesus. The art and architecture of later years attest to the faith of the people of Greek culture.

* Stop Here *

We cannot speak of this Eastern Christianity without veneration. In many ways it was the origin of our own faith. It is impossible to calculate how much Christian thought—theology, exegesis, and philosophy—owes to it, what great gifts the liturgy received from the marvellous ceremonies which developed within it, or how much Christian piety inherited, even without realizing it, from those admirable believers in the East. . . . The Christian East was a kind of granary which sent forth innumerable seeds. . . . and it was to the East that devout souls turned in search of spiritual wealth. . . . This tradition of fervour permeates the history of Byzan-

tium. It is a history scattered with saintly figures, whose first desire was to serve God, in whatever human situation they find themselves.*

The Christian intellectual and spiritual movement in the Eastern Church of this era was part of the evolutionary development of the emerging Church. It prepared the way for the development of knowledge and piety of later years, and led to a broader, deeper understanding of the meaning of Jesus, and enabled the Christian message to be more

_____

* Henri Daniel-Rops, *The Church in the Dark Ages.* Translated from the French by Audrey Butler. Copyright 1959 by E. P. Dutton & Co., Inc. and reprinted with their permission. Pp. 169, 170.

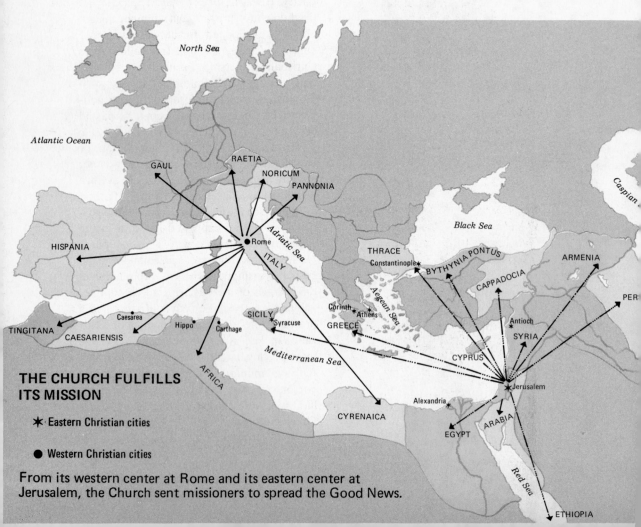

THE CHURCH FULFILLS ITS MISSION

✳ Eastern Christian cities

● Western Christian cities

From its western center at Rome and its eastern center at Jerusalem, the Church sent missioners to spread the Good News.

clearly presented as civilization itself developed in the next few hundred years.

By the end of the fourth century, the Christian population in the East was great—much greater than in the West—spreading out from its center of origin, Palestine. In many areas, Christians made up the majority of the population, and, in some areas, its total. Christianity extended beyond the boundaries of the Roman Empire, past Egypt into Arabia and Ethiopia, into Mesopotamia, Persia, and Armenia, and into areas we now know nothing about. In truth, the Church was fulfilling its mission to be witnesses to Christ "in Jerusalem, throughout Judea and Samaria, and indeed to the ends of the earth." (*Acts* 1:8)

The Spread of Christian Influence to the Western Roman Empire

Although the majority of Christians were living in the Eastern half of the Roman Empire, Christianity was steadily moving to the West. There is no doubt that Christianity was preached in the countries east of Syria, but we don't know for sure what happened there. Perhaps the reason that the Christian influence spread westward is that the real Greek world was west of Jerusalem and the problems of language and travel in the Greek world were minimal compared to the same problems in the areas east of Jerusalem. It was natural for Greek-speaking Christians to move into those areas with which they were familiar.

Christianity had been brought to some of the major cities of the Roman West as early as St. Paul.

Christians in Rome seem to have become numerous first among the Jewish population of the city. The Roman historian Suetonius mentions an edict of Emperor Claudius (died c. 49 A.D.) ordering the expulsion of certain "Chrestes", probably an error for "Christus." According to Acts 18,2, Aquila and Priscilla (or Prisca, as in this epistle [to the Romans]) were affected by this edict; cf. Rom. 16, 3. Since neither early Christian tradition nor Paul's letter to the Romans mentions a founder of the Christian community in Rome, it may be concluded that the Christian faith came to that city through members of the Jewish community of Jerusalem who were Christian converts. About 57 A.D., when Paul wrote the letter, most probably from Corinth, the Christians in Rome were predominantly Gentile, with a Judeo-Christian minority . . .

At this time Paul was considering a missionary journey to Spain and wanted to make Rome his headquarters for the project. He was informed about the Roman community . . . and it may be assumed that he in turn was known to the Christians there . . . [who] were aware of his apostolic role and his whole remarkable history, and would receive his reflections with corresponding interest.*

The story of Christianity's development in the West is fragmentary at best. About all we know is that by the end of the first century the Christians were able to say that their religion was "universal,"** and that by 107 A.D. the famous martyr, St. Ignatius, referred to the Christian Church as "Catholic" and most people knew what he meant and to whom he was referring.

Almost by accident—in an occasional reference to a meeting, in an argument about

---

* From the "Introduction to the Epistle of Paul to the Romans," *New American Bible*, p. 223.
** By this they meant, of course, the universe they knew: the Greco-Roman world.

some aspect of Christian faith, in a record of some small presentation here or there— we discover Christian communities in Spain, Portugal, France, the Germanic territories on the rim of the northeastern Empire, and in Roman Africa. Most of the territory was still pagan, of course, but Christians wielded great influence in the cities where they lived in the Roman Empire of the West.

Christianity was eventually successful in the Western Empire for the same reasons it was successful in the East. It made much more sense to the sophisticated and educated than the pagan and mystery cults did, and had a much stronger base than the humanistic philosophies that were popular at the time. And it appealed to the poor, the uneducated, the slaves, and the common people because of its message of love and hope. Christianity was "everyone's religion." Rich and poor, freeman and slave, men and women were all proclaimed equal. All were encouraged to share equally, and all participated in the Lord's Supper. There were, ideally, no divisions, no classes, no places of honor. As St. James said in his epistle:

My brothers, do not try to combine faith in Jesus Christ, our glorified Lord, with the making of distinctions between classes of people. Now suppose a man comes into your synagogue, beautifully dressed and with a gold ring on, and at the same time a poor man comes in, in shabby clothes, and you take notice of the well-dressed man, and say "Come this way to the best seats"; then you tell the poor man, "Stand over there" or "You can sit on the floor by my footrest." Can't you see that you have used two different standards in your mind, and turned yourselves into judges, and corrupt judges at that? Well, the right thing to do is to keep the supreme law of scripture: *you must love your neighbor as yourself;* but as soon as you make distinctions between classes of people, you are committing sin, and under condemnation for breaking the Law.

Take the case, my brothers, of someone who has never done a single good act but claims that he has faith. Will that faith save him? If one of the brothers or one of the sisters is in need of clothes and has not enough food to live on, and one of you says to them, "I wish you well; keep yourself warm and eat plenty," without giving them these bare necessities of life, then what good is that? Faith is like that: if good works do not go with it, it is quite dead.

James 2:1–4, 8–9, 14–17

St. Paul's celebrated words to the Christians of Galatia were no empty phrase. They were the working principle for Christian communities. St. Paul wrote:

All baptized in Christ, you have all clothed yourselves in Christ, and there are no more distinctions between Jew and Greek, slave and free, male and female, but all of you are one in Christ Jesus.

Galatians 3:27–28

The effect among those who became Christians was felt almost immediately, for it changed the attitude and the actions of the rich and the educated toward the poor, and afforded the poor the things they needed the most: understanding, sympathy, and the practical things of life—food, clothing, and shelter. There was a noticeable difference between Christian and pagan communities in the way the poor were treated.

The center of Christianity in what was

THE BETTMANN ARCHIVE

called "The Western Empire" (which was, in effect, the western half of the Roman Empire which controlled all the land surrounding the Mediterranean Sea) was Rome. Politically, militarily, and economically, Rome was the heart of the empire. It was in Rome that the emperor lived, and it was from Rome that the legions took their orders. It was natural, therefore, that Paul would establish the headquarters for his missionary work in Rome, and it was natural for Peter to come to Rome to function there as the "chief bishop of the Christian Church." It was from Rome that western Christianity spread to the Empire of the west, and it was from Rome that the Church was to develop the characteristics peculiar to it in the western half of Christianity. There were, in effect, two centers of Christianity—the East and the West—and though it was to remain the one Christian Church, "the Church of the Apostles and Martyrs," there were two distinct strains developing, each a product of the predominant culture in which it developed.

Roman Persecutions

Christianity's success, however, produced its severest trial, for it ran head-on into the power of the Imperial Roman government. Almost as soon as it gained a foothold in the cities of the Empire, it ran into trouble because of what it preached and what it stood for. It was not simply because it was a religion that Christianity suffered persecution from various Roman rulers (the Romans were the most tolerant of all people at that time), but because Christianity, unlike many religions the Roman government encountered, required involvement in people's earthly life. For Christians, religion was not an "extra-natural" segment of life. It was for real. It required a radical change in thinking and acting. For pagans, on the other hand, religion did not deal with their real lives; it dealt with a spirit world, with a "reality" that was only remotely connected with human life, with gods that had to be honored, appeased, or compensated for by rites and ceremonies that had very little to do with the business of living.

It must be understood, however, that most people in pre-Christian Greece and Rome were religious. Every city and state had its own special gods whom all citizens were expected to worship in countless ways both public and private. In doing so, they not only performed a spiritual act, but demonstrated their loyalty to their city. Atheism was regarded as a crime against the state as well as against the gods, and an atheist (that is, one who denied the gods of the city or the state) might be executed or exiled.

When Rome conquered the people of the Mediterranean basin, it allowed them to continue their previous religious practices. Rome's attitude was one of toleration. But it did insist on one thing: to help unify all its different subjects and to insure their loyalty to Rome, it insisted that they add an extra

god to their own group. This was either the goddess called Roma to represent the Roman state, or it was the emperor himself. This action indicated loyalty to Rome. For the monotheistic Christians, however, compliance with this demand was impossible; thus, they came to be considered as traitors or as disloyal subversives who threatened their country's safety. *This is the chief reason why Rome persecuted the Christians.*

Another reason was the mystery that surrounded early Christianity, especially in its liturgical practices. Because non-Christians were excluded from the liturgy, the Church was thought of as a secret society. All kinds of rumors were circulated about the Christians, and the Roman people came to believe that Christians practiced evil and inhuman rites which no decent society could tolerate. Besides, when a person became a Christian, he often had to change his personal life, giving up former friends because they were pagans, or staying away from the immoral or blood-thirsty theaters and circus games. This made Christians unpopular; people called them "enemies of the human race." Minority groups always suffer from

prejudice and discrimination because their style of life sets them off from their suspicious, often ignorant neighbors. As such a minority group, accused of vile crimes and treasonable tendencies, Christians lived in a hostile environment, which sometimes employed physical violence against them.

It was human spite which first enlightened it, or, in some areas, the sordid self-interest of some specific business concern. The natural instinct which whips up the masses' hatred for the nonconformists in their midst, and especially for those who fail to conform in matters of the spirit, played the role of policeman here, as in so many like cases. Undoubtedly the fact that their own trade in sacrificial animals or pagan statuettes was suffering was enough to make certain folk hostile to the Christians. In addition a thousand and one ugly rumours were popularly circulated concerning the new sect's alleged indulgence in human sacrifice and secret immorality. But at the back of its mind the pagan mob sensed that the new doctrine was about to demand of it a dramatic transformation, a complete change of heart. It hated all those changes which the 'new race' wanted to make.

In this way, urged on by the *vox populi,* the public authorities were forced to take action. In very many instances, at least in the early days, they did so only with extreme diffidence and real moderation. Thus Trajan's instructions on the subject to Pliny, his representative in Bithynia, were highly circumspect. For a long time to come a number of imperial officials were to retain an attitude of sceptical indulgence and scorn towards the Christians; and by confusing certain expressions, such as 'Son of God' and 'Supreme King,' made out that they were not, in fact, committing treason. But as the Empire went further and further along the road of authoritarianism and absolutist centralization—as, in effect, it became more totalitarian—it grew increasingly aware of the gulf which separated the Christians from official conformity, and recognized them as its enemies. This evolution became very marked from the end of the second century onwards, and by this period it can be seen that it is the best rulers, those who see the demands of their imperial office and the fundamental needs of the regime most clearly, who are the Christians' fiercest persecutors.*

* Henri David-Rops, *The Church of Apostles and Martyrs, Vol. I* (Garden City, N.Y.: Image Books—Doubleday, 1960), p. 195, 196.

Catacomb
fresco
FREDERIC LEWIS

The Gods of Rome

Religion in Rome wore many faces and had many names: each new people the Romans encountered through conquest or trade seems to have added to the Roman pantheon. And yet for many centuries, almost until the birth of Christ, Roman religion, whatever its guise, had certain unchanging qualities. It was, to begin with, a religion of form, of ritual, with little emphasis on the spiritual. The Roman made a compact with his gods—you do something for me and I will do something for you—and his religion was largely a meticulous observance of that bargain. Second, it was an external, communal affair, rather than an internal experience. At first the religious community was the family; then, as Rome grew, it became the village, the city, the state and finally, the Empire. Only when these public formal observances became mechanical and meaningless did Rome turn, in reaction, to other kinds of religion whose appeal was intimate and emotional.

In its earliest form, when the ancestors of the Romans were still simple shepherds and farmers, this religion was almost pure animism. The gods were not persons, but impersonal spirits, and they resided in everything—in trees, in rocks, in birds and beasts, in the grass of the fields and the lightning in the sky. These spirits, or *numina,* were totally amoral, neither good nor bad, and with no special affinity for man. They could help or harm, depending on how they were treated, and it was the job of religion to deal with them in such a way that their powers would benefit man.

At first these dealings, or observances were probably handled by the head of each household, the *pater familias.* Later they were taken over by the head of the community, the *rex,* and by groups of men, rather like priesthoods, who understood the often complex ritual of pleasing a particular *numen.* The king himself was advised on the proper conduct of religious matters by colleges of wise men called *pontifices* and *augures;* the first were specialists in religious law, the second in the interpretation of omens.

The earliest of the *numina* were the spirits that inhabited each Roman family and farm: Vesta, whose concern was the hearth fire, the Lares, who guarded the home and the boundary of each family's fields, the Penates, spirits of the larder. Also dating from very early times were the *numina* of Jupiter and Mars: Jupiter in the days of the Italic tribes was an Indo-European sky god, but the Romans assigned him a home in a particular oak tree on Capitoline Hill; Mars was the spirit of the season of growth and harvest, which was also the season of warfare.

Finally, there was the spirit of a man himself, his *Genius,* which inhabited only the men of his family or clan. A man's *Genius* was a kind of spiritual double; it was his *Genius* that was being honored when he was tendered a banquet or a birthday gift. Many centuries later, when Augustus took for himself the role of central authority, making Rome Augustus and Augustus Rome, it was his *Genius* that received the homage, not Augustus himself.

Gradually, as the rites of propitiating the *numina* were taken over by the king and the priests, the *numina* proliferated until their number, origin and duties became a confusing welter. Many centuries later St. Augustine, making a case for Christianity, ridiculed the multiplicity of the Roman deities still honored by country people:

> Do you think they dared trust one god with their lands? No, Rusina must look to the country, Jugatinus to the hilltops, Collatina to the rest of the hills, and Vallonia to the valleys. Nor could Segetia alone protect the grain: when it was in the ground Seia must look to it; when it was up and ready to mow, Segetia . . . Proserpina they made goddess of the grain's first leaves and buds, Nodotus of the knots, Volutina of the blades, Patelena of the forming ears, Hostilina of the beards, Flora of the blooms, Lacturtia of the blooms whitening, Matuca of their being cut, and Runcina of the cut flower. . . . Their entry-ways had three gods: Forculus for the door, Cardea for the hinges, and Limentius for the threshold.

Imperial Rome by Moses Hadas and the Editors of TIME-LIFE Books (New York: Time, Inc., 1965), pp. 121–122.

The Roman persecutions lasted for about two and a half centuries. They did not continue steadily throughout this period, however, and for many decades and in most places Christians lived in relative peace and security. The usually tolerant Roman government was reluctant to use force and in most cases avoided any open or systematic attempt to search out and persecute the Christians. However, in this case, as in so many other cases involving political motivation, everything depended on the circumstances.

For example, it was an accident that the first real persecution began in 64 A.D. Emperor Nero was blamed by his people for a great fire that destroyed much of the city of Rome. Knowing how unpopular the Christians were, and that the people would believe almost anything about them, Nero insisted that it was they who had started the fire. He arrested and executed several dozen Christians in the city, including, tradition tells us, St. Peter and St. Paul in 67. "Their executions became sports events," wrote Tacitus, a Roman historian. "They were covered with wild animal skins and torn

Durer: *The Martyrdom of St. Catherine*   RELIGIOUS NEWS SERVICE

apart by dogs." But Nero did not order an attack on Christians outside of Rome itself, and the persecution soon ended.

Until about 250 A.D. the persecutions were sporadic and haphazard. But then a series of reforming emperors, Decius (249–251), Valerian (253–260), and Diocletian (284–305), anxious to strengthen the decaying empire, initiated three general persecutions designed to wipe out Christianity completely. These emperors regarded the Christians as a dangerous, disloyal group. In Egypt, Syria, and Asia Minor the government executed Christians, sent them to prison, enslaved them, and confiscated their property.

"The blood of martyrs is the seed of Christians," one of the early Christians wrote, for the persecutions failed to halt the Church's growth. Impressed by the Christians' piety and courage and by their loyalty to their beliefs, more and more people joined the Church. Besides, their fellow citizens now realized that the Christians were not really a threat to the Roman way of life,

Nero   BROWN BROTHERS

for the Christians showed that they were quite willing to accept most of the great cultural and political achievements of the Greek and Roman people. In other words, because the People of God demonstrated that their secular culture did not have to be rejected when they professed belief in Christ, opposition to them died down.

In 313 A.D., Emperor Constantine issued the Edict of Milan, which cancelled all anti-Christian laws and granted complete toleration to the Christians. (By now, they made up about ten percent of the Empire's population.) Constantine himself became the first Christian Emperor, and all following emperors except Julian (360–363) also took up the Christian faith. At the end of the fourth century, Emperor Theodosius (378–395) proclaimed Christianity the only legal religion within the Empire.

Not everything was a bed of roses, of course. There were selfish and cruel people who called themselves Christian (who had become Christians for one unworthy reason or another) and there was lying, and cheating, and adultery. The important thing, however, is that the conditions for the improvement of society were present. Slowly paganism began to disappear from the Western half of the Empire and **by the end of the fourth century (approximately 400 A.D.) to be a Roman and to be a Christian were for all practical purposes identical.**

Because the Roman West represented law and order, and because most of those who eventually became Christian leaders were "Roman thinking," they organized the Western Churches along the lines of the Roman Imperial government. The Christian Churches of the West were somewhat more highly organized than those in the East, and although the bishop of Rome was a bishop like every other bishop, he had more prestige because he was the successor of St. Peter. As such he was the accepted leader of the Western Church regardless of his ability or his learning. He was called upon so often to settle both doctrinal and jurisdictional problems—because it was felt that he best represented the "apostolic tradition"—that he began to be looked upon as unique in his position.

Conversion of Constantine

Theology in the Western Church

Even though the cultural center of Christianity was located in the Eastern Empire, the Western half of Christendom was not without its centers of influence and learning. As far as we know, the intellectual center of Christianity in the West was located in Roman Africa, in cities along the northern coast of Africa which were already tied to Italy by commerce, culture, and government.

Western schools of theology gave more attention to practical theology than did the Eastern schools. Western Christian scholars, schooled in the Roman tradition of practical government, put most of their efforts into changing people's lives and dealing with immediate problems of this world. A significant, though secondary factor in the difference between Eastern and Western theology was that from about 160 A.D. Western theology, for the most part, was written and preached in Latin and used Latin modes of thought to express its cultural ideas.

There were many great Christian teachers and preachers in the West. However, generally speaking, the period of the Western Fathers of the Church was about a century later than the period of the Eastern Fathers. Outstanding in the West were Tertullian (about 160 A.D.), Saints Ambrose (340–397), Jerome (340–420), and Augustine 354–430), and two outstanding popes, Leo (pope from 440–461) and Gregory (pope from 590–604), whose leadership did much to shape the form of the papacy and make Western Christian doctrine the "official" doctrine of the Western Church. The greatest of the Western Fathers was St. Augustine.

Augustine was born in 354 A.D. in Northern Africa. His mother was a Christian, his father a pagan. He was a bright, impulsive, restless student who led an uninhibited life for about twenty years. Dissatisfied with his life and with the small opportunities for advancement he found in Africa, he went to Rome where he was a teacher for about ten years.

Under the influence of St. Ambrose, the popular and scholarly bishop of Milan, Augustine turned his attention to the study of Scripture. The enlightened and practical advice of St. Ambrose finally brought Augustine into the Church, and he was baptized in April 387 A.D. when he was thirty-three years old.

Shortly thereafter, he returned to Africa and began his career as a writer. In 396 he became bishop of Hippo, a small diocese in Northern Africa about 300 miles to the east of Carthage. For the next thirty-four years, he produced the great books which were to make him one of the most influential men who has ever lived.

St. Augustine

St. Augustine was a unique genius. He was an intellectual of unquestioned brilliance, a writer of extraordinary ability, a first-rate theologian, a top-notch administrator, a great humanist, and a saint. Volumes have been written about him, yet each author says that no words can adequately portray the man or his influence. Of Augustine, more than of any other single man, it can be said that his ideas and his life were the principal (some say the saving) inspiration in shaping Western civilization.

He was a prolific writer. We still have most of his writing, which includes 232 books, over 350 long sermons explaining the Faith, and 260 lengthy letters explaining his viewpoints on the Faith. Among his ninety-three major works like *On the Trinity, On Teaching Christian Doctrine, On the Faith and the Creed,* and commentaries on the epistles of St. Paul and the gospel of St. John, two acknowledged masterpieces remain on everybody's list of the greatest works ever written. The first, and still considered the greatest autobiography ever written, is his *Confessions,* his own story of God's saving action in his life. The second, *The City of God,* is Augustine's concept of the destiny of the world. It is because of this book that we refer to St. Augustine as "the prophet of history."

The City of God, the first "salvation history" book, is the work of a genius who could synthesize all of the aspects of history into a comprehensible whole. It is a philosophy of history, a theory of the state and of social life, and a summary of the complex relationships between spiritual and temporal authorities. At its center is the idea that Christ is the answer to the dilemma of human history, and the Church—the body of Christ—is the beacon light to guide civilizations in their self-expression. (Augustine's magnificent presentation of evil in society, and of its worst expression, war, is one of

the very great passages on the existence of evil ever written.)

For thirty years Augustine was *the* voice of the Church in the West. His influence grew to such proportions after his death that everything in Western Christendom—in theology, philosophy, culture, and politics—was measured by its conformity with Augustine's ideas. His influence has been so great that the famous Protestant scholar Adolf von Harnack has said that "The inner, living piety found in Catholicism, and its expression, are essentially Augustinian." In the turbulent years that followed his death, in spite of the barbarian chaos and the theological upheavals in the Eastern Church, Augustine's theology and political philosophy shaped the theology and culture of the West.

This intellectual giant dominated Christian theology in the West for 800 years, until the time of St. Thomas Aquinas.*

---

* The influence of these two men on Western thought has been so great that the first "theological age" of Western Christendom might be called Augustinian, and the second Thomistic. You will see later that perhaps a third Christian thinker, Teilhard de Chardin, may assume a similar position for our own age.

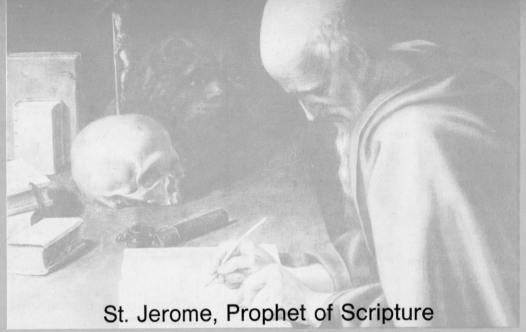

St. Jerome, Prophet of Scripture

RELIGIOUS NEWS SERVICE

Eusebius Hieronymous Sophronius ("the reverend, holy-named wise man") was born at Strido about the year 340 A.D. As a young man, Jerome (that is how Hieronymous is translated) was educated at Trier and in Rome. His principal interest in school was the Latin classics which prepared him for the work for which he was to become most famous, his translation of the Bible from Hebrew and Greek into Latin.

He was a dedicated, even passionate, Christian. He and some of his friends established a monastery that was so strict in its observance that, we are told, the local bishop told them to be more reasonable and more sensitive to the natural frailties of the people among whom they lived. Jerome, always impulsive, left Italy because of this and went to Asia Minor, where he entered a monastery outside of Antioch, then one of the most famous Christian cities in the world. In 379 he was ordained a priest, and in 382 he was called to Rome to serve as secretary for Pope Damasus. It was at this time that the Pope appointed him to make an improved Latin translation of the New Testament.

After Pope Damasus died, the new Pope, Siricius, did not reappoint Jerome, so in 385 he left for Bethlehem where he founded a monastery, a convent, a church, and a place for pilgrims visiting the Holy Land to stay. He made his own room in a cave, gathered his books and papers, and devoted himself for the next thirty years or so to his translation of the entire Bible. His translation, known as the Vulgate, became the standard Bible for Christians of the West (because it was in Latin) for nearly 1600 years. It still remains as the "official" Latin translation, though, of course, translations made in the last twenty-five years or so, have added vast stores of knowledge and more accurate translations to the Bible now in use in all Christian Churches.

Doctrinal Understanding Develops Out of the Christian East

As the Church grew in numbers and prestige in the Roman Empire, so did her understanding of herself and her mission. As the message of Jesus reached new cultures and transformed them, the preaching of the message and the understanding of the meaning of Jesus for the world developed.

As we have seen, it was obvious to the great teachers and preachers that the role of Jesus as Messiah had a much different meaning and application to non-Jews than it did to Jews. St. Paul recognized this early in his own ministry; and in every succeeding age, the church has had to face the challenge of this fact.

After the question of how Christians were related to Jews had been settled, the next doctrinal discussion centered around the Person of Jesus.

At this early stage of its development, as we have pointed out, the political center of Christianity was Rome, but the cultural center of Christianity was in the Mediterranean East and its leaders were Greek-speaking and Greek-educated. It was natural, therefore, that in the schools where Christians were teaching, the chief question asked was a theoretical one: "How is Jesus related to God?" The answers which various Christian scholars proposed to this question, created "schools of theology" in the major cities of the Eastern Roman Empire. As time went on, these schools of theology tended to polarize the answers to the question, and major differences arose which had an effect not only on the Church's understanding of Jesus and her formulations of her faith, but also upon the political scene at the time and for the next several hundred years.

It is impossible to understand this effect unless you understand the political and cultural developments taking place at the same time. During the last three-quarters of the fourth century, the Emperors took the Church under their protection, granted it concessions, and began to enact laws reflecting Christian principles. Because the Roman Emperor had been the supreme head of the pagan religion, he naturally felt that he had supreme power over Christian affairs also. Some of the Emperors acted as if they were bishops, even though they were not ordained. This assumption of power created many problems for the Church. While the Emperors helped win converts and donated much wealth to the bishops, their interference in the doctrinal affairs of the Church complicated things immensely.

As we have said, Rome was the undisputed ruler of the entire Mediterranean world. It reached the peak of its territorial expansion during the reign of Trajan (98–117 A.D.). Because the territory was so vast, changes in governmental administration were necessary. When there were strong Emperors, the territory could be ruled by one man; when there were lesser men, the territory on the rim of the Empire required strong local rulers to keep it in tow. Eventually two major centers of government were established, one in Rome, the other in Constantinople about 1000 miles to the east on the straits between the Aegean and the Black Seas. By the end of the century (395 A.D.), the Empire was permanently divided with an emperor in the East and an emperor in the West. Culturally, the East and West were poles apart. This difference was to have a great effect upon the emerging Church—such an effect, in fact, that the Christian Church would eventually split into two different expressions of Christianity: the Roman Catholic Church and the Greek Orthodox Church.

The Greeks were a more thoughtful, inquisitive people than the Romans. They had a natural talent for rational analysis, and were always asking questions about the

Modern day Istanbul (Constantinople)

meaning of life, the nature of people, truth, goodness, justice, and so on. They produced some of the world's greatest thinkers in literature, political science, philosophy, physics, and mathematics. One historian has put it simply by saying that the Greeks taught mankind how to think.

The Roman people, on the other hand, did not create fine theories and rational interpretations, but they could get things done. Their talents were practical: engineering, building great highways, organizing armies and winning wars, and forming laws for the government of a world-wide empire. When the Romans conquered the East, they united in their single state and under one citizenship both kinds of talents: the speculative skill of the Greeks and the practical ability of the Romans complemented each other neatly.

These natural differences between the Latins and the Greeks were reflected in their Christianity.* The Greeks approached Christianity as if it were a system of philosophy. They wanted to think about their beliefs. They tried to understand them as

thoroughly as possible. They received from the missioners the traditional fundamentals of Christianity, and then they turned their trained minds on these beliefs in order to understand them better. They believed that Christ was both God and man, for example, but they wanted to know exactly what this meant. They accepted the idea of the Trinity, but they tried to understand how the three divine Persons of the Trinity could be one God. In other words, the Greeks represented the Church's search for self-understanding. In trying to use their minds to comprehend as much as possible of their faith, they created the science of theology.

Important Greek Christian thinkers became fascinated with particular parts of the Church's teaching. They asked themselves questions, and they asked other Christians too. Debates were held. Books were written. Different explanations were suggested.

---

* It is important to recall that great cities like Alexandria in Egypt, Antioch in Syria, and later Constantinople were as much Greek centers as were Athens and Corinth.

Lively discussions developed everywhere as evidence of the vitality of the Faith among these intense searchers for truth.

This sort of thing was not new. We have already seen that the Christians discovered that they were not a Jewish sect and that they were not Gnostics. They were now discovering that they were not a state religion. This attempt at self-understanding is a process that goes on all the time within the Church, either on the part of individual Christians or on the part of the entire tribes or nations which contemplate accepting Christianity. Through this process Christianity becomes meaningful to different people at different periods of history. By their discussions the Greeks came to understand the meaning of the Faith and at the same time they contributed immeasurably to the total growth of Christianity, for all Christians since then have benefited from their probing and questioning.

While the Greeks were probing the depths of the gospel message, the Roman influence on the Christian Church became evident in its organizational structure. Roman Christians accommodated the Church's organization to the already existing political subdivisions of the Empire. Every major city became the headquarters of a bishop, who was the chief administrator of the Church. Some of the greatest cities such as Rome, Constantinople, Alexandria, and Antioch were governed by bishops with the honorary title of patriarch. This meant that he supervised a number of bishoprics in his area. St. Peter had gone to the capital of the Empire, Rome itself, and thus his successors as the Church's chief leaders came to live in Rome.*

Although the bishop of Rome was generally recognized as the Church's supreme authority on earth, the great distances and the poor means of communication in those days left much of the actual business of the Church in the hands of the scattered bishops. When questions of the meaning of the Faith arose, people turned to the bishops for guidance. The bishops met together at different times to consider such question as were raised by the Greek thinkers. These meetings, called "councils," were held rather often during the fourth century. The more important or difficult the questions, the larger the councils became as more and more bishops were brought into the discussions. Since most of the great theological debates occurred in the East, it was there that most councils met.

The debates on the nature of Christ serve as a classic example of how the Church arrives at an understanding of itself. The formulas of explanation indicate the Church's thinking at a particular time and in a particular place. As in any human attempt at meaningful explanation (for example, in Einstein's theory of relativity), there is an experience of a situation or an awareness of a reality, then there is an examination and a discussion of the reality, finally there is a theoretical expression of the experience as it is understood at the time. The resulting formulation into a theory then conforms to what some thinkers today call "the law of complementarity": the theory is held in a kind of suspension, accepted as the best explanation until a better explanation can be arrived at through clearer understanding of more data. The same process is followed when the matters under consideration are religious.** The debates on the nature of

* The title "papa" or "pope" was originally used for all bishops, but eventually it came to be limited in the "Western Church" to the bishop of Rome. It is still used for the Patriarch of Alexandria and for Russian priests.

** For example, the Church's new insights about its role and mission in the twentieth century resulted in the discussions and documents of Vatican Council II.

Christ held in the second half of the first 500 years followed this pattern.

For over one hundred years the Eastern Church had had running debates on the nature of Christ and the meaning of the traditionally accepted conclusions about the Trinity. These debates were carried on by sincere, zealous, and learned men. They were searching for meaning; they were reacting to what they considered false or misleading interpretations of the meaning of Christ. In almost every school of thought, the basic idea was formulated and fostered by a single person of very persuasive character. When the debates got serious, that is when factions arose on either side of the argument and differences created human problems, meetings were held by local bishops to determine whether or not this or that idea was in keeping with the traditional understanding of the Church. The history of this time is filled with examples of meetings of bishops in a particular area to discuss one or another of the proposals presented by the major schools of theology in Egypt, Syria, Palestine, and Greece.

Once Christianity ceased to be a religion in hiding and came under imperial protection, the debates were no longer local; they were the concern of the whole Church. Because the Emperor took it upon himself to enter the discussion, the debates assumed a political dimension as well.

These expanded debates on the nature of Christ arose at the end of a severe period of persecution. They were brought to a head by a brilliant and persuasive Eastern priest, Arius (?260–336 A.D.), who, overwhelmed by the majesty and grandeur of God, preached that Jesus was not the Son of God (in the traditional Catholic sense), but was a man with certain divine characteristics and attributes. He argued that, if God was not material, he could not show himself humanly; therefore, Jesus was not God.* If

Fresco: Arius anathematized   RELIGIOUS NEWS SERVICE

this was so, then people were not really redeemed. This teaching was contrary to the entire Christian tradition, but, because Arius was so forceful and persuasive, he had a great following. Many powerful men, both churchmen and political leaders, defended him. Arius was no fool, and he did not just put out ideas to create a sensation. He firmly believed that God was so completely outside of the created world that he could not possibly enter the world. (At this time, you will recall, most people believed in the heavens as a place for the gods, the earth as a place for people, and the underworld as a place for the dead.) Arius said, therefore,

---

* This was similar to the old Gnostic argument discussed on page 60.

that Jesus could be no more than God's highest creature.

Arius' ideas created such controversy in the East that physical violence developed. Emperor Constantine decided to call a General Council of the Christian bishops to settle the issue. The Council met in May 325 A.D. in Nicaea (present day Iznik), a small town near Constantinople.

It is impossible to recreate the emotional atmosphere of this occasion. For the first time since the apostles met in Jerusalem in 49 A.D., bishops from all over the Christian world assembled. For the first time bishops were able to meet together under the sponsorship of an Emperor who personally endorsed Christianity. It was inevitable that Constantine would dominate the Council, not by his theology, of course, but by the force of his person and position.*

Bishops from Egypt, Syria, Palestine, north Africa, modern Turkey, Persia, Greece, Italy, and Spain, gathered together —men as diverse as the races and cultures from which they came. They were divided, not only by Eastern and Western modes of thought, but also according to what they understood of Arius' doctrinal expressions. What information we have tells us that 318 bishops assembled at Constantine's invitation together with experts in all fields, and priests, laymen, soldiers, and dignitaries from all professions and vocations.

Among the bishops on both sides of the issue under discussion—and adding drama to the whole scene—were men who had suffered persecution (the highest mark of honor among Christians) because they were Christian. There were bishops who had been branded with hot irons, men whose bodies bore visible scars of horrible torture, of scourging, mutilation, stretching on the wrack, men whose eyes had been gouged out, whose hands had been cut off, and men who had been galley slaves for years. There were

intellectual giants, astute and crude politicians, parish priests, hermits, and monks. There were powerful bishops from large dioceses and bishops from unknown towns. *But they all came with one purpose in mind: to preserve what they understood as the message of Christ.* They might respect the Emperor but they did not fear him. They might use politics to help their cause, but there was no doubt in their minds as to why they had assembled. This was a serious religious meeting. Its end and aim were religious.

When the Council finally opened, debates were held between those who believed that Arius was right and those who believed that his teaching destroyed the very meaning of Christianity. After a month's time the dele-

---

* It is difficult for us in the twentieth century to understand the absolute power of the Roman Emperor. He was supreme in every detail of life. He had full legislative power, was the final judge in lawsuits, controlled currency, economics, and politics, and dictated the religion that was to be practiced by his subjects. He was "emperor" because he was commander-in-chief of the armies (emperor comes from the Latin *imperator* which means "commander"); and he maintained his power and prestige as long as he controlled the army. Constantine, whose father had been "subemperor" in the West, succeeded to the throne because he controlled all the armies in what is now Portugal, Spain, France, Belgium, and the southern half of England. From this power base he defeated the Emperor of the East, and thus controlled the entire Roman world. His word was absolute law; he controlled the destiny of every man, woman, and child in the Empire. It was by his favor that any form of life was openly allowed; hence, the Christians, newly relieved from their persecutions and sensitive to the prestige of the Emperor, were anxious not to do anything that would upset the status of freedom they so lately acquired. Philip Scharper, a noted Catholic writer, says that Constantine changed Christianity as much as any pope, theologian, or martyr in the history of the Church.

Council of Nicea

gates were able to draft a formula which, they felt, expressed the traditional belief of Christianity. This formula, amended later to include items from later Councils, is the expression of faith that Catholics recite at Sunday Mass to the present day. At the present time, almost every Christian Church recites this formula or one nearly like it to express its beliefs. (It is well to note that the Nicene Statement does not attempt to prove a fact but to formulate a Catholic belief.) In its approved form in 325 A.D., it looked like this:

We believe in one God,*
the Father almighty, Maker
[of heaven and earth, and]
of all things visible and invisible,
and in one Lord Jesus Christ,
the only-begotten Son of God,
Light of Light, true God of true God;
begotten not made; consubstantial
   with the Father,
by whom all things are made,
who for us men, and for our salvation
came down [from heaven,] and was
   incarnate
[by the Holy Ghost of the Virgin
   Mary];
and was made man;
[He was crucified also for us],
suffered [under Pontius Pilate, and
   was buried].
The third day He rose again
   [according to the Scriptures];
and ascended into heaven
[and sits at the right hand of the
   Father];
and He shall come [again with glory]
to judge both the living and the dead
[of whose kingdom there will be no
   end].
And I believe in the Holy Ghost.

Once this "Nicene Creed" had been publicly signed by all the bishops and promul-

gated by Constantine, it became the official creed for all Christians. To deny the divinity of Christ in any way was to put oneself outside of the Christian community and was a crime against the state. However, the dispute did not end with the close of the Council. Powerful friends of Arius appealed to the Emperor, and some Eastern bishops withdrew their signatures. This dispute continued for several years and created other doctrinal discussions because various theologians and bishops, attempting to explain the meaning of the Nicene formulas, exaggerated now one aspect, now another. As a result, succeeding ages wrestled with such problems as the role of Mary, the nature of the Holy Spirit, and the meaning of salvation. As each discussion became heated, successive Councils were held (381, 431, 451 A.D.). At each the Nicene formula was reaffirmed and statements were added reaffirming the traditional Christian belief.**

Although Christian doctrinal formulations were born in the intellectual contro-

---

* The words in italics have been changed in some modern creeds to suit local conditions. The words in brackets were added to the original formula by later Councils, which also added certain statements to affirm a Christian belief.

** In Roman Catholic history there have been twenty-one General Councils, not counting the meeting of the Apostles in Jerusalem in 49 A.D. The first eight (from 325 to 870 A.D.) were dogmatic, that is, Councils which defined Christian doctrine to counter the heresies that cropped up about the meaning of Jesus. The eight Councils of the medieval period (1123 to 1417 A.D.) were largely political or reform Councils. The three Councils of the Renaissance Age (1439 to 1563 A.D.) were reforming Councils, whose purpose was to change the moral and religious tone of Christendom. The two Vatican Councils (1870 and 1965 A.D.) attempted to define the nature of the Church in a scientific age. (For a detailed and human account of the Councils, see Philip Hughes, The Church in Crisis [New York: Doubleday, Image Books, 1964.])

versies of the time, and although the parry and thrust of these minds and the personality conflicts involved are of little concern for us today, what did come from these controversies is important, for they are the basic formulas in which we modern Christians have taught the Mystery of Christ.* We believe *what* we do and we understand *as* we do because the intellectual giants of the first 500 years of the Christian era wrestled with the problem of the meaning of Christ.

The End of the Second Era

Once Constantine had officially granted religious freedom in the Roman Empire and succeeding Roman Emperors had taken an active part in the affairs of the Church, Christianity was finally established on firm ground. In the entire Roman Empire, it was no longer an outside sect, a religion practiced by a minority group. It was, unofficially at least, the religion of the Empire. The Mediterranean world was, to all intents and purposes, Christian.

By the same token, Christianity too had changed and developed. It had outgrown its Jewish beginning, had acquired an institutionalized form to function in society, and had developed a rather settled theological framework. It was, in the best sense, a religion for the world, for it preached in Greek and Roman concepts a Saving God who had entered the world in the Person of Jesus. It embraced people from every walk of life in every tribe and nation known to the Greco-Roman world (and beyond), and its principles all but dominated the thought and actions of an entire empire.

Never before had a religion so captured the religious sense of so many people. Christianity had survived the opposition of Jewish religious leaders, the paganism of the Roman world, the disdain of the sophisticated, and

Constantine   RELIGIOUS NEWS SERVICE

the predictable odds against survival. But there was much to do. Even though the people of these times were only vaguely aware of the vast number of people who lived on the fringes of the Roman Empire, and though they were not at all aware of the cultures that flourished in India, China, Japan, and the continent of Africa, and did not even dream of the existence of the Americas, the Church was conscious of its mission to all people and pushed ahead by sending missionaries to the known lands outside the Roman world.

The Church was also conscious of its religious force within the world in which it

---

* The term "mystery," as in "Mystery of Christ" or "Mystery of the Church," means a divine reality inserted into history. The use of this term indicates that the reality cannot be fully explained or "captured" in human language.

operated. It knew that, even though it was deeply involved in the politics of the time, it was not a political party, a dependent group, a national, or imperial religion. It knew that it should not pursue economic, political, or cultural concerns primarily for their own sake, but for the sake of leading people through them to the divine. Christians knew that, though religion is a human way of expressing people's relationship with God and, as such, has economic, political, and cultural interests, it is more than any of these alone and more than all three together. Christians knew that the meaning of Christ for their world went beyond the aims and purposes of human society and its institutions; it made people conscious of cooperating with a personal, Saving God.

As we look back into history to better understand our Faith, we can see the social and political progress of civilization. We can also see the development of its understanding in its ideas of God, the meaning of religion, and the expression of worship, and its ethical sense. Jesus did have an effect upon society: the greatest single force for change in the Western world was the entire Christian Church he founded.

Mosaics in early Christian tomb under St. Peter's

RELIGIOUS NEWS SERVICE

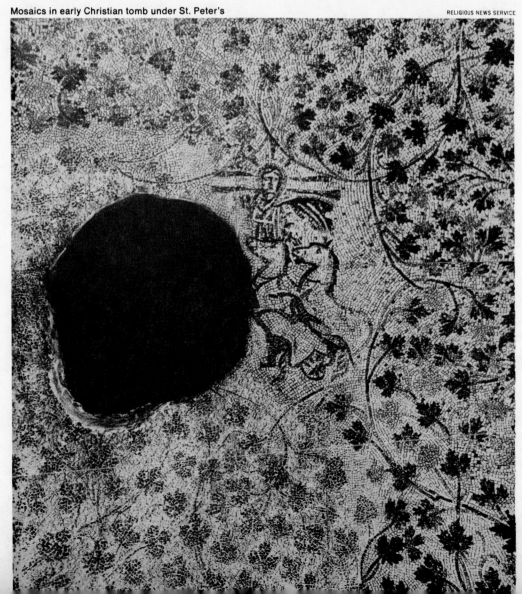

1. After Christianity had faced the question of its relationship to Judaism, what challenge did it face in its search for self-understanding?

2. Why did Christian missionaries go out to preach Christ to other people? (See *Romans* 1:1–15.)

3. What affected the growth and expression of Christianity during the second phase of its development? What was the effect? Why was it so affected?

4. What is meant by "The Roman World"? What kind of world was it? What was the Greek influence in this world? What was the Roman? Explain each in some detail and give examples.

5. Prepare a report on Socrates, Plato, and Aristotle.

6. Why did Paul select Rome as the headquarters of his missionary journeys in the West? Why were the major cities of the Roman Empire also cities for Christian communities?

7. Explain why an "Eastern" and a "Western" expression of Christianity developed. What were some of the differences between them?

8. What reasons does your book give for Christianity being accepted by so many Greeks and Romans?

9. Read *Acts* 17 to see what approach Paul used when speaking to educated Greeks about Christ. How did this approach differ from his approach to the Jewish people as described in this chapter of *Acts*? Why did he use different approaches? Did other Christian missionaries ever do this? Can you give examples?

10. Read *1 John* 4:7–21. How does what John says agree with what James and Paul say in page 76? Why was Christianity called "everyone's religion"? Does this agree in any way with the material in your book on the Church as the people of God? How?

11. What effect did Christian intellectuals have on the expression of Christianity? What role did Origen, Athanasius, Basil, and John Chrysostom play in the development of Christianity? What is the meaning of "Father of the Church"?

12. According to the map on page 74, what cities were the principal centers of Christianity?

Why was Jerusalem no longer the principal center?

13. What does Henri Daniel-Rops say about the Eastern Church?

14. Prepare a report on monasticism in the Eastern Church. Include in your report a paragraph on asceticism.

15. Why were Christians persecuted by the Roman authorities?

16. Prepare a report on the Roman Coliseum.

17. Prepare a report on the catacombs.

18. What is the substance of St. Augustine's satire as given in the selection "The Gods of Rome," page 81?

19. Read *Romans* 12 and 13. Does what Paul says to the Roman Christians justify what was said about them in some Roman circles? Why? Why not?

20. Explain the role of Constantine in the development of the Church.

21. St. Cyprian, a famous and saintly Father of the Western Church, is reported to have said, "We have built buildings, now it is time for us to build Christians on the model of the gospel." What do you suppose he meant by that?

22. Why does your book refer to St. Augustine as "the prophet of history"?

23. Prepare a report on the role of St. Augustine in the history of the Church. Include in your report a brief presentation on his *Confessions* and his *City of God.*

24. What was St. Jerome's major contribution to Christianity?

25. How and why was the Nicene Creed developed?

26. What is the purpose of Church councils?

27. What major development in the Christian understanding of the meaning of Jesus for people developed during the second half of the Church's first 500 years?

Reconstruction
Christianity

9

Christian Communities
Rebuild Civilization
During "Dark Ages"

The third phase of development in the Church's emerging consciousness of itself and of its mission occurred in the western half of the Roman Empire. Although Rome controlled the Mediterranean basin, its frontiers were never really secure. Beyond the fortifications, and held in check by the Roman armies, thousands of restless people were on the move. Time and again these "barbarians" tested the strength of Rome on the frontiers, and, eventually, finding a weakness, overran the Roman civilization established in what is now England, Ireland, Germany, France, Spain, Italy, Yugoslavia, and North Africa.

It is the end of the Second Century B.C. The place: the northern borders of the Roman Republic in what is now Austria. On the edge of a deep forest that stretches—no man knows how far—beyond the Alps, a well-disciplined garrison of Roman legionnaires is suddenly attacked by a mob of howling, spear-waving warriors. Who they are, where they come from are as much a mystery as the forest from which they have emerged. Tall and sturdily built, with blond hair and fierce blue eyes, they wear ani-

BROWN BROTHERS

98

mal totems on their helmets and strip themselves naked for battle, throwing themselves into the fray with the relish of men who love combat and have no fear of death. To the small, dark-haired Romans they look like demons.

Frightened and confused, the Romans fall back before the onslaught of this wild horde and are swept to defeat. The invaders push westward into Gaul, plundering as they go, overwhelming one Roman division after another. In the spring of 102 B.C., they cross the Alps into Italy itself, shouting their war cries and sliding on their shields down the snowy slopes of the mountains into the Po Valley. Rome, in a panic, finally sends an army to crush them in 101 B.C. and carries off their chieftains in chains.

But the vanquished were yet to be the victors. This episode marked the first appearance in recorded history of a people—the Northmen—who would eventually overrun the Roman world and help shift the center of European civilization from the Mediterranean to cooler lands beyond the Alps. They would also play a major role in shaping the laws, languages and customs of all Europe—and hence of America too. And from the startling remains of their culture, uniquely preserved in the soil and bogs of their northern homeland, would finally come, in the 20th Century, one of the most detailed pictures ever assembled of life in prehistoric Europe—from 10,000 B.C. to the beginning of the Christian era.

The homeland of these invaders lay along the shores of the Baltic and North seas in what is now Denmark, Norway and Sweden. In 500 B.C., when the weather pattern in the north turned unbearably cold and damp after a prolonged warm cycle, the Northmen began pouring south in search of a more hospitable domain. The first to terrorize the Roman world in the Second Century B.C. were Cimbrian and Teutonic tribesmen from Denmark's Jutland peninsula. In the centuries that followed, other Northmen swept across the continent in successive waves to pillage and conquer—and, incidentally, to leave behind evidence of their tribal identities in a host of European place names.

From Sweden—perhaps from the Swedish provinces of East and West Gotland—came the Goths, who first broke Roman power in the West. From the Danish island of Bornholm in the Baltic, once called Burgundarholm, may have come the Burgundians who founded the modern French province of Burgundy. From Vendsussel in the northern part of Denmark's Jutland peninsula may also have come the Vandals, who gave their name to the Spanish province of Andalusia—once Vandalusia. Lombards, from the region just below the Jutland peninsula, made northern Italy their home, and their fair-haired descendants may be seen there today strolling the streets of Verona and Milan. The Franks—whose kingdoms gave birth to France, Germany, Holland, Belgium and Switzerland—were originally a loose confederation of northern tribes that settled along the lower reaches of the Rhine. It is even possible that the first rulers of Russia were expatriate Swedes, descendants of a Scandinavian people who called themselves the Rus and who established trading settlements along the Volga and Dnieper as far back as 1800 B.C. No wonder the Sixth Century A.D. monk Jordanes, a Goth, proudly referred to Scandinavia in his *History of the Goths* as "the cradle of peoples" and "the womb of nations." *

---

* From *The Northmen,* Thomas Froncek and the Editors of TIME-LIFE Books (New York: Time Inc., 1974), pp. 9–10.

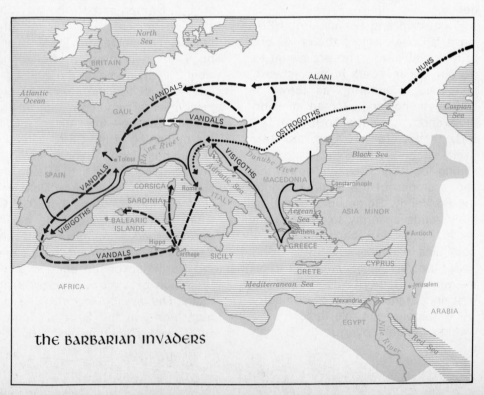

the BARBARIAN INVADERS

For over 500 years, Rome had been relatively successful in holding off the barbarians and building a Roman civilization in the northern parts of the Empire. The average Roman citizen was undisturbed by the frontier skirmishes, and the Church, secure in the heart of the Empire and working ceaselessly to convert what barbarians it came in contact with on the fringes of the Empire, continued its mission of bringing the message of Christ to the people. It was not until the reign of the last of the "great emperors," Theodosius, who died in 395 A.D., that the threat of a barbarian takeover became a possibility. Finally, during the fifth and sixth centuries the Roman Empire, so glorious and so strong in its golden years, collapsed in the West, and a half dozen barbarian kingdoms took its place.

At one time, historians referred to the period between the decline and end of the Roman Empire in the West and the emergence of the Middle Ages (approximately 476 A.D. and 1000 A.D.) as "The Dark Ages." They did so because, rather simplistically, they viewed the "light" of Roman civilization and culture (that is, urban civility, art, music, drama, architecture, sculpture, painting, reading, writing, and the rule of law which brought peace) as having been extinguished—replaced by barbarian "darkness." Although the term is generally discarded by historians now, we have retained the term in order to illustrate a point: the effect of Christianity on the barbaric culture, and the effect of the barbaric culture on the expression of Christianity.

During this period of transition, the Church remained as the principal civilizing, unifying force in the turmoil that is inevitable in any period of cataclysmic change and in the period which followed. The transformation of this society into a "new" Roman society was a slow process, but it was accomplished in great part through the dedication and hard work of hundreds of Christian missionaries, monks, and lay people, who in the midst of untold hardships brought the message of Christ, the liturgy of the Church, and Christ's way of life to the thousands of barbarians who finally made up modern European peoples.

In order to understand what the decline and end of the Roman Empire in the West meant for the story of Christianity, two facts should be kept in mind. The first is that *the eastern half, the Greek-speaking section of the Roman state, survived under the name of the Byzantine Empire.* Here, then, the forces of continuity were not interrupted. A strong, cultured, deeply religious state continued its existence as a Christian bulwark for another one thousand years, although in time it too lost important bits of territory.

Among the Christians of Byzantine, the dynamic traditions of an intellectually alert Christianity flourished vigorously. Constantinople, the noblest Christian city in the world, took pride in its splendid churches, such as the magnificent Hagia Sophia, and Christian art in sculpture, painting, and mosaics reached a high degree of perfection. Many of the old theological disputes contin-

Hagia Soph
in Constant

himself as his duty to stamp out heretics and convert pagans. It was he who built Hagia Sophia with a splendor that had never been seen before. The church still stands today, although it is now a public museum.

The second point to remember about the decline of Rome is the difference between *the Roman state,* which disappeared, and *Greco-Roman culture,* which survived. In fact, Greco-Roman culture as an essential ingredient of Western civilization is still with us today.

As we have seen, Christianity had come to terms with Rome and its culture so thoroughly that it had identified itself with them. The Empire and its civilization were the vehicle for the preservation of Christianity. Christ had been born into the Roman Empire, and this was interpreted as a divine sign of approbation. By establishing Christianity as its official religion, the Empire had been "baptized." Pagans had spoken of "eternal Rome" even before the time of Christ; not long after the end of the persecutions, Christians were using the same language.

Typical was the attitude of St. Jerome. When he learned that the Visigothic barbarians had captured the city of Rome in 410 A.D., he predicted that the end of the world was at hand; the world, he thought, would last only as long as Rome endured. Obviously things did not work out that way, but this mental block lasted for a long time among the People of God. The Byzantines in fact called Constantinople "New Rome" for this very reason, and they saw the hand of God in their survival.

But if Christianity could not save the Empire, it could save Greco-Roman culture. In fact, it had to, for Christianity, in the West at least, had been completely Romanized. It thought and spoke and acted Roman. Thus, when the barbarians took over Roman territory, the Christian Church found itself with

ued into the 500s and 600s, and others were added, but this was evidence of the vitality of its faith. The old Greek habit of philosophizing and questioning continued.

This Byzantine Empire was the completely Christianized remnant of old Rome. It represented a combination of Greek learning, Roman legal and political ideas, various artistic values adopted from the Oriental peoples of Syria (such as the use of the crucifix), and the teachings of Christianity. The Byzantines thought of themselves as the foremost upholders of Christianity, its defenders against the forces of paganism.

One significant feature of the Church in the Eastern Mediterranean was the powerful control exercised by the government in religious affairs. Emperor Justinian (527–565 A.D.), who did much to put this state on an enduring foundation, exemplified this tradition of what came to be called Caesaro-Papism. Justinian meddled in the doctrinal disputes of the times, appointed bishops, even a bishop of Rome, and took it upon two jobs to do: it had to *evangelize* the barbarians and baptize them into the Christian community, and it also had to *civilize* them by introducing them to the cultural achievements of the Romans. The two tasks went hand in hand.

The barbarians were not savages. They had their own culture, though it was on a much lower level than that of the Mediterranean peoples. They had enough sense to admire much of Roman life and to desire to share in it rather than to destroy it. Much, very much, physical damage was done to Roman civilization during the barbarian migrations, but a great deal of this was due to the excitement and the fears of the moment, not to deliberate policy. In fact, some of the most destructive barbarians, for example, the Visigoths, were already Christians when they entered Roman lands. Thus, when the Visigoths captured Rome, they spared all churches and granted safety to all who took refuge in them—even if the refugees carried great wealth into the churches.

The Christianization of the Barbarian Nations

Historians distinguish among three main groups of the barbarian heirs of Rome: the Celts, the Germans, and the Slavs. Rome had long ago subdued many Celts when it conquered northern Italy, Gaul, and Britain, and these people had been Romanized and Christianized for centuries. Only the Celts of Ireland remained outside of the fold.

The Germans had begun their great migrations around 500 B.C., and these continued until almost a thousand years later. Some Germans had been allowed to migrate into the Empire during its better days, but large tribes had remained outside the rim of the Empire until the fourth and fifth centuries. When internal political pressures on Rome forced the withdrawal of the Roman

St. Bede

legions from the outlands, the German tribes invaded and forcefully seized Roman lands. Here they established their independent kingdoms.

Far off in northeastern Europe lived the Slavs, the ancestors of the Russians, Poles, Czechs, and other peoples of modern Europe. The Slavs were so far removed from the Mediterranean that they did not move onto Roman soil except in the Balkan peninsula. Roman civilization had to go out to reach them; they did not come to it as did the Germans and Celts.

Each of these three groups represented a distinct challenge to Christianity. Because Roman Christianity was eventually replaced by these barbaric cultures, particularly in the territory outside of Rome itself, the Church was forced to new missionary efforts in the territory which had already been somewhat Christianized. The Celts and the Gauls had been exposed to Roman Christianity but they had retained, for the most part, their barbaric religion. The Germanic tribes, too, though they had experienced Christianity were largely pagan. The Slavic nations had not been exposed to Roman culture or Christianity; they required special missionary techniques. The guiding principle in all cases was the advice given by Pope Gregory (590–604 A.D.): disturb the regular life of the barbarians as little as possible; missionaries should, he said, try to reconcile Christianity to the customs and mentality of their converts.

For centuries, the Church put great effort into the missionary endeavor. The transformation of Europe from barbarism to Christianity took many centuries. The names of several famous missionaries have come down to us, but those by no means tell either the story of conversion, the human sorrows and disappointments, or the concentrated effort of the many who went to foreign lands to bring the message of Jesus to the people. We recall the names of a few, more to show the passage of time than to glorify individual efforts.

Ulfilas converted the Visigoths during the fourth century. St. Patrick baptized the Irish around the 450s. In 496 Clovis and many of his Frankish followers accepted baptism from St. Remigius. St. Augustine of Canterbury came to Anglo-Saxon England in 597 with a band of followers to begin the conversion of these barbarians. The Englishman Boniface visited central Germany in the 740s and won many of these people to Christ. St. Cyril and St. Methodius are known as the "Apostles of the Slavs" because they came to Bohemia to spread the Gospel during the ninth century. About 988, Vladimir, ruler of Russia, allowed himself to be baptized along with many of his people living around Kiev. These are only a few of the eminent missioners; there were dozens and dozens more.

At the same time that they brought the Gospel to the barbarians, the missioners brought Roman culture. There was no choice; the two were inseparable. Because Christianity wore a Roman garb, it appealed strongly to the backward barbarians, who had a lively admiration for the intellectual and material achievements of the Romans. The acceptance of Christianity was a step toward winning these achievements for the converts.

From the missioners' point of view, they could only communicate the full meaning of the Christian message through its contemporary Roman form. To read the Scriptures, the barbarians had to be taught how to read; even more basic than that, an alphabet had to be invented for those tribes that had no written language at all. Hence, we see that Bishop Ulfilas invented a system for writing the Gothic language as a prelude to translating the Bible into this written form for his converts; similarly Cyril and Methodius devised the first written Slavic language for the same reason.

Everywhere the coming of Christianity brought the beginnings of literary education, sometimes in the vernacular languages first, but eventually always in Latin. Books and schools were the next things that the missioners introduced, and these came quickly into Ireland, England, Germany, Bohemia, and Russia. Usually it was only the clergy who had the time and the inclination to take advantage of the cultural tools that were put at their disposal, but at least there were soon to be found in every land some scholars who understood the meaning of culture, and who could preserve it for better days.

Detail from early Celtic manuscript

offenses. They began to distinguish between different degrees of sinfulness, established categories of sins, and tried to list specific penances that atoned for the various degrees of evil. (This penance fits this sin, that penance fits that, and so on, is the way they talked.) From the Celtic monks of Ireland thoughts and practices concerning penance and reconciliation eventually spread to the continent, and finally had a profound influence upon the Christian sacrament of reconciliation.

The Germanic people, for their part, carried over from their past a deep feeling of awe and wonder at the great power and majesty of God. They developed a special fascination for things like relics, the cult of the saints, miracles, intervention by saints and by God himself in daily life, and so on. These ideas seemed to be a carryover from the Germanic past when the people believed that their pagan deities loved the mysterious, dark, haunting forests and misty swamps of their country. The Christmas tree is a specific example of how this Germanic mentality passed into the framework of Christianity.

Thus, once again Christianity was affected by culture, and culture was affected by Christianity. Born into an Hebraic milieu, nurtured in the Greco-Roman philosophical and political atmosphere, and modified by the primitive religious heritage of many barbaric nations, Christianity comes to people today filtered through the cultural prism of many civilizations and the historical development of people. Throughout its long history, the Church has not only exhibited the principle of change, but also maintained its principle of continuity: the meaning of Christ for all people.

One of the most effective instruments for spreading Christianity during the Dark Ages was monasticism, which probably originated

While Christianity was uplifting the barbarians in both a cultural and a religious sense, it was itself undergoing subtle changes in emphasis. This development came from the peculiar psychology and history of the barbarian races. The essential doctrine of Christ, of course, remained unchanged; it was just that certain aspects of Christianity interested the barbarians more than others. The result was an interaction between the culture of the new converts and their faith. Each affected the other.

The Celtic monks, for example, became fascinated with the question of reconciliation and how people made retribution for their in Egypt during the third century. Men, and eventually women too, who sought to lead a more nearly perfect Christian life left the villages and cities in which they lived and moved into hilly or deserted areas where they could be alone to meditate and pray. They often stayed for years in these remote places, living off of the roots and berries and insects that they could find, since the warm climate of Egypt kept a supply of food available all year. St. Anthony of Egypt and St. Paul of Thebes are among the first and most famous to adopt this style of life.

These early monks felt that a good life involved having as little as possible to do with material things. The idea probably arose from the Eastern primitive religious idea that material things were essentially evil and from some of the Greek philosophers, who disdained the body as a prison for the pure soul. They saw the Christian's struggle for perfection as a battle between the evil body and the imprisoned soul. To win the battle, the body had to be punished, deprived, and whipped into submission. They fasted rigorously, scourged themselves, and devised

many other methods of keeping their bodies under control so that they could open themselves to the influence of spiritual forces.

When these monks lived alone, they were called hermits. Eventually groups of them began to gather in communities or monasteries* under the guidance of an abbot, who usually prepared a set of rules for them. St. Basil among the Greeks of Asia Minor wrote such a monastic rule. He suggested that the monks might be able to attain salvation by serving their fellow Christians occasionally instead of always running away from them. Thus, St. Basil ordered his monks to teach poor children, care for the sick, and aid orphans. St. Jerome, another famous monk, suggested that scholarly labor and study were suitable occupations that might please God along with prayer.

In the West, the community form of monasticism was always more popular than the hermit life, and the man who gave it shape was St. Benedict of Nursia, who lived from

---

* From the Greek *monazein,* meaning "to be alone" or "to live in solitude."

EDITORIAL PHOTOCOLOR ARCHIVES   Monte Casino

St. Benedict
RELIGIOUS NEWS SERVICE

about 480 to 550 A.D. After some early years of trial and experimentation, Benedict took his followers into southern Italy to the place called Monte Cassino. Here he wrote his Benedictine rule, which became the guide for monasticism for hundreds of years, and has endured down to the present.

What made Benedict's rule so successful was its moderate spirit. "Nothing too heavy or too rigorous" is the way the rule reads. Benedict knew that the average person was not capable of the heroic mortifications and extremes of the Egyptians, so he prescribed for his monks at least seven hours of sleep per day, enough food (although little meat), even small quantities of wine to drink, and a balanced program of work and prayer. The work served to make the monastery self-sufficient by providing food, building materials, and clothing. Although an abbot of a Benedictine monastery was in full charge of everything in the monastery, he too lived under the rule. The monks could own no property of their own, and they could not marry or have a family.*

Benedict, who seems to have remained a layman all his life, had no intention of en-couraging intellectual activity in the monastery. He provided for reading of Scripture and lives of saints, but nothing more. But someone had to teach novices how to read; Bibles and other books had to be copied in order to have enough to go around; and pamphlets and such things had to be written to explain theological matters and secular subjects to the monks. Therefore, it was not long before the monasteries became small-scale centers of learning. They never were intended to preserve Greco-Roman culture and education, but they did so accidentally. Because almost no one else was doing anything at all in this line, their achievement was eminently important.

Generally monks lived in the countryside. Their monasteries were not only centers of learning and prayer; they were an example to the rural population of the benefits of hard work, the Christian moral life, and the celebration of the liturgy. For many centuries the monastic orders were the chief source for the preservation of learning and Christian culture.

Sometimes, monks took on missionary activity as part of their work. The Celtic monks from Ireland were famous for this; for centuries Irish monks travelled all over Europe spreading the Gospel. (A popular but uncertain legend arose that St. Brendan even reached North America in his travels.) But the Irish monks never stayed long in one place. Unlike the Benedictines, their influence was only temporary. Even so, they contributed to the reconstruction of European society after the decline of the Roman Empire. Their courage and zeal for the faith should not be minimized; nor should their achievements.

9th Century Irish monastery   RELIGIOUS NEWS SERVICE

---

* This way of life established the pattern for all future religious orders. The vows of poverty, chastity, and obedience and the living together in a community constitute the essentials of religious life in the Western Catholic Church.

Two Giants of the Reconstruction

There were many Christians who contributed to the reconstruction of civilization after the decline of the Roman Empire in the West. Two men who contributed much to this reconstruction were Pope Leo I and Pope Gregory I. Their principal contributions were strength and leadership, the two most important ingredients in making any movement a reality.

Pope Leo I, called "the Great," was pope from 440 to 461 A.D. He was born in Tuscany, a Roman state north of the city of Rome. He was called a "true Roman" because he so well represented what Roman education and culture hoped to produce. He was very bright, very personable, very religious, and had a strength of character and determination that marked him as an unusual person. From his first days in the ministry he was entrusted with important and delicate missions to both the barbarian chieftains and the Eastern Empire leaders. He had the characteristics of a born leader: he was forceful without being arrogant, diplomatic, far-seeing, honest, and trustworthy. He could see, when others could not, what was happening to Roman civilization in the West, and knew how to cope with what was happening. When he became pope, Rome was without an effective political leader—the emperor, Valentinian III, being virtually useless as a ruler—against the invading Huns under the famous Attila.

Pope Leo took charge of the situation, and one of the historic confrontations of all time is his meeting with Attila and persuading him not to attack and destroy Rome. Leo is remembered in history for this incident, but his accomplishments as spiritual head of the entire Church and political leader of Rome are far more important. So great was Leo's influence that from his time to the present, and chiefly because of him, the papacy has occupied a unique and important place in political and religious affairs.

S GREGORIO MAGNO

Pope Gregory I, also called "the Great" by Church historians, was the second most important figure in the reconstruction of civilization during the Dark Ages. He was pope from 590 to 604 A.D. Like Leo, Gregory was well educated in the Latin classics, and like Leo, he was a born leader. Some historians have called him the most qualified man ever to be pope, combining political wisdom and spiritual depth in such harmony that he became known as the model pope —the one against whom all other popes are measured.

When he was elected pope, Rome was in a virtual shambles, its political health nearly destroyed by the barbarians and its physical health threatened by a plague. Without a good leader, Rome was in danger of becoming a second-class city. That it did not was due, in large measure, to Pope Gregory I.

Gregory, the descendant of a long line of distinguished Romans, had been prefect of Rome and a judge of criminal cases before he retired from political life to become a monk. He was a monk when he was asked to become the bishop of Rome. Reluctantly he left his monastery, but once he did he took complete charge. His experience in government enabled him to see the political problems of Rome and solve them. His experience as a monk had made him a deeply religious man, and his piety and his organizational ability enabled him to reestablish the papacy as a strong political and spiritual force. Where Leo had saved Rome from the barbarian devastation, Gregory used his position as bishop of Rome to Christianize the barbarians and begin the process of rebuilding a unified Europe.

Gregory's ability and accomplishments are without parallel in Church history. He not only enabled the transformation of society to take place, he revitalized the spiritual forces of the Church through his sermons, his letters, his commentaries, his books, and above all, through his "Gregorian chant" (or plain song, as it is known) which was the characteristic music of the Western Church for fourteen hundred years. Gregory's impact on the Church and on Western civilization was so great that his spirituality, moral force, and liturgical approaches were to be the mark of the Church during the "Ages of Faith"—the thousand years of Church life which followed his reign as pope.

A Christian Europe

The process of reconstructing a new civilization never slackened. The impact of an educated clergy and hard working, deeply spiritual monks gradually transformed the barbarian tribes into a Christian society. Eventually, a new Christian Europe burst into full bloom during the reign of Charlemagne,* king of the Franks (768–814 A.D.), the founder of both France and Germany. Although Charlemagne built on the achievements of his predecessors and of many lesser men, he towers over all other European leaders for hundreds of years. By inheritance and conquest, he ruled over more territory than any other king since the fall of Roman Empire. Yet he was more than a mere conqueror, for he worked hard to raise the cultural level of his empire and to instill a love of learning in his people. Barely able to read and write himself, he nevertheless understood that no state could last and

Charlemagne and the Scholars   BROWN BROTHERS

no people could accomplish significant deeds without education. Above all, Christianity motivated his actions, stirred his imagination, and benefited from his support.

To spread Christianity, Charlemagne conquered new pagan lands in Germany, and invaded Spain to drive back the Moslems. (See p. 113.) Typical of his times, he believed that the sword was a suitable instrument for the missioner—but not all of those who embraced Christianity at this time did so from fear of punishment.

From all over Europe Charlemagne recruited scholars wherever he could find them, and brought them to his court, where they were employed to teach others or where they were encouraged to think and write. The English Benedictine monk Alcuin was the greatest scholar whom Charlemagne encouraged, but there were dozens of others who made up the finest collection of scholars brought together anywhere in Europe for centuries. Generally they studied Scripture, or the liturgy, or the writings of St. Augustine, St. Jerome, or other Fathers of the Church. But some of them wrote fine poetry, interesting essays, books on geography, history, and even mathematics and the sciences. Whatever they did, they did it as their way of praising God and leading people to Him. It was Charlemagne who established the tradition of scholarship for which Europe is famous.

Because of his power and his huge empire, Charlemagne received the title of Roman Emperor from Pope Leo III in the year 800, when he was crowned king of the Holy Roman Empire.** So firmly was the Church still attached to the idea of Rome that the

---

* That is, Charles the Great.

** Called "holy" to indicate that it was founded as a *Christian* empire, distinct from the previous "pagan" empire. It was called "Roman" because it was viewed as the successor of the empire whose capitol had been Rome.

111

pope thought he could bestow on the Frankish king no more noble title than this. This honor implied that Charlemagne was the special protector of the papacy and of the Church. As a matter of fact, Charlemagne made serious efforts to preserve the Church's teachings free from error, and he did not hesitate to meddle, perhaps a bit too much sometimes, in church councils and debates.

It was at this time that the pope acquired his own territory, the Papal State, which he was destined to rule for over a thousand years and which survives today in the tiny remnant known as Vatican City. This came about when the pope was threatened by the Lombards, the Germanic conquerors of Northern Italy, who wanted to extend their control over all of Italy. The Byzantines still owned Italy in the sixth to eighth centuries, but at this time they were busy fighting the Moslems and could not spare soldiers or money for their western lands. They told the pope to do the best he could by himself. For a while he stalled the Lombards by diplomacy, but finally he had to have soldiers.

Charlemagne's father, Pepin the Short, listened to the pope's plea. Pope Stephen II even crossed the Alps into Frankland, the first pope ever to do this, to talk to Pepin in person. Pepin came to Italy, drove back the Lombards, and then drew up a document called the Donation of Pepin. In this document, dating from 756 A.D., the Frankish king gave the pope the lands taken from the Lombards for the pope to govern himself. This Donation marked the beginning of the Papal State. Because of renewed troubles, Charlemagne later had to repeat his father's intervention in Italy and to issue a second Donation, with an implied promise of further protection if needed.

The Europe of Charlemagne was a Christian Europe built on the principles of Christianity. Even though by our standards, Charlemagne's territory was unsophisticated and racked by political and military upheavals, it was Christian in its intent and philosophy. The Christian ideal was never reached, of course, but Europe had come a long way from the confusion, agitation, and terror that marked existence after the decline of the Roman Empire in the West. Christianity was to be confronted with other threats and challenges—the trials and difficulties of changing civilizations—but through them all, the Church kept its mission uppermost in its endeavors. Through all its ups and downs, in spite of occasionally less than inspiring leadership and the natural limitations it experiences from its members, the Church continued to try to establish the kingdom of God on earth.

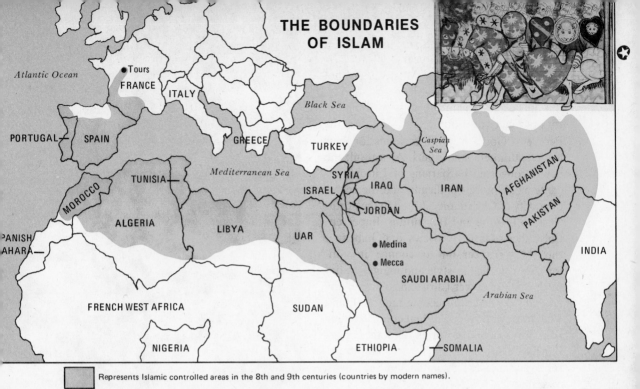

THE BOUNDARIES OF ISLAM

Atlantic Ocean

Tours
FRANCE
ITALY
Black Sea
PORTUGAL SPAIN
GREECE
TURKEY
Caspian Sea
MOROCCO
TUNISIA
Mediterranean Sea
SYRIA
ISRAEL
IRAQ
IRAN
AFGHANISTAN
ALGERIA
LIBYA
JORDAN
PAKISTAN
SPANISH SAHARA
UAR
Medina
Mecca
INDIA
SAUDI ARABIA
Arabian Sea
FRENCH WEST AFRICA
SUDAN
NIGERIA
ETHIOPIA
SOMALIA

Represents Islamic controlled areas in the 8th and 9th centuries (countries by modern names).

The Rise of Islam

One group of invaders who took possession of much former Roman territory steadfastly resisted all efforts at conversion. These were the Arabs, who had a religion and culture of their own.

By the time Mohammed was born in 571 A.D., the entire Mediterranean area was firmly Christianized. Vast areas of the inhospitable Arabian desert, however, had never experienced Christianity, just as they had never been penetrated by Greek or Roman civilization. Here wandering, primitive tribes practiced a mixture of superstition and idolatry. Then came Mohammed. He preached to them of Allah and persuaded them to accept him as their single leader. He gave them one faith and political unity for the first time.

Within a century after Mohammed's death in 632, the Arabs controlled a huge empire

along the southern shores of the Mediterranean, stretching from the Indus River Valley to the Atlantic Ocean.* Furthermore, they converted millions of people to Islam. Within this vast area, the Arabs quickly built up a flourishing culture, a mixture of the civilization of the Greek and Roman lands that they conquered, the civilizations of Persia and Mesopotamia and the religion of the Hindus. Materially and intellectually, their empire was far in advance of Europe.

For Christianity, however, Islam was a catastrophe. All the cradle lands of the Christian Faith passed under Moslem control: Palestine; Egypt that had produced great saints like Athanasius and Cyril; North Africa, the home of Augustine, Cyprian,

---

* It was descendants of these same Moslems who controlled the shipping lanes in the Mediterranean, harassed American vessels in the early 1800s, and provoked the famous line: "Millions for defense, not one cent for tribute."

Tertullian and others.* Spain too was lost, at least for the next 500 years.

Within these lands the Moslems did not deliberately set out to eradicate Christianity, but life became so hard there that Christianity practically died out. No longer could the People of God look to these lands for their leaders, thinkers, and saints. As a result the newly converted barbarians of Europe became much more significant, and the center of gravity of Christianity shifted to the northwest, to Europe and Byzantium. Imperceptibly, then, Christian views and habits of thought were certain to change in conformity with the life-style and mental equipment of these newer Christians. Christianity was also destined to become more militant. The threat of further Moslem conquest hung over Europe for centuries, and the Christians were forced to learn to defend themselves and thus to fight in the name of Christ.

Invaders from the North

If there is any part of the 500 years between the decline of the Roman Empire in the West and the emergence of a Christianized Europe that deserves to be known as the Dark Ages, it is the time from about 850 to 1000 A.D. Europe had seemed to be thoroughly rebuilt by Charlemagne's time, but his state and civilization were much more fragile than they looked. Charlemagne had accomplished much because he was a genius; his sons and grandsons were not. That was the root of the trouble.

On top of this came a second wave of barbarian invasions that struck Europe and almost completely wiped out much of the good work of the past centuries. Wild Hungarian horsemen devastated Eastern Europe. The south suffered under scattered but destructive Moslem incursions, as in the year 846, for example, when the Moslems destroyed the suburbs of Rome and looted St. John Lateran. But the most destructive

THE BETTMANN ARCHIVE

of all the barbarians were the Vikings, who swept out of Scandinavia and descended on Europe in every direction.

For over seventy-five years these Vikings preyed on Northern Europe, attacking coastal cities and villages along the great rivers in their longboats. Cities and towns were destroyed: villages of three hundred homes became ghost towns of perhaps five or six houses. Fortified cities were destroyed, great merchant ports were abandoned, monasteries were laid waste, and in-

---

* The loss of North Africa to the Moslems continues to mystify Church historians. North Africa, of all the territory invaded by non-Christians, is the only one that was not eventually re-Christianized. It remains to this day a stronghold of Islam.

tellectual ruin was added to the physical destruction when monastic libraries, art treasures, and the cultural achievements of centuries went up in flame.

Nothing was spared. Whereas in previous centuries churches and monasteries were preserved and protected, these marauders learned quickly that churches and monasteries always contained vessels of gold or silver, fine cloth, and stores of food, all of which could easily be carried off from the defenseless monks. Therefore, church property suffered especially much, and when efforts at resistance were made the invaders slaughtered anyone they could catch and burned down the buildings. Since these ecclesiastical centers were also centers of civilization, Europe experienced dreadful blows both to its faith and to its culture.

Here and there a Christian champion stemmed the tide temporarily. Alfred the Great of Wessex, for example, between 871 and 899, managed to save much of England from the Danes. Like Charlemagne he even began the reconstruction work. And in Germany Otto the Great fought the Hungarians to a standstill. But so much damage had been done, society was so badly dislocated, so much wealth had been destroyed, that it would take centuries to recover.

The End of the Third Era in Church History

The most devastating effect of the Viking invasions, however, was the fragmentation of "The Holy Roman Empire." Before the Vikings, what is now Europe was united politically and religiously. With the destruction of the churches and the monasteries and the slaughter of Christian leaders, Europe did not have bases to work from nor leaders to bring unity to society. It was a case of every man for himself.

The threat of invasion and the lack of a unified political force to deal with the invaders caused a new system of politics and landholding to arise in Europe, called feudalism, that developed somewhat spontaneously to meet the needs of the times. Feudalism put government on a personal basis between lords and vassals. Political authority split into minute fragments. Everyone who held a sizable piece of land became the ruler of that land, with only vague obligations to any superior. The common people living on the manors that became the property of the feudal lords were supposed to be protected by their lords, but many of the rough, ignorant nobles violated the rights of the serfs as often as they protected them.

The Church owned much land, and the bishops were members of the rising noble families. Inevitably, then, the Church became involved in feudalism too. Bishops and abbots became vassals of some lord as a means of holding their possessions, and they, in turn were overlords of those who were vassals to them. As vassals, however, they were obliged to fight in their lord's army, and they became involved in all the problems of government and warfare. Lords would only give power to their ecclesiastical vassals when they felt sure that they would do their feudal duty. And so the lords often simply appointed this or that faithful warrior or reliable follower to positions of leadership in the Church. As a result, the churchmen often had little time for, or interest in, their spiritual functions.

If the bishops and abbots became involved in war and politics, what happened to the clergy beneath them whom they were supposed to supervise? They became lax and disinterested. Poorly prepared candidates were ordained or received into the monasteries. Often laymen owned the right to appoint the pastor of the parish churches, and there was no one to see to it that good men got the positions. Not all of the prince

bishops or prince abbots were entirely worldly—some in fact were later canonized as saints. But even with the best of intentions, they simply did not have the opportunity to concentrate on their spiritual work. A pattern in both church and state had been established in which the ruler's will was everything, and some bishops of the system, who combined religious, military, and civil power into one force, were often brutal, licentious, illiterate barons who took over a territory, and appointed abbots and influential clerics cut from the same cloth as they.

Even the papacy became involved in the general decline, because the pope had to govern the Papal State. It quickly became evident that this entailed many nonspiritual duties. Since the papacy was a political power, greedy noblemen schemed to get control of the papacy by securing it for their children or relatives. Teenage popes and corrupt politicians in ecclesiastical positions let church matters slide, and the rivalries among the military aristocracy in Italy to control the papacy became notorious. Good men were murdered, reformers were run out of town, and pious, sincere people were at the mercy of the tyrants.

Everywhere there was corruption and decline. Christianity seemed to provide little leadership for society. Instead, society and the world and its problems seemed to overwhelm Christianity.

Yet somehow, the Church survived. It survived because there had always been in the community of Christian believers people who are sensitive to the message of Jesus. These people—many good popes, many good bishops, dedicated monks, and a vast number of lay people who retained a strong religious sense—understood the meaning of religion and worked for the reform of the Church.

It was in them that the Christian message survived, and it was from them that the Church was to receive its strength.

1. Why were the second 500 years of the time after Christ called "The Dark Ages" of Western civilization?

2. Select one of the barbarian invasions as the subject for a lengthy report. Be prepared to make an oral presentation with names, places, and a map. In the oral report, mention at least three of the other invasions giving the movements of the tribes, some of their customs, and what happened to them.

3. Check the map on page 100 and be prepared to chart the general movements of the migrating tribes.

4. Describe the difference between the Eastern and Western Church situation during the time of the collapse of the Roman Empire in the West.

5. In an encyclopedia or good resource book, find what causes are given for the collapse of Roman power in the West.

6. What double task faced the Western Church when the Roman Empire in the West succumbed to invading tribes?

7. If your ancestors are from one of the European countries, prepare a special report on the Christianization of that part of Europe from which they came. Include both your mother's and your father's ancestors' countries.

8. What effect did the barbarian cultures have on the Western expression of Christianity?

9. Prepare a report on Western monasticism as it was lived in the first 700 years of Christendom.

10. Look up the legend of Pope Leo's meeting with Attila.

11. What is "Gregorian chant"? Look up its history, and, if you can, bring an example of this plain song to class.

12. What role did Popes Leo I and Gregory I play in setting the tone and character of the papacy? How did each approach the task of preserving and developing Christianity?

13. What role did Clovis, Pepin, and Charlemagne play in the development of a new civilization in Europe?

14. Prepare a linear chart giving the names and dates of important people mentioned in the last two chapters.

15. Prepare a report on Vatican City giving its origin, development, present dimensions, and what it now contains.

Catholic Church - west.
Roman C. C - affairs of Christianity.
western - Islamic, eastern

117

16. Look up information on Mohammed and the origins of Islam. How far into Christian territories did the Moslems move and what has been the greatest effect of Islam on Christianity?

17. Why was the second invasion by the barbarians worse than the first?

18. What effect did the invasions by the Vikings have on the political situation in what is now Europe? What effect did it have on the Church?

19. What is feudalism? Prepare a report on a typical overlord-vassal relationship around the year 1000 A.D.

20. Write a short report on the Christianity as it developed in the second half of the first 1000 years of Christianity.

21. Discuss what kept Christianity alive in Europe during the Dark Ages.

10 Medieval Christianity

**Western Civilization
becomes Christian
in Philosophy and Practice**

By the year 1000 A.D. the split of what we might call the Christian sphere of influence into three parts (Eastern, Islamic, and Western) was a matter of practical reality. From this time on, the term "Catholic Church," for all practical purposes, meant the *Western* Christian Church, and the affairs of Christendom were described by historians in terms of what eventually became known as the *Roman* Catholic Church.

This terminology is important for students of history to remember for it will help them to understand Church history as it is written by Western Christians, and will enable them to appreciate the richness and autonomy of both the Eastern Christian Churches and the Islamic spheres of influence as well.

It must also be remembered that beyond the borders of these three areas there were other civilizations, such as the Indian, the Chinese, and the African, as well as the vast areas of the yet undiscovered Americas and Oceania. People living in these areas had their own cultures and their own religions, and were progressing at their own rate toward their particular level of civilization.

Be that as it may, for the purposes of this book, the Church history being presented is the history of the Western Christian Church because that is the history of the Church in whose traditions we have been raised. Therefore, when we speak of "The history of the Church," or "The emerging Church," we are speaking of the history of the Church in Western Europe and in America.*

By the year 1000 A.D., Europe was again "Catholic," except for pockets of non-Christianized people, for example, in Spain and Portugal, which were almost completely under Moslem control. Most Europeans professed to believe in the doctrines of the Church and followed the liturgy of the Western Church. Most philosophical, literary, and artistic expressions were Christian in subject and tone, and moral conduct was measured by its conformity to Christian standards of morality. How did this happen, when so much of society's leadership was morally corrupt and there was so much suffering and injustice experienced by the average person? What forces did God put in motion to rescue His people from the forces of evil which threatened to engulf them? There were five: the Church's influence in morals, the reform of monasticism, a revitalized papacy, the new religious orders which sprang up to meet new religious needs of society, and the appearance of the "prophet of the intellect," St. Thomas Aquinas.

The Church's Influence in Morals

In spite of the general malaise that afflicted Christianity just prior to the year 1000 A.D. (brought on by the moral corruption of many persons in positions of leadership in politics and the Church), there were many good people dedicated to Christian living and worship, and some good leaders who recognized the need for reform in society's high places.

The reform began where it would be most effective: in the moral life of the feudal lords. Slowly but surely, and always with the realities of the possible in mind, reform leaders passed laws which, over the long haul, would affect the course of society. They did not expect instant perfection nor instant conformity; they hoped only to move society toward the ideal, step-by-step, by removing the most serious causes of evil first, then by promoting the good which would result from the change.

The Second Barbarian Invasions had spawned political corruption, almost incessant war, murderous feuds, vendettas, mass murders, banditry, hatred, violence, rather wholesale destruction, widespread and constant fear, and a kind of caste system that kept the majority of people virtually enslaved. It was these evils that the Church attempted to correct first. How it did is described by Henri Daniel-Rops, the prizewinning French historian in his classic works on the history of the Church.

In the year 1000 there was yet another quarter of the sky where dawn appeared, faintly, dimly, but full of promise; a quarter in which the night had seemed darkest, that of morals. Here we can best study the determi-

Council of Clermont

EDITORIAL PHOTOCOLOR ARCHIVES

gration of the Carolingian Empire would be solved. In spite of appearances, the Church would never allow the bases of civilization, with which she was entrusted, to dissolve in a sea of barbarism.

She began by continually insisting upon the evangelical principles. Look at any of the canons of any Council held between 900 and 1050, and you will find that they contain excellent provisions with a truly Christian ring. Were they voices crying in the desert? Certainly not. When a bishop or a monk told a prince that his sole duty was 'not to allow the continued existence in his realm of any iniquity,' the person addressed fully admitted that he was right, even though in practice he behaved himself otherwise. A profound observation of Hugh Capet deserves to be quoted: 'The sublimity of our devotions is of no avail unless we render justice by all means and to all men.' Vast numbers of the great feudal lords said and thought likewise; it was highly significant that, even when violated in fact, the principles of charity and justice were admitted by all as superior.

The Church did not limit herself to this Platonic reminder. By every means at her disposal she tried to act. Homicide, that plague of the 'Dark Ages', in which human life counted for so little, she denounced unmercifully; no Council ignored it or failed to chastise those guilty of a crime that had at all costs to be prevented. The Church was well aware that she possessed a weapon capable of subduing those souls which, however gross, were still subject to the dictates of religion. She was the

nation of the Church and her fidelity to the message of Christ. In the savage world of nascent feudalism, where, as one preacher said, 'men have claws and live with the wild beasts,' she alone was prepared to recall the existence of certain higher principles. Despite the evils to which she was herself a prey, she applied herself to this task and, small results notwithstanding, would not be discouraged.

About the year 1000 it became certain that the grave problem which had faced Europe since the disinte-

121

guardian of oaths; she gave a solemn character to those which the warriors swore to their suzerain, and she had more than once to remind a vassal that such undertakings must be treated as sacred. Could she not use the same method to enforce obedience to her principles?

It was in answer to this question that there were born, during the tenth century, those magnificent ideals in which were founded the grandeur of the Middle Ages—*the Peace and Truce of God.* It is a splendid thought that the primary purpose of the Church was to protect from unbridled force those humble, weak, and insignificant folk who could not defend themselves. Never perhaps in the history of this age did Mother Church reveal herself as so truly a mother. The crusade for peace dates chiefly from the Council of Charroux, on 1st June 989, and from that of Puy-en-Velay in the following year. Those Councils inveighed, in noble language, against the excesses of violence and denounced as sacrilegious any scoundrel who destroyed or stole the goods of the poor. Very soon, and almost everywhere, the Church introduced treaties of peace to which the feudal lords swore obedience by solemn oath. This oath was first exacted at Verdun-sur-Saône in 1016. Resistance was inevitable: noblemen fought shy, even such bishops as Gerard of Cambrai (1013–51), a too faithful servitor of princes, would not take it, rejecting, as they said, the necessity of excommunicating too many barons! This striving after peace, in a society that loved war, was a splendid dream, perhaps an

example of midsummer madness, and certainly a paradox; but at least it expressed a justifiable Christian hope that would spread gradually throughout the world.

It is necessary to distinguish within this great movement two separate institutions: the *Peace of God* and the *Truce of God.* The express purpose of the first was to protect the clergy, the poor, and their property, in fact to limit the havoc that might be caused by outbreaks of violence. The text of the oath of Verdun-sur-Saône, very precise and amusing in its details, states the matter clearly. The influence of the assembled bishops had to be such that the secular lords would be ready to take the oath of peace, and indeed many of them took it. Sanctions were provided against those who violated their oath, even going so far as to impose an interdict on the whole region within which the breach had occurred: no public masses, no baptisms, marriages, burials, or sounding of bells. . . . This movement towards peace, starting from Auvergne and Poitou, gradually extended to the whole of France. We may guess it was welcomed by the people, and Raoul Glaber says: 'Those present at the Council shouted with joy: Peace! Peace! Peace! symbol of the everlasting alliance that had been made with God!' Towards the middle of the eleventh century the movement extended beyond the Rhine, the Alps, and the Pyrenees; it was favoured almost everywhere by kings, who realized that this invention of the bishops would help to control the anarchical tendencies of feudalism. Thus Robert the Pious, in France,

2nd century fresco figures from the catacomb of Lucina, Rome.

7th century mosaics decorate the Church of San Apollinare Nuovo, Ravenna, Italy.

Christian Art through the Ages

Detail from altar frontal, *The Life of the Virgin,* in Barcelona, 13th century.

Tympanum over main portal of Cathedral of St. Maurice
in Angers, France, 12th century.

Rose window in
Cathedral of Chartres,
13th century.

Entrance into Jerusalem by Giotto,
a 14th century Florentine painter.

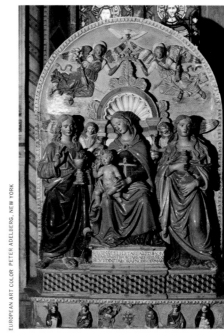

Virgin and Child, a polychrome
by Robbia, a 15th century
Florentine artist.

Supper at Emmaus by Rembrandt,
a 17th century Dutch painter.

The Agony in the Garden by Gauguin,
an early 20th century French painter.

Contemporary New York setting
highlights primitive *Madonna and Child.*

wished the conciliar decrees to have the force of law. Was he not dreaming of a universal peace? Did he not speak of it seriously to the German emperor Henry II when they met at the Council of Ivois in 1021? In 1023 the Emperor Henry III promulgated a 'day of indulgence' (an amnesty), undertook not to seek vengeance for wrongs suffered by him, and invited all rulers to do likewise. Such trends of thought indicated well enough that all was by no means lost in that age of darkness. On the one hand there was perpetual war, shedding of blood on the slightest pretext or none, and the horrors of invasion and famine. On the other there were generous attempts to secure a more happy state of affairs. Hope remained of better things to come.

A second step towards the realization of this ideal was the *Truce of God,* the *treuga Dei,* which had a different end in view. The 'Peace of God' was intended only to protect the helpless from the sufferings of war; the Truce forbade war itself within certain periods of time. It was first suggested in 990 by Pope *John XV* (988–96), during the conflict between the Duke of Normandy and

the King of England, but without success. In 1017, at Elne, the episcopal city near Perpignan, a synod ruled that all military operations should cease 'from the ninth hour of Saturday until the first hour of Monday.' Twenty-four years later, when the great famine of 1041 had terrified the hearts of men, the Council of Nice went further and ordained an absolute truce from Wednesday evening to Monday morning. The good bishops who made this wise decision explained why those four days should be days of peace: Thursday because of our Lord's Ascension, Friday because of His Passion, Saturday because of His burial, and Sunday because of His Resurrection. With a little care it might have been possible to celebrate every day of the week in this manner! Their example was followed. In some dioceses the Truce was extended to two great parts of the liturgical cycle, Advent and Lent; elsewhere it ran from the Rogations to the octave of Pentecost. Certain feasts of our Lady and the vigils of ember days were also to be observed in peace. In 1054 the Council of Narbonne would codify all these regulations. While the Truce of God spread in northern France, then to Liége, Rhenish Germany, England, Italy, and Spain, the Papacy took up this initiative by associating it with a new purpose.

In practice what were the results of this fine teaching? Not many, to judge by appearances. The threat of excommunication did not suffice to prevent brutal excesses. The eleventh century still wallowed in blood and violence. The chronicler Lambert of Waterloo, for example, states that his father's ten brothers were killed on one day in a private war against a neighbouring lord! Nor was this case unique. To strive for peace and brotherhood had never been an easy task. It sometimes happened that such attempts had consequences exactly opposite to those intended. For example, Aimo, Archbishop of Bourges, had, in 1038, instituted a 'militia of peace,' composed of volunteers who would punish those lords who violated the Truce of God and who in fact, so it seems, did chastise quite a number of them; but after some time this pious militia began to imitate those whom it pretended to attack, and committed innumerable depredations for which, according to the *Miracles of St Benedict,* God punished it by causing their utter defeat at the hands of a better armed force. But, however slight the results may now appear, the creation of these pacific institutions was important: what progress may not such good intentions have effected in the human soul? . . .

There is another point of view from which we can observe the Church's influence upon morals. She offered men of humble conditions a means of rising to the top. Adalbero, Archbishop of Rheims, says in his famous *Satirical Poem:* 'The divine law recognizes no distinction in nature among ministers of the Church. She grants them all an equal status, however unequal they may be by rank and birth; in her eyes the son of an artisan is not inferior to the heir of a monarch.' Nor was this assertion merely theoretical: on episcopal and abbatial thrones, even on the very throne of Peter, we find both princes and men of the common people. St Peter Damian, as a boy, had herded swine, and in his youth Gerbert, the great Pope Sylvester II, had been a shepherd. The Church thus helped, in feudal society, to preserve for those who could not attain to nobility by force of arms the indispensable opportunity of personal success; and this made possible a constant renewal of the upper ranks.

The same conception of Christian equality before God induced her also to fight for that most oppressed of all classes, the *serfs.* True, serfdom was not slavery as known to the ancient world; beginning in the fifth century, its evolution was now complete. The slave was treated as a chattel; the serf was a man possessing family, hearth, and property. He was 'tied to the land,' of which, however, he could not be deprived. But certain limitations restricting his freedom appeared more grievous, notably the law which forbade him to marry a woman belonging to a different lord, i.e. outside his master's own fief. The Church fought vigorously against this rule which affected family freedom; numerous councils and synods concerned themselves therewith, and during the tenth century a custom arose of allowing a serf to marry outside the fief on his paying a fine for having, by marriage in another fief, 'lessened' his master's estate. The Church went much further in this matter of equality. She demanded for serfs the same liberty as that enjoyed by other peasants. . . .

A profound social transformation was on the way.*

_____

* Henri Daniel-Rops, *The Church in The Dark Ages,* pp. 330–335.

The Reform of Monasticism

As often happens, God inspires someone with an idea that, if carried out, affects an entire society or even a whole civilization. Such was the idea that inspired the founding of the abbey of Cluny (in 910 A.D.) in south central France in the province of Burgundy. This monastery stood out like a beacon amid the general political and religious corruption that infected Europe in the tenth century. Like the reform in the moral life of the people, the reform in monasticism initiated by the monks of Cluny enabled Western civilization to move from the barbarism of the feudal period to the Christian expression of what it means to be human.

Many of the monasteries which had played so vital a role in rebuilding civilization after the fall of the Roman Empire in the West fell victim to the abuses of the feudal system. Because each monastery was autonomous, it depended for its life on the local feudal lord in whose territory it was. Many times feudal lords appointed corrupt cronies, or inept or irreligious relatives, to the post of abbot and prior, the two most important posts in a monastery. When this happened, the religious life of the monastery came to a virtual standstill and its public image and effect faded.

There were, of course, good monasteries, but because they were isolated from each other and had no common purpose or government, their overall effect was limited. When monasticism was at its lowest ebb, God inspired William, Duke of Aquitaine, to deed some of his land to a monk, Berno, the abbot of a monastery in Baume, for a new monastery. Berno brought twelve good monks with him and began a monastery of strict observance of the Benedictine rule. In a surprisingly short time, it gained a reputation for being what a monastery should be.

Three things enabled Cluny to become

THE BETTMANN ARCHIVE

the center for monastic reform. The first was its total dedication to a religious life whose center was the liturgy. Every action of a monk's life in Cluny was directed to the praise and worship of God through private prayer and meditation and the solemn celebration of the Eucharist carried out with all the perfection possible. The second was its form of government. Instead of being subject to an abbot who might be the tool of some feudal lord, Cluny was under the direct supervision of the pope—the abbot being only the delegate of the pope. (Fortunately, there were only six abbots in 250 years, and every one of them was a truly religious, highly organized person dedicated totally to the ideal of monasticism.) This centralization of authority under the pope took the monastery out of the jurisdiction of a feudal lord or a feudal bishop, and, when more "daughter monasteries" sprang up, each subject to the pope, a group of interrelated monasteries uncontrolled by local authority was established.*

The third thing which made Cluny the center of reform for civilization in the tenth century was the dedication of its monks to the gospel idea of charity. Not only was there a new spirit of fellowship in the monastery, this spirit was carried over to the poor, the sick, and the unfortunate in the lands surrounding the monastery. Every day, hundreds of poor were fed from the resources garnered from the monks' well-kept farms, the sick were cared for, and travelers were housed. No one was turned away, and every person was treated with respect and courtesy, the so-called "least deserving" receiving special attention. Because the people experienced the effect of a truly lived religious life, they, too, began to devote themselves to living in charity.

So great was the fame of Cluny that its abbot was called on to assist in the reform of other monasteries and to help in the training of the local clergy. Experienced, dedicated monks were sent from Cluny to help in the reform of monastic life, and others went out to start other monasteries in the image of Cluny. Because the reformed monasteries and the new ones were all closely associated with and subject to Cluny, a network of reformed monasteries sprang up all devoted to the expression of monasticism in its best form. The Cluny approach to monastic life affected the religious life of all the people because the monks, noted for their piety and learning, and the local clergy, trained by the monks of Cluny, dedicated their lives to upgrading the material, moral, and liturgical life of the people. The influence of Cluny on the development of the Christian life that flourished in the next four centuries is immeasurable. "Cluny," said a

---

* There were over 300 monasteries attached to Cluny at one period of its history.

Daily Life in the Monastery

During the Twelfth Century there were more than 2000 monasteries in Europe all following to a greater or lesser degree the Rule of St. Benedict. The life of a monk was controlled and directed to achieve the purpose of the monastery: the praise of God removed from the turmoil of the world. Daily life in the monastery consisted in:

Rising between 1:30–2:30 A.M.
Community prayer highlighted by the community Mass
Community meeting for reading the Rule, commentary on the Rule by the abbot, and discussions on the business of the monastery
Work in the fields or at special jobs for about six hours per day, interrupted by community prayer about every hour or so
Private devotions and Scripture study for about four hours per day
Final Divine Office sung before retirement
Retire at dark

There was one main meal per day consisting of fish, vegetables, bread, and a beverage. Meat was served only rarely and then only to the sick. Two other sparse meals were served in most monasteries usually consisting of nothing more than bread and a beverage.

noted French writer-historian, "was the new force, pure and relentless, that was to smash the decaying framework of Christian society, and despite simoniacal and immoral bishops, to introduce everywhere the reign of virtue. . . ."

The Revitalized Papacy

The third force in the Church which contributed to the development of Western civilization and the expression of Christianity for over five hundred years was the revitalization of the papacy. The popes of the eleventh, twelfth, and thirteenth centuries were of a far higher caliber than many popes of the preceding two centuries. Many of them, due to the influence of the monasteries in education, were men of piety, learning, intelligence, and vigor. Following the example of men like Leo IX (1049) who had been a monk of Cluny, men like Gregory VII (1073), Urban II (1088), Alexander III (1159), and Innocent III (1198) were giants of the medieval period who not only revitalized the papacy; but who also had tremendous influence in shaping the political, economic, and social life of medieval Europe.

For a long time, the papacy had been in a state of eclipse. Various feudal lords and powerful Roman families tried to make the pope their own vassal (as they had done with local bishops), and more often than not they succeeded. For some years the papacy was bought and sold by various Roman noble families, and at one time, three men claimed the papacy as their family right. So intense were the rivalries for the office of bishop of Rome that murder, torture, exile, and imprisonment were used to get a favorite "elected" pope. At one period, the average reign of a pope was a bit less than three

Lateran IV convened by Innocent III

years! During this time the papacy exercised little effective control and almost no influence outside of Rome itself. The pope was still head of the Church—virtually no one in the West denied that—but in practice it meant little.

Beginning with Leo IX and the reform popes, however, the papacy rapidly developed a big centralized government that took more and more of the affairs of the Church into its hands. If decentralization had been the cause of the long period of decline, the popes now felt that the new momentum toward improvement could best be maintained by a highly centralized government. And so they tightened their hold over the bishops, who were summoned to Rome frequently or kept in line by the pope's ambassadors who traveled all about Europe to keep in touch with things. The right to issue significant indulgences and to canonize saints was taken from the bishops and reserved for the pope. The pope's court became a supreme court, to which cases could be appealed from the diocesan courts. The popes launched the crusading movement and granted special papal protection and privileges to all who took the cross. They started to tax bishops and dioceses, and to punish recalcitrant clergy and nobles by excommunications and other penalties. Ecumenical Councils were summoned in Rome so that the popes could play a prominent part in their deliberations—a very different situation from that of the Councils of the primitive Church when the popes deliberately stayed away.

In the area of Church-state relationships, the strong popes of the period initiated moves to curb the power of the rulers of the emerging states of Europe in both religious and secular affairs. The ensuing struggles, in which the popes were most often victorious, enhanced the prestige and power of the papacy, but resulted, finally, in the troubles of the fifteenth and sixteenth centuries which destroyed the unity of Christianity in the West. For the moment, however, the strength of the papacy at this time in history played a necessary role in shaping Western civilization. Without it, the economic, political, social, religious, and cultural gains of the next era of Western civilization would not have been achieved.

The New Religious Orders

Out of the reform movement came a great increase in vocations to the monastic life, and many different kinds of monastic orders were founded. Like the Cluniac order, many of these new groups used versions of the ancient Benedictine rule. The Cistercians, whose most prominent member was St. Bernard of Clairvaux, became especially numerous during the twelfth century. Other new monastic orders were the Carthusians, and the Premonstratensians or Norbertines.

Monasticism was a very flexible institution; it could be shaped to meet many different kinds of needs. That it did so is proof of the continued vitality of monasticism. As long as it responded to the needs of the people, it flourished. Nowhere is this more evident than in the establishment of the mendicant orders of friars during the thirteenth century—Dominicans, Franciscans, Augustinians, and Carmelites.

Three features distinguished the mendicants* from the older orders. One was their place of operation. The Benedictines, Cistercians, and others had always considered their ideal to be withdrawal from the world, isolation from the larger society, and concentration on their own spiritual perfection. In the days when most of Europe's population lived in manors and villages scattered all around the countryside, this monastic practice had the effect of keeping before the people examples of dedication to Christian renunciation and spiritual perfection. However, from the eleventh century on, towns began to spring up everywhere, then to grow into cities, and then to keep on expanding. More and more, the people of Europe began to live in closer contact with each other, often in tightly packed areas with little privacy and with all the hustle and bustle of shops and trading centers. The mendicant orders were founded specifically to serve the people of these crowded centers. The ideal of these "new monks" was not to get away from society, it was to become involved with the people in society. This made the mendicant orders revolutionary.

The second thing that distinguished the mendicants from the monastic monks was their reliance for their livelihood on the gifts of the people among whom they worked. The monastic monks had a self-contained society; they produced what they needed. The mendicants depended on alms. Inevitably, this led to abuses in the next period of civilization, but the idea was to make the mendicants servants of the people.

The third difference between the mendicants and the monks was in the makeup of the community. The mendicant orders were more democratic than the monastics; they accepted almost anyone from any class among the people they served. Previously, many monasteries preferred to have noblemen or people of higher rank rather than peasants as recruits. If they did accept "commoners," they were generally assigned to lower positions in the monastery. By accepting people from all ranks of society, the mendicant orders tapped a pool of previously neglected talent. Within a few years, the mendicant orders surpassed the monastic orders in numbers and influence—they became a common part of the medieval society.

A whole host of small religious orders for men and for women grew up in Western Europe who vowed themselves to poverty, chastity, obedience, and specific charitable works. They cared for the poor, widows, and orphans, and opened hospitals for the seriously sick. They taught school, preached, gathered people into pious societies, and formed organizations whose purpose was to upgrade the religious life of the people. Some men formed themselves into religious

---

* From the Latin expression for begging or living on alms.

CONTEMPORARY CHRISTIAN ART

groups of soldiers whose purpose was to protect people from roving groups of bandits, invasions from the seas, and the violence that flared up between competing lords and nobles.

The two most successful of the new religious orders were the Order of Preachers (called Dominicans* after their founder, St. Dominic) who concentrated on preaching and teaching, and the Friars Minor, popularly known as Franciscans.

St. Dominic, a Spanish priest (1170–1221 A.D.), disturbed by the influence a heretical sect (the Albigensians) had on the peasants of southern France, organized a group of priests who went into the area to influence the people through the holiness of their lives and their learning. At first they were only a confederation of interested priests, then they organized themselves under Dominic into a congregation. Finally they became a reli-

---

* Some say that they are so called because they are the *domini canes,* that is, "watchdogs of the Lord."

gious order approved by the Pope in 1217 A.D. They were the first group to give attention strictly to the study of theology for the purpose of preaching. So famous did they become that the major intellectual effort of the medieval period was Dominican-led.

The other great order to spring up at this time, the Franciscans, was started by John Bernardoni (1182–1226), a young man of Assisi who was nicknamed "Francis" (*Frenchman*) because of his early imitation of French ways, manners, customs, and language.

Italian Christianity was in a state of serious moral decay in the twelfth century, and John Bernardoni was an example of the typical adolescent of his time. He was witty, talented, and high strung. By the time he was twenty, he was easily the most popular person in Assisi.

He gave up a promising career in his father's prosperous business and, appalled by the conditions of the poor, the sick, and the unhappy drifters he saw everyday, decided to dedicate himself to the ideal of the Christian life as he saw it come through the pages of the gospel. He gathered a few of his friends, persuaded them to his way of thinking, and determined "to preach by his actions." His few followers formed themselves into a group they called the "Friars Minor"* in protest against the worldly ways of some of the wandering friars of the time. In 1208 A.D. they received approval from the pope. From that time on the Franciscans, as they were later called, grew to become the most popular and most widely known religious order the Church has even seen. They exerted tremendous influence in the medieval society in which they lived.

From these two religious orders came literally dozens of others.** By their twin assault on the evils of the time—ignorance and immorality—the Dominicans and the Franciscans were a unique force for the transformation of medieval society.

THE BETTMANN ARCHIVE

Thomas Aquinas, Prophet of the Intellect

A major development of the medieval period was the rise of the universities. From them came the "new" philosophy and theology, which in turn created the period in history known as "The Renaissance" which developed chiefly in Italy in the latter half of the five hundred year period from 1000–1500 A.D.

Centers of learning had always been a part of civilization, but the growth of learning complexes called universities really became a major part of Western civilization during the medieval period when population centered in the towns. Important schools

---

* From the Latin term for small or of relatively little importance.

** There have been hundreds of congregations based upon the Rule of St. Francis.

arose in every major town, and each vied with the other for fame. All had the usual colleges, but each seemed to specialize or become famous in a particular area, and each had its famous master or principal teacher. At the same time new interest was aroused in the philosophy taught by the famous Moslem scholars, the philosophy based upon the Moslem "discovery" of the works of Aristotle, one of the most famous of all the ancient Greek philosophers.

Western Christendom had lived comfortably under the influence of St. Augustine's interpretation of history presented in his *City of God*. His views pointed unmistakably to heaven. In the eleventh and twelfth centuries, Aristotle's philosophy—which pictured "heaven" as the life of a good person here on earth, "God" as the ultimate good, and morality as the possession of human virtue—threatened to replace the Augustinian philosophy under which Europe had lived.

Intellectual battles raged, and while the other avenues of learning (the *trivium:* grammar, logic, and rhetoric, and the *quadrivium:* arithmetic, music, geometry, and astronomy) flourished, a theological philosophy and a philosophical theology were the characteristic phenomena of the age. Some scholars dismissed Aristotle's views as trash, some as trivia, and some as contradictory of much that was known. By far the larger number, however, considered his ideas dangerous and a threat to the whole of society. Fortunately, however, the great thinkers of the time, like St. Anselm (1033–1109) and Peter Abelard (1079–1142), and later St. Albert (1193–1280) and St. Thomas Aquinas (1225–1274), saw Aristotle's philosophy as a boon to medieval learning and set out to champion it.

St. Thomas Aquinas was the brilliant son of a nobleman of Italy, the nephew of the Holy Roman Emperor, and the cousin of Frederick II. His family position offered him almost unlimited opportunity for prestige and wealth. When he was fifteen, he shocked his family by wanting to join the Dominicans, a new religious order with no prestige, no land holdings and, apparently, no future. He became a Dominican anyway.

This extraordinary intellectual genius ("the brightest mind in the history of Western civilization") did for his age—and the following 700 years—what Augustine had done for his. Thomas was essentially a teacher at the University of Paris, but he was also a prolific writer and adviser to men in every walk of life. His reputation as teacher made him one of the most respected men of his time; his reputation as philosopher-theologian as presented in his writing made him one of history's most respected thinkers.

Thomas' greatest work, the *Summa Theologiæ,** is a monument of learning. It has been called the most comprehensive book ever written. Basically, it is supposed to be a summary of or introduction to theology. *Actually, it is a synthesis of much of the learning of the time, directed to theology.*

Thomas came on the scene at the height of the university battles about Aristotle's philosophy. He saw it, not as a threat, but as a means to a whole new understanding of the faith. Just as Augustine's *City of God* showed that history had an explanation in faith, Thomas' *Summa Theologiæ* showed that faith had its foundation in reason. **Augustine made sense out of history; Aquinas made sense out of faith.**

Thomas started out with the idea of giving his students a concise and systematic body of teaching in the light of the "new" philosophy. He wound up with the most monumental philosophical-theological work ever produced. He did not set out to "prove"

---

* That is, *Summary of Theology.*

the faith. It was *there,* hence it deserved an examination in the light of reason. In effect, Thomas showed that it made sense to believe. He tried (and succeeded) to explain the phenomenon of faith in the light of what a person can reason to. In this attempt, he systematized learning and, using what data was already available, focused his attention on the object of faith: God.

[In the *Summa*] God, the object of all theology, is present in every chapter; He alone is always in question, directly or indirectly. In the First Part He is studied as *Being,* first in Himself—the One and Triune God—then outside Himself as principle, i.e., in so far as He can be known in His Works (God the creator and ruler of the world) and through the behaviour of the spiritual and temporal universe, including man. The Second Part treats of God as the *Good,* i.e., as the end of rational creatures; and this leads the author to examine not only human acts and passions, but also the principles of conduct, the law by which God teaches us, and the grace by which He assists us. Then, viewing together those moral obligations to which man must submit if he is to attain God, St. Thomas analyzes the virtues (theological, cardinal, and human) together with the vices opposed to them. This leads him to conclude by analyzing various ways of life and those gifts which enable us to practise virtue and avoid vice. Finally, in the Third Part, he meant to show God as the *Way,* not only for man as such, abstract and theoretical, but for *fallen* man, a creature of sinful flesh, but redeemed by Christ's Incarnation and Sacrifice.*

This great genius died at the height of his career (he was forty-nine) with much of his work still unfinished. What he did do in a relatively short span (from 1251 to 1274 A.D.) was to examine the Mystery of Christ in the light of his own culture and civilization and to give Western Christendom a new understanding of itself. His works remained as *the* classical work in Catholic philosophy and theology until the rise of modern science and the evolutionary theory raised questions for which a new style of answer was needed.**

An Age of Faith

The forces of good which changed the barbarism of the Dark Ages into the civilization of the medieval period of Western civilization produced, in the twelfth and thirteenth centuries, what many historians call "An Age of Faith." Almost every aspect of human activity in that period in the West was permeated by the faith of Christianity. People were not perfect, by any means, but they were willing, at least, to govern their lives by the principles of Christianity.

In economics, people tried to understand how the principles of Christian justice applied to the growing problems of commerce. In literature, whatever they wrote about— adventure, Knights of the Round Table, love or war—the Christian ideals of salvation and the redemptive action of Christ provided the norms that controlled human activity. When

---

* Henri Daniel-Rops, *Cathedral and Crusade,* Vol. II, D154B, pp. 40–41.

** See pp. 201 ff. for a description of the work of the Jesuit priest-scientist, Father Teilhard de Chardin.

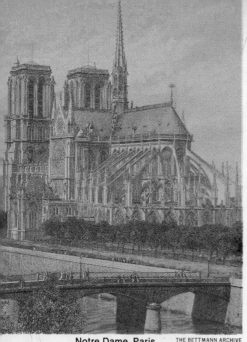

Notre Dame, Paris

Cologne Cathedral

the guilds were formed to serve as social organizations as well as to protect the craftsmen, they always had the religious welfare of their members as part of their program.

Almost all the art and building of this period was associated with the faith in some way or other. This was partly due to the fact that the Church was the only institution with sufficient funds to erect huge structures or to buy statues, stained glass windows, or pictures. But it was also due to the fundamental faith of the people that they cooperated in the building of the great cathedrals that sprang up all over Europe at this time.* Gothic architecture, which was the style used, symbolized by its pointed arches and upward-reaching buttresses the eternal struggle of people to reach heaven.

Even medieval warfare felt the influence

---

* So popular did cathedral building become in France that 500 major churches were built between 1170 and 1270 A.D. The greatest of these is at Chartres which was consecrated in 1260 A.D. after 100 years of building. During this time it is estimated that 1587 churches were built in France alone!

Great Door of the Cathedral, Beauvais

of Christianity. The Church tried to check the numerous petty but costly wars of the troublesome feudal nobles, as we noted on page 122, by customs such as the Peace of God, which insisted that noncombatants should not be harmed, or the Truce of God, which stipulated that fighting should be suspended during sacred seasons and on holydays. When fighting could not be prevented altogether, theologians tried to determine when wars were justified and under what conditions they might be carried on.

The crusades* were a special kind of medieval warfare. They had as their aim the recovery of the Holy Land from the Moslems. Their justification rested on the medieval belief that it was permissible to kill people of other faiths for "the Faith." Such standards are regarded as barbarous and intolerant today, and we thoroughly reject the idea that motivated them. But it is a fact that they did truly believe that they were serving God by killing non-Christians, and that because of this belief medieval Christians were willing to run the risk of being killed themselves.

To understand this aspect of history, you must look at these "Holy Wars" with the eyes of those living at the time. From the point of view of historical analysis, it does no real good to decry the horrors of war, and the treachery, the self-seeking, and chicanery

of selfish men who, at any period in history, exploit a situation for their own ends. Neither does it do any good to glorify a horrible period regardless of the motives of those who engaged in its treachery. Further, as any student of history knows, what may be done for a perfectly good end, may be the very worst thing that could happen.

The Crusades must be looked at dispassionately. Often those who write about them do so from a point of view that brings out their own bias. To those engaged in them, they may be holy wars; those who are on the receiving end are persecuted. For example, for the Romans, the classic persecutions were holy wars; for Christians they were "the Roman Persecutions." The Mohammedans engaged in holy wars for Allah; on these occasions the Christians saw themselves as persecuted. The Crusades were initiated "for the Holy Cross"; those being attacked were of a different mind.

---

* Meaning, literally, "for the Cross."

At the time of the Crusades, Western Christians looked upon them as the only means to rescue the Holy Places (in Palestine) from the Moslems. The first waves of the armies recruited throughout Europe moved toward Constantinople and Jerusalem in 1097 and 1098 A.D. They succeeded in capturing Antioch and Jerusalem and setting up Western states for a short period of time. But the Moslems looked upon their own efforts to recapture these territories as holy wars too (Mohammed's "Holy Hill" was in Jerusalem). Battles raged for more than two centuries. Great and good men on both sides championed their causes; but the fact remains that the Crusades in the East were a dismal failure, and contain some of the blackest pages in Western Christian history.

If anything good came from the Crusades, it was the exposure of Western Christians to other cultures. The circumstances of the period from 500 to 1000 A.D. had insularized Western Christendom. For them, the world outside of the European perimeter was an unknown land of "infidels" and pagans. The Crusades taught them that there was a whole world outside the boundaries of Europe with flourishing cultures and exciting people. Western Europe was never the same. The exposure to other cultures and the "knowledge explosion" of the universities gave rise to an entire new stance in Western civilization which we call the "Renaissance."

When we look closely at the religious life of medieval men and women, we can discern various distinctive characteristics that give us an insight into their interpretation of Christianity. Six points in particular stand out.

In the first place, medieval people had a very pervasive sense of God's presence and action in the world. While retaining vestiges of past superstitions, and even while inventing some of their own, the great mass of Christians believed firmly in the Christian God. His reality was as much a part of their lives as the air they breathed. They were conscious of his majesty, his power, and of his vengeance.

A second characteristic was their conviction of the destiny of Christianity to eventually take over the world. They knew that their faith would triumph over all obstacles, for Christ was the Lord of the world, who ruled all people and controlled all human history. This belief explains not only the missionary compulsion of the Middle Ages but also the motivation for undertaking the Crusades.

Thirdly, we notice the involvement of the people in the practical liturgy of the day. The pageantry of the celebration of the feasts of the Church gave spark to their daily lives at the same time that it instructed their minds. Plays were sometimes enacted in the churches in connection with the observances of Holy Week and Christ's passion and death in order to make these historical events more real and meaningful. When we realize that in those days there were no movies, no television, no magazines or newspapers, few books, few sporting events or regular forms of recreation to distract from the daily routine, we can understand how important participation in religious ceremonies was to the people.

A fourth characteristic of medieval Christianity was that the people were thoroughly immersed in scriptural events. Even though most of them could not read and many were not wealthy enough to purchase a copy of the Bible, they heard the biblical stories in the gospels read at Mass and in the sermons of the preachers. Biblical heroes were familiar to the common people: their expressions were biblical, as were their patterns of religious thought and their art.

Medieval people also felt a strong attraction for the human side of Christ, that is, for the human events of Jesus' life and death. They did not fully understand how the hu-

man Christ could still be present to them, but they were interested in those aspects of the historical Jesus that showed him as truly man. Every aspect of his life was depicted in painting, sculpture, and stained glass, especially the nativity and the passion.

But the understanding of the role of Christ as mediator between God and people seems to the present observer, to have been obscured in the vision of the average person. The sixth characteristic, then, of medieval spirituality was the strong devotion of medieval Christians to the saints, and to relics as the visible, miraculous heritage of the saints. Saints' lives were a very popular form of literature. The saints were the folk heroes of medieval times, just as singers, or actors, or baseball or football stars are the heroes of people today. The saints were considered the instruments for bringing God's graces to bear on one's profession, home, city, or special problem. Each city, each profession, each problem had its special patron.

A particular aspect of the veneration of the saints was the cult of the Virgin Mary. Reverence for Mary as the Mother of God is as old as Christianity. Mary's role as the Mother of God had been carefully enunci-ated at the Council of Ephesus in 431 A.D., but it was not until the Middle Ages that Mary came to hold a really unique place in Christian daily living. The cult of Mary reached vast proportions. She was everyone's saint and patron. There was a flood of poetry, art, sculpture, and theology whose central theme was the perfection of Mary. This cult of Mary gave rise to various practices which resulted in new social expressions, the chief of which was greater respect for women in general. The codes of knightly virtue and the troubadours' songs and romances expressed this theme of the proper conduct toward women.

Although Christianity did succeed in Christianizing medieval people and developing Christian thought processes, a student of history must not romanticize any age, as great as it may be in its general expression or thrust. People are still people. They are limited by the realities of their own existence and by the realities of the existence of others. They are products of their times, their culture, the forces at work in any historical event or era, and the tensions of conflicting ideologies, and the dynamics of civilizations around them. No age, however great, is better than the people who live in that age can possibly be at any given stage of history.

So it is with "The Age of Faith." It was an age of faith it is true, but tremendous gaps existed between actual human practice on the one hand and fine theories on the other. Whether or not their armies were fighting the battles of the Lord, the crusaders committed horrible atrocities against innocent victims. Professing a faith founded on love, medieval men burned to death their fellow Christians who held unorthodox views. The splendid cathedrals proclaim God's beauty and power to the world, but what do we really know of the faith or the charity of those who worshipped in them? We must presume that then, as now, there was a great gap between ideals and practice.

The Church Succeeds

Some 500 years have passed since the close of the chapter of Western history known as the Middle Ages, yet its evidences survive and flourish. The European of today may pay his taxes in the same town halls as his medieval forebears; vote in the same parliament buildings; buy and sell in the same marketplaces; change his money in the same streets; roam the same castles; study within the same college walls; listen to the same bells; and worship in the same cathedrals.

Even to the casual tourist from across the seas, the imprint of the Middle Ages is inescapable. He finds it in the great blue and red windows of Chartres, in the walled battlements of Carcassonne, in the half-timbered houses of Nuremberg, along the Ponte Vecchio in Florence. At Nottingham he may drink an ale at the Trip to Jerusalem, an inn where 12th Century English Crusaders slaked their thirst

R. GATES, FREDERIC LEWIS

en route to the Holy Land. At Santiago de Compostela in Spain, he may lodge at a hospice founded by the same Ferdinand and Isabella who financed the journeys of Columbus. At Ypres he may witness a festival, first celebrated about 960, in which cats are flung from the town belfry to symbolize the Belgians' abandonment of pagan gods for Christianity. (In deference to modern sensibilities, stuffed toys now take the place of live animals.)

Beyond the material legacy left us by the Middle Ages, institutions of far more moment in our daily life have come down from that time. Trial by jury, assemblies of elected representatives, middle-class society, universities, banks, the capitalist system itself—all had their roots in an era still often misconstrued as totally bleak and barren, as a thousand years of dark slumber between the grandeur of Rome and the glory of the Renaissance.

The very name, Middle Ages— covering a period from about the second half of the Fifth Century to the first half of the fifteenth—was a label attached ex post facto by men eager to proclaim their own intellectual advance. This somewhat patronizing designation implied a rekindling of the light of classical times after a prolonged interim in deep shadow. Modern historians reject this view of the medieval era. While much of it was benighted, much of it was spirited and creative. Among the products of its culture were the masters of polyphonic music and of cathedral architecture.

Alighieri Dante
BROWN BROTHERS

Dante's Inferno
BROWN BROTHERS

The works of Dante and Boccaccio, of Giotto and Fra Angelico, heralded the Renaissance.

Along with Dante's lyric genius, it is true, there was wide illiteracy, and below the soaring Gothic spires was the squalor of hovels. For the essence of the Middle Ages lay in its extreme paradoxes. Corruption coexisted with saintliness, ignorance with erudition, bestiality with chivalry, unimaginable devices of torture with exquisite works of artistry.

Beyond these was the greatest paradox of all. Of political unity, medieval Europe actually had little or none. There were successions of kings and dynasties—the Merovingian, the Carolingian, the Capetian, the Ottonian, the Hohenstaufen—but their power was generally short-lived, and

their kingdoms uncertain. Of these rulers only the great Carolingian, Charlemagne, wielded his scepter long and well enough to fuse vast areas of the Continent into a cohesive empire. For the most part a central authority was unknown to medieval man. His world was local, sequestered, circumscribed. He was accountable only to his own lord of the manor, understood none but the accents of his own region, and rarely had cause to communicate with his fellow man in another region.

Yet for all their isolation from one another, people of the Middle Ages enjoyed a common bond of surpassing strength: the Christian faith. However physically disjointed, medieval Europe was spiritually a commonwealth—a quasi-real, quasi-ideal entity called

Christendom, under the suzerainty of the Pope of Rome. This entity was never static. The forces of another great faith, Islam, continually had to be reckoned with. In time they reft Christendom of most of the eastern Mediterranean lands which it had included at the beginning, and for five centuries they controlled much of Spain, yielding it up to complete Christian reconquest only as the Middle Ages drew to an end.

But whatever might be at any given moment its geographical extent, fundamentally medieval Christendom was a unity—the *Respublica Christiana.* This unity was never absolute; it was forever being marred by power struggles between popes and emperors or kings or nobles. Even so, the very fact of its existence pervaded medieval life. All over Europe, there was one Church only. If a man were not baptized into it, he was not a member of society. Anyone excommunicated by the Church lost his political and legal rights as well. At the same time it was the Church which provided sanctuary for those endangered souls who took refuge within its walls. It was the Church which insisted that the poor did not have to fast as much as the rich, and which forbade servile work on Sunday. It was the Church which provided the poor with social services—free food and free hospitalization. There was, for a long while, no other source of education.

The hold the Church had on men's affairs, no less than on their minds, was enormous. Many a king or emperor had a prelate at his side. Charlemagne had his Alcuin, Edgar of England his Dunstan, Charles the Bald of West Frankland his John Scotus Erigena. The occupant of the throne was sometimes as unlettered as his lowliest serf. Charlemagne, though his realm reached from the Elbe to the Adriatic and from the Danube to the Pyrenees, slept with a tablet under his pillow so as to be able to practice the alphabet whenever he woke. Alcuin served him, as other churchmen served their kings, in the capacity of tutor and mentor.

Through its scholarship the Church could also preserve and nurture what was left of the heritage of Roman culture. The Roman pontiffs had remained in the city even after Constantinople had replaced it as the political seat of empire. The Church and its representatives were thus the sole actual link between the medieval present and the classical past. Among other bequests they transmitted were the Latin language; a respect for the written word; and a corollary zeal for record-keeping based on the Roman concept that *scripta manent*, "what is written endures."

Because from the first Christianity emphasized the value of the individual, in the medieval scheme every person had his place. He had his duties and responsibilities; he also had his rights. All these were scrupulously detailed and recorded in the manorial rolls in England, the accounts of French abbeys, the ledgers and chronicles of Flemish or Italian towns. The survival of such annals has made it possible to know more about the unique way of life of the Middle Ages, in terms of the firsthand, than about any preceding period.

The ten centuries spanned by the medieval era can be divided, roughly, into halves. The first half was a time of alternating chaos and torpor. The second was a time of growing stability, purposeful institutions and individual awakening. In these later upward-soaring centuries the Roman Empire and the tribes that had overwhelmed it together became Christendom. Once they had settled down, these pagan peoples, with astonishing speed, developed into brisk, busy nations, complete with arts and artifacts. In some cases, Poland and Denmark and Hungary for example, they became admirable examples of forward-looking Christian states within a few decades after the conversion of their leaders. The foundations of the modern world were thus built by former barbarians whose initial entry onto the stage of history had caused terror and upheaval.

The Age of Faith by Anne Freemantle and the Editors of TIME-LIFE Books (New York: Time Inc., Books, 1965), pp. 11–13.

Mont St. Michel

The Final Separation Between the Latin and the Greek Christians

One of the great tragedies of Christianity during the medieval period was the final separation of the Church into the Eastern, or Orthodox,* and Western, or Roman, Churches. What makes it particularly tragic is that what separates the two is not doctrine or belief, but the concept of authority. Its roots go back into primitive civilization and into the cultural, philosophical, and sociological developments that each civilization experienced.

The Greeks and the Latins were always different, even before Christianity came along. They spoke different languages. They viewed the world differently, and they had dissimilar talents. Thus, they approached Christianity from their respective points of view. We have already discussed this. The two peoples drew further apart culturally when the West was overrun by the barbarians and fused with them, while the Byzantines preserved much of their original culture unchanged.

Petty disputes marred relations between Greeks and Latins on a number of occasions. The problem created at the Council of Nicaea and the growing importance of the pope in Western civilization created tensions which caused numerous disputes through the centuries. One such argument broke out in the 860's over the activity of the Greek missionaries in Bohemia and Bulgaria: the Greeks allowed their converts to use their own language, while the Westerners insisted that everyone use Latin in church services. The Greek liturgy also differed from the Latin on various other points. The Latin added the word *"filioque"* meaning "and from the Son" to the Nicene Creed, contrary

---

* From the Greek words *orthos* and *doxos*, meaning "right opinion" or "sound doctrine."

141

to the Greek insistence that the Creed could only be changed by an Ecumenical Council like the one that had originally formulated it. These were things that, because of the underlying cultural and political feelings, assumed proportions that they otherwise would not have had.

But much greater problems developed from the Cluniac and Gregorian reform. The Latin reformers insisted that priests be forbidden to marry, and they gave the pope a much more active role in church affairs. The Latins believed in conformity; they wanted everyone to act alike. The Greeks claimed that these Latin ideas were all right for the Westerners, but they did not want them to apply to themselves. They insisted on the right to keep their old way of doing things.

The real break came about 150 years later when the Patriarch of Constantinople, Michael Cerularius, began his violent anti-Latin campaign by raising all the issues of the previous era and by closing all the Latin churches in Constantinople. The fateful day of complete separation came July 16, 1054, when the papal delegates solemnly excommunicated Michael. Michael, in turn, excommunicated the papal legate. Both parties were stubborn and unsympathetic and both, as so often happens in religious disputes, forgot the major things they had in common and concentrated their anger upon the very minor issues at stake.

The damage had been done. The Eastern Patriarch took virtually all of the East with him,* for, although the external grounds for the decision had been very debatable, it was at heart a political judgment. The Eastern churches considered the delegate's action an affront to their dignity, a disregard of their ancient rights, and another example of Western domination.

---

* The Greek Orthodox Church is the dominant Christian Church in Eastern Europe, Asia, and Egypt.

Historic meetings occurred when Athenagoras, Patriarch of Constantinople and Pope Paul VI met in 1967. Athenagoras was the first Patriarch of Constantinople to call on a reigning Pope at the Vatican in some 500 years. Pope Paul's visit to Istanbul was the first by a Pontiff to the See of Constantinople in 1000 years.

The whole mess was further complicated by the fanatical, barbarous attack on Constantinople in 1204 by the Western Crusaders. The city was destroyed, a Western Emperor was crowned ruler of Constantinople, and a Latin bishop was placed over this ancient Eastern city. The separation of Eastern and Western Christianity remains to this day.*

This Greek schism shows very clearly how important nonreligious concerns can be in religious affairs. Medieval men did not understand that cultural differences and varying customs are of little significance to true Christianity. What a person believes, not how he worships or expresses that belief, is what makes a person a member of the Christian community.

* It must be noted that: 1) sporadic attempts have been made from time to time to heal the separation, and 2) there are certain Eastern Christians who are in union with Rome. These last are called "Catholic Churches of Eastern Rites" and are in full union with the papacy but retain their own rites, ceremonies, customs, worship, and privileges. (See *Documents of Vatican II*, "Decree on Eastern Catholic Churches.")

Of importance for American Catholics also is the fact that American Catholics, having been raised in Western Catholicism, may tend to view Eastern Orthodox Churches in the same way that they view Protestant, humanistic, or Oriental religions (Buddhism, Hinduism, etc.). Such a lumping together is not only unfair to Western Catholic tradition and understanding, but it is unfair to the Orthodox and the other religious traditions. Each has its own sacredness and dignity, and each must be considered on its own terms. It is well to recall, also, that the Orthodox churches retain the tradition of Christianity, have the complete sacramental system of the Roman church, have bishops with apostolic traditions, and a clergy dating back to the earliest times. Orthodox Christians are Christians in whatever way Christianity is defined.

The Dawn of a New Age

The impact of the universities which had attracted thousands of scholars, the broadening horizons of culture resulting from the crusades, and the effect of the mendicant orders upon all classes of society speeded up the tempo of European life considerably in the fourteenth and fifteenth centuries.

As Europe moved out of the medieval into the early modern world, changes of many kinds took place in all aspects of human existence: *political, economic, social,* and *intellectual*. All of these new ideas and developments affected the church considerably.

Political Changes: Stronger Monarchies and Increased National Consciousness

As the feudal system disappeared, the power of kings became greater. They took over from the dukes and counts many of the tasks and much of the authority that men in these positions formerly had. Just as the popes had earlier centralized religious authority in their own hands, kings now began to do the same thing in their nations. Powerful rulers such as Philip IV in France and Edward I in England determined to assert their rights, and by this they meant getting a tighter hold on everything within their territory, including the clergy and the church's property. In feudal times clergymen could not be tried in the regular courts of their own country, no matter how serious a crime they might commit. Church property could not be taxed by the secular government regardless of how badly the state needed revenue. But the new kind of king wanted to change these customs.

When Pope Boniface VIII (1294–1303) and King Philip IV of France argued about such matters, the king hired a band of thugs to go to Italy and arrest the pope. They tried to do so and failed, but the shock was too much for the old pontiff, who died shortly afterwards. Boniface's successors were too frightened to protest; they made concessions instead. Thus, the kings learned that they could bully the pope and get away with it. *In medieval times, the Church had tended to dominate the state, but now the pendulum was beginning to swing in the opposite direction.*

Christianity had grown up and flourished in the cosmopolitan world of the Roman Empire and of the Middle Ages. Then people were not much aware of the differences between Frenchmen and Germans and Italians. They had thought of themselves as members of small tribes or groups, or else as citizens of one great Christian Commonwealth. The Church had helped Charlemagne to revive the Roman Empire in 800 A.D. because it accepted the theory of a universal citizenship of all Christians within a single state. Christ's message made no distinctions between nations and races of people.

By the 1300s, this cosmopolitan spirit was breaking down. People gradually became aware of their differences and proudly jealous of them. National feeling was beginning to grow. Latin, the international language of scholars, was beginning to lose out to national language—Chaucer and Dante showed that English and Italian could be used for serious, deep thought. The English government passed laws prohibiting the pope from appointing Italians to positions in the English church; they wanted English bishops, not foreigners—an idea that had not occurred to them before. When Philip IV's men mistreated the pope, most Frenchmen condoned this outrage because they thought that the pope had insulted France. Joan of Arc came along claiming that God had in-

structed her to fight the English and drive them from France, despite the fact that they were as Christian as the French. It seemed as if even God was beginning to recognize national differences!

During the years from 1309 to 1377, the popes lived in Avignon, a city located in Provence, where the people were mainly French. All seven popes of this period were Frenchmen, as were most of the cardinals and other officials in the pope's service. Rumors swept across Europe that the popes favored French Christians over all others. Because the Hundred Years' War between England and France occurred during this period, the English suspected the pope of helping their enemies, and national hostility developed against the pope. At the same time, Italian patriots denounced the popes for not coming back to Rome, and Germans objected to what they called Italian meddling in German affairs.

The Avignon period of the papacy led directly to the *Great Western Schism*. When the pope finally got back to Rome in 1397, only to die in the next year, an election had to be held. The Roman people rioted and threatened the conclave of electors, trying to force the cardinals to elect a Roman pope who would not go back to Avignon. The cardinals elected an Italian, not a Roman; but because many of them did want to return

to France and the new pope would not fall in with their plans, they tried to depose him by electing another pope, a Frenchman. Now there were two popes, Urban VI in Rome and Clement VII in Avignon.

Europe split into two camps. The French naturally backed Clement VII, as did the Scottish allies of France. The English disliked the French, so they supported Urban VI, as did many of the Germans. Nobody could figure out who was the real pope. Even Christians who were later canonized as saints were found in the camp of each pope. For forty years this situation continued. In fact, it got worse when some of the cardinals from each group finally came together in 1409 and elected Alexander V as a compromise; but the other two would not yield to him. It is easy to imagine all of the troubles that came out of this confusion. The papacy became a laughing-stock, with each pope excommunicating and denouncing the others, and with bishops and priests not knowing whom to obey. Some people even began to ask whether it was necessary to have any pope at all.

Finally, in 1415, a great Council assembled at Constance, Switzerland. The bishops and cardinals persuaded one pope to resign, another voluntarily abdicated (the Roman pope, Gregory XII, whom later historians have come to recognize as the legitimate one), and the Council declared the third to be a usurper whom they deposed. Then in 1417 they elected Martin V as the first universally recognized pope in forty years. But papal prestige had suffered irreparable damage, all of which was largely due to bad feeling among the nations of Europe who put national interests ahead of the welfare of the universal Church. This rise of nationalism and the hostility directed against the papal office were to result in the second major break from the Catholic Church. But more of that in the next chapter.

Economic Changes: Commerce and Capitalism

Although most people continued to earn their living from agriculture, the manorial system was beginning to be replaced by an economic organization based on money instead of land. Rather than pay rent by performing services, people had more money and began paying cash. This was due to the increase of commerce and trade which brought money into circulation again and made economic life more flexible. Serfs were able to emancipate themselves by commuting their former services into yearly money payments. More goods were available, too, and prices gradually rose. The body of economic practices that goes by the name of capitalism began to take shape. Banks, business firms, insurance companies, wholesale and retail buying and selling, and manufacturing provided new sources of employment and income.

While the Church possessed a great deal of wealth, which was necessary to pay for all its services, this wealth consisted of land and of manorial and feudal rights. These sources of income had to be transformed into the newer kind of investments to produce cash. Inevitably, the pope, the bishops, and all the clergy found themselves, like the other leaders of society, in a financial bind. More and more time and energy had to be devoted to raising money.

Soon people began to object that the Church was giving too much attention to money. The methods that it used provoked criticism: imposing taxes and excommunicating those who could not or would not pay; demanding payments for all offices from cardinal's hats to bishop's dioceses; asking for tips and bribes from anyone who had any business to conduct in the church's courts; and the usual fees that were requested for some of the sacraments. Some of the criticism was unfair, and many of the abuses were not as bad as rumor made them, but people objected anyway.

Another source of difficulty was the new question of ethics and morality raised by the new business practices. *For a thousand years the attitude of Christianity had been to condemn money.* "Where money exchanges hands, sin is involved," is the way the traditional theologians expressed their opinions. But obviously in the new economic order based on money, sin was not automatically involved. Money-lending, an essential part of the new capitalism, had traditionally been condemned as the sin of usury by the theologians. Would they now stand in the way of the new economic system? The theologians, in other words, had to rethink their teachings to bring them into line with the current practices. They had to study these practices carefully before they could decide. All this rethinking proceeded slowly and with much effort.

Meanwhile society again seemed to be leaving Christianity behind. Businessmen felt that the Church was out of touch with reality. They did not become less religious, but they paid less attention to the Church's laws. Christianity seemed to be so closely entwined with farming and the rural life that it could not adjust to a businessman's way of doing things. The Church exerted less and less influence in people's daily lives.

Social Change: the New Middle Class

Since the new economic practices sprang up chiefly among the people who lived in the cities, these members of the "middle class," came increasingly to dominate European life. Money talks; and the middle class had money. Their ideas were now more important than those of the old nobility. They set the standards for social behavior.

For hundreds of years the Church had

been very closely associated with the nobility, and like the nobles, churchmen misunderstood and even feared the middle class with their interest in making money through buying and selling. But the Church's bias in favor of those who lived from agriculture—the noble landowner and the peasant—had to yield in the face of the steady rise in numbers and the prosperity of the middle class. It had to learn to trust them and to make them feel welcome in the Christian community.

The balance of social and economic power shifted from the nobility and the Church to the new middle class who were distinguished from the nobility by their personal drive, their individualism, and their interest in the affairs of the world. The new middle class, as opposed to the older aristocracy, earned their livelihood by their skill in dealing with the goods of the world. Individual ability, enterprise, and industry rather than place and condition of birth determined a person's worth within the new middle class.

Inevitably, the rise of the new middle class to positions of power brought a change in outlook to all of society. Where early medieval people were taught to distrust the world and to consider it as part of the devil's scheme to distract them from their spiritual duties, later medieval people began to use the world and its goods to achieve their destiny and better their lot. Prior to late medieval days, withdrawal from secular affairs into monastic seclusion and a life of contemplation had been the ideal; now, interest in the world, in art, luxury, and the things that money could buy, was the goal. Fewer and fewer persons joined the monasteries, for in the middle classes, men and women felt that monasticism no longer represented a vital, realistic Christian attitude.

What did this mean for traditional Christianity? It did not mean that Christians were less religious than before; it simply meant that they were beginning to see that they could use their talents to serve their fellow men and to worship. It made them realize again that Christianity was not wedded to any particular system, class, or way of doing things. In other words, society was emerging into a new stage of human history, and Christianity was being challenged to emerge with it. It did, but not without suffering the tensions of continuity and change.

Intellectual Changes: the Renaissance

By far the most important effect of the speeded-up tempo of life in Europe was the giant leap forward in learning which brought about the period in history called the Renaissance.* Although the term is used most often to express all the attitudes and customs of the late Middle Ages, it applies most precisely to the intellectual achievements of the age and to the new attitude concerning human nature. For this reason it is often called "humanism."

The Renaissance was the culminating effect of the forces of learning which began in the universities in the twelfth and thirteenth centuries. The philosophical-theological disputes about Aristotle's view of the world had brought about a tremendous increase in the study of Greek culture. The effect was to inject in Western Christianity the practical aspects of Greek politics, law, logic, and government. There was a "rebirth" of the Greek view in life, politics, economics, and culture. The result was a new direction in intellectual interests.

Whereas, in previous centuries in Western Christendom, people's attention had been turned "heavenward" and "toward eternal values," it was now focused on earth, on the "city of man." People and their earthly exis-

---

* From French, meaning "to be born again."

Michelangelo's Masterpieces:
Moses and *Virgin and Child*

tence occupied the attention of scholars and an entirely new culture arose which centered upon the concerns of people in this earthly life.

In the Middle Ages to praise man was to praise God, for man was a creation of God. But Renaissance writers praised man for himself as a creator. They played down the sinfulness he was born with and emphasized his ability to think and act for himself, to produce works of art, to guide the destiny of others. They freed man from his pegged place in the medieval hierarchy, half way between matter and spirit, and allowed him to roam at will, through all the levels of being, sometimes identifying himself with the brutes, sometimes with the angels. He was seen as the ruler of nature—the lord although not *The* Lord of creation.*

Taking hold in Italy chiefly, and at first about 1350 A.D., the Renaissance brought life and human warmth into every aspect of living, and found its expression principally in culture. If the early days of the Middle Ages could be called the age of cathedrals, the last half could be called the age of painting and sculpture.

The building of cathedrals had inspired art forms of various kinds. Stonecutters, masons, glassworkers, and sculptors vied with one another to perfect their art. Sculptors and artists developed new styles accommodated to the soaring architectural themes, and musicians began to write polyphonic music and employ large choirs to fill the cathedral with sound. As time went on, new art forms emerged and under the inspiration of the Renaissance studies, artists first began to bring warmth and humanness to painting, then abandoned almost entirely the religious themes of previous ages. Religious art, how-

---

* *Renaissance*, John R. Hale and the editors of TIME-LIFE Books (New York: Time Inc., 1965), p. 17.

148

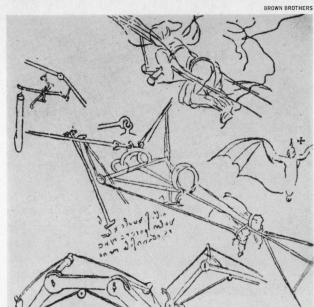

Flying model sketches
by da Vinci

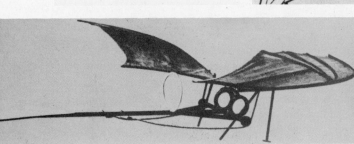

ever, still occupied the attention of the masters, and this age of culture produced two of the most outstanding geniuses the art world has ever produced: the famed Michelangelo (1475–1564) and the multiple genius Leonardo da Vinci (1452–1519), who designed the first airplane!

In addition to these great cultural changes, which gave society a new view of the world and turned its attention away from religious matters, there was a general rise in the level of education.

By the close of the Middle Ages, the clergy had lost their monopoly on education, which was now shared by the laity in large numbers. There were still plenty of intelli-

gent, well-educated priests, but there were also many with almost no training in theology. The medieval church had never set up a regular course of study for the clergy. Priests were ordained first, and then, if the opportunity presented itself, they went off to the university to study; but many never were able to do so. Educated laymen often became scornful of the poorly trained priests with whom they came into contact.

Many of the laity now knew not only what the Church taught but also how it arrived at its opinions, and often they could see alternatives that appeared more logical or attractive. The spirit of individualism which permeated late medieval society

of the Church. Everything seemed to be in a state of ferment; no one seemed sure any more of what he should believe.

Unfortunately there were no outstanding theologians alive at this time to help people solve their problems concerning the relationship between the old and the new ideas about the meaning of the faith. The theologians seemed stuck in the past. All they could do was to repeat old phrases and opinions in the hope that they would make sense as they had centuries ago. But often these ancient formulas had no relevance for Renaissance people. Theology fell behind the general thrust toward learning; and as society moved into a new era, religion played a less important role in people's lives than it had for centuries.

tempted many to ignore the traditional interpretations of the Bible and to formulate their own. New methods of thought, different theories of education, and new ideals were suggested. All of this was accomplished through a spirit of questioning and skepticism. People discovered that, unless they doubted, unless they raised objections to accepted theories, no intellectual progress could be made. This was the lesson that Abelard had taught in the twelfth century, but it had been forgotten until the Renaissance revived it.

Some Renaissance scholars rejected various Christian doctrines and moral standards, but others became zealous to put the new learning at the service of Christianity. Thomas More, Pico della Mirandola, and the great Erasmus of Rotterdam insisted that deeper wisdom would make people better Christians by giving them a fuller understanding of their faith. Everyone wanted to question and discuss and probe the teachings of Christ and the writings of the Fathers

The End of the Fourth Era

Looking back on the history of the Middle Ages, we can see another step in the Church's self-understanding. Through the sufferings entailed in the death of one era and the birth of the next, the Church was to learn that it was *not* inevitably tied to one political system or another; that the Christ-event was larger than one political or philosophical system; that religion is bigger than the concerns of the moment. It was a hard lesson, and it was not learned overnight. The philosophical, cultural, economic, and political evolution of the period was to have its effect in the new age which was just dawning.

It must not be overlooked, in the midst of all that was going on, that Europe at this time was one in its Christian outlook. There was "one Lord, one Faith, one Baptism." But it was not to be so for long. The economic and political realities were to have serious repercussions in a very short time, for on the stage of history a new character was to enter who would leave it a different sort of drama. That man was Martin Luther.

Three Profiles in Courage

THE BETTMANN ARCHIVE

Thomas a Becket (1118–1170), called St. Thomas of Canterbury, was appointed Lord High Chancellor (that is, the highest ranking officer in the kingdom after the king) of England by King Henry II. Four years later, while he was still Chancellor, he was consecrated bishop of Winchester. When he was consecrated, the archbishop whom he replaced (who was retiring because of age) said: "I give you a choice. Now as arch- bishop and chancellor you must lose the favor of your earthly or your heavenly king." Thomas replied: "I will never forfeit the grace of the kingdom of heaven."

For ten years Thomas was the staunch defender of the rights of the people and the rights of the Church against a strong, determined, and egotistical king. Henry became so angry with Thomas that he banished him from England. After four years in exile, Thomas returned to his episcopal work in spite of the King. His presence in England was a reminder to the king that personal and religious liberty were safe as long as Thomas remained alive. On December 29, 1170, Henry, infuriated by Thomas' opposition, said, we are told, "Is there no one in my kingdom able to free me of this stubborn man?" Five or six of Henry's supporters went to the Cathedral where Thomas was reciting the Office with his monks. Just before he was beaten and hacked to death with swords, as he stood in front of the altar, he said to his murderers: "For the name of Jesus and in defense of the Church I am ready to die."

The history of the Christian Church is filled with people who have remained faithful to their Christian commitment in spite of threats to their social, civil, economic, and psycho- logical welfare, to their physical well- being, and to their lives. The early martyrs are the exemplars of such courage. Every age, however, has presented Christianity with heroes. Some are canonized saints, some are not. Three such heroes of the third period of development in the Church are St. Thomas à Becket, St. Catherine of Siena, and St. Joan of Arc.

151

Catherine of Siena (1347–1380) was born in Siena, a small town about thirty miles southwest of Florence, Italy. When she was sixteen, she became a member of the "Third Order of St. Dominic." (The "first" was the Dominican priests; the "second" was the regular Dominican nuns.) She lived at home following the rules for nuns living outside a convent, and worked hard caring for the sick and the poor and the victims of the almost constant warfare among the "families" that controlled the Italian city-states.

By the time she was eighteen, she was the acknowledged leader of a group of men and women trying to restore the spiritual life of the people of Siena. Her influence was so great that in a short time she had a reputation for deep, practical spirituality throughout Italy and France. Although she was "a poor, little nun," she exerted influence on all who met her. People persuaded her to try to get the pope back to Rome.

She, too, was convinced that the troubles of Italy were directly related to the pope's living in Avignon, France, rather than in Rome, and devoting more time to political and secular matters than he did to the Church. She wrote a letter to Pope Gregory XI and told him (she did not ask!) to return to Rome immediately. The cardinals and diplomats around the Pope laughed when they heard about the letter, but the pope, intrigued by her audacity, asked her to come to Avignon. She did, and although her appearance disappointed the "worldly" court of the pope (she wore the simple black and white habit of the Dominican nuns, and she was small, frail, and quiet), her demand that the pope return to Rome startled the court and frightened the pope. He did return to Rome "solely at the insistence of Catherine and over the protests of his cardinals and the people of France." This tough minded, determined, courageous woman succeeded in bringing the papacy back to Rome where kings, cardinals, diplomats, and economic czars had failed.

Joan of Arc (1412–1431) was born in Domremy, France, about 140 miles southwest of Paris, during the infamous 100 Year's War between England and France. The story of Jeanette, or, as she is called in France, Jeanette d'Arc, is one of the most famous and romantic stories in history.

In 1428, when she was sixteen and France was all but ready to surrender to England, Joan, at the insistence of her "voices," went to the king of France to tell him that she would lead France to victory. She was, naturally, laughed at by the king's advisers, and considered completely insane by the king's generals. (Can you imagine a sixteen year old, uneducated girl from your home town going to the White House to tell the President that she should be the chairman of the Joint Chiefs of Staff!) Somehow Joan convinced the king and, in spite of the fierce opposition of the generals, she led the French troops to victory in the celebrated battle of Orleans and broke the back of the English forces in subsequent battles. On May 24, 1430 she was captured—betrayed by the spies of the Duke of Burgundy, who was secretly in league with the English. She was humiliated, tortured, and questioned for four months. In July, 1430, she was brought to trial *as a heretic* and condemned to death by a traitorous bishop named Couchon. She was burned at the stake on May 30, 1431. She was, of course, eventually cleared of all charges against her, but the bishop who condemned her has been in disgrace in France ever since her death. His name, from that time on in France, has been used to call pigs!

RELIGIOUS NEWS SERVICE

1. Discuss the general cultural, economic, political, moral, and religious atmosphere of Western civilization in the century before 1000 A.D. (*Refer to the end of chapter 9.*)

2. What is the meaning of the subtitle of this chapter?

3. Why were some bishops less than they should have been during the feudal period? Can "the Church" be blamed for this? Why? Why not?

4. What forces in Christianity were brought to bear on Western civilization to Christianize it during the tenth and eleventh centuries?

5. On page 120 in the discussion on the Church's influence in morals, the phrase "with the realities of the possible in mind" is used. What does this mean? Can you give examples from modern American experience which bring out the idea of the paragraph in which this sentence appears?

6. According to Henri Daniel-Rops, how did the Church influence morals in the medieval period? What sanction did the Church have which enabled it to influence the moral practices of the feudal lords?

7. What was the distinction between the "Peace of God" and the "Truce of God"? Was the Truce of God at all effective? What would be the effect of a universal Truce of God in modern society?

8. What was the difference between a serf and a slave?

9. One historian has said that the Church was able to change society because it always took a practical rather than an idealistic approach to problems. What does he mean? Is this a good idea? Why? Why not?

10. How was the monastery at Cluny able to effect so great an influence on medieval society?

11. Why was the papacy in a state of eclipse in the eighth and ninth centuries? How did it revitalize itself? Why was the bishop of Rome considered more important than any other bishop?

12. What changes in monasticism did the mendicant orders bring about in the medieval Church? Explain what the vows of poverty, chastity, and obedience mean for those who become religious in the Catholic Church.

Why does your book call St. Thomas Aquinas the "prophet of the intellect"? What is his

Summa Theologiae about? Compare St. Thomas with St. Augustine.

13. Why are the later Middle Ages called "an age of faith"? Were they? Why? Why not?

14. Why were the Crusades called "Holy Wars"? What was the rationale behind them? What was their effect on Western civilization?

15. What were the principal characteristics of the religious life of medieval people?

16. What is the reason that Mary is so honored in the Catholic Church?

17. Discuss the separation of the Latin and Greek Churches. Was the reason given in your book on page 142 the principal reason or a contributing factor? Why? Why not? (*Refer to chapter 8 for background.*)

18. What is the difference between Orthodox Christian Churches and Eastern Catholic Churches?

19. The Middle Ages came to an end because of drastic changes in society. Discuss the changes and why they affected the religious outlook of Western European people.

20. At the direction of your teacher, select one of the following topics for a lengthy report to be presented to the class. Be sure to bring visual materials to demonstrate.

Cathedrals of medieval Europe
The Crusades
St. Francis of Assisi
Michelangelo
Leonardo da Vinci
Renaissance art
The Divine Comedy
The Canterbury Tales
Monasticism in the Middle Ages
St. Thomas Aquinas
Medieval religious plays
Town life in medieval Europe

Renaissance Christianity

11

Otto Brauseinetter: Copernicus

Christianity Faces a New World

If the separation of the Eastern and Western expressions of Christianity can be considered a tragedy because it affected the unity of the Church, it can also be considered a blessing for it taught the Church that the expression of Christianity is not limited to one form, one political system, one set of ideas, or one culture. The church is "catholic," or universal, not in numbers but in its salvational aspects: it is for everyone.

This lesson was to be learned again in the Western Church in the political and cultural upheavals resulting from the Renaissance. Once again, the Church was to learn that God uses human means to achieve His goals. He used the political, social, economic, cultural, and human aspects of the Renaissance to reform His Church.*

As civilization moved into the 1500s, the

---

* It must not be thought that the "Roman" Church alone suffered from what we might call religious myopia. Protestant and Orthodox Christianity also experienced tunnel vision— seeing only what they want to see. It probably results from the tensions that exist when the forces of change meet the need for continuity. It may be a kind of pride, but it also comes from a sense that everyone has that not every change proposed necessarily means progress.

cultural impact of the Renaissance was affecting all of Europe. The forces for change were reshaping the economic, political, and cultural face of Western civilization, and in the process were influencing the European expression of Christianity, the Catholic Church. Three developments particularly affected the role of the Catholic Church in Western Europe: the fact of self-determination in politics, the discovery of America, and the emergence of the divergent expressions of Christianity which we call Protestantism.*

As we have seen, the economic picture of Europe was changing. The feudal system, which had kept people in the economic and social class into which they were born, was slowly dying out and a new class of people was rising to power, the merchants and the bankers. Although most of the people were still farmers, the European economy was beginning to respond to the growth of mining, manufacturing, and trade. Money, rather than social position, was becoming the medium of influence; people with money controlled the political and cultural destinies of the new Europe.

The political scene in Europe was changing rapidly too. The Holy Roman Empire was an empire in name only. France, England, Spain, and Portugal were independent of it. Italy was divided into separate states, and Germany, supposedly the seat of the Empire, was controlled by more than 300 Church and family units, seven of whom elected the Emperor. Europe was beginning to experience the strong feelings of nationalism and independence which were to characterize the Europe of the next four centuries.

Only the Church continued as a unified political body, though it had no determinate territory outside of the Papal States. The comprehensive authority of the Church, though based on religious necessities, was political in the extreme, for the Church

---

* The term *Protestant* is used here with reservation and great respect. It is *not* used to designate dissident elements in a negative way or to indicate that all "Protestants" had the same Christian expression. It is used as an umbrella term to indicate those groups which professed what they believed to be the authentic Christian message. It is a commonly understood term and expresses a movement.

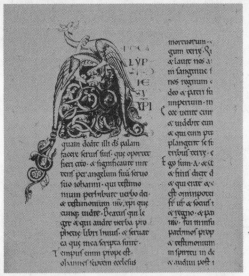

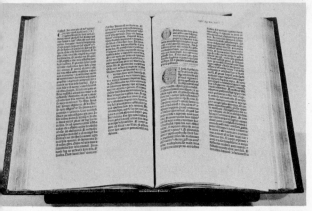

12th Century New Testament
and the Gutenberg Bible

handed treatment by court-appointed bishops, and the poor resented the triple tithing —of grain, fruits and vegetables, and livestock—that was exacted before they could care for the needs of their own families.

The unrest in politics and the changes in the economic scene were preceded and accompanied by the rise of humanism. The interest in learning sparked by the Renaissance and made possible by the invention of printing with movable type soon made itself felt in all classes of society. More and more people began to read and to think for themselves.* New ideas in theology, philosophy, art, literature, and science were being spread. Bold theories on government, on the rights of individuals, and on the primacy of reason were published. Sculpture and art reached their Renaissance height in the works of Michelangelo and Leonardo da Vinci. European cities outside of Italy, like Antwerp and Brussels, Seville and Lisbon, London and Paris, became centers of commerce, banking, and culture.

With the rise of educational opportunity came independence of mind and the development of science and the scientific method. Copernicus, Galileo, and Kepler, all pioneers in astronomy, moved earth from its previously assigned central position in the universe to a subordinate place as one of the satellites of the sun. Francis Bacon spearheaded the development of natural science; arithmetic, algebra, geometry, and calculus were perfected and put at the disposal of the new scientific discoveries. A whole new "world" was opening up. Civilization continued to move forward; as it did, there was an ever-increasing emphasis upon a new order based upon the worth of every individual and his right to self-determination.

waged war, negotiated treaties, collected taxes, and settled boundary disputes and marital problems.

The authority of the Church in purely secular matters had always been challenged, but rarely successfully until the sixteenth century. Kings and powerful local rulers opposed both the influence of the Church in internal politics and the heavy taxes which diverted money much needed at home to the papal court. Scholars chafed under what they considered interference in their scholarly pursuits, the middle class resented high-

---

* At the beginning of the seventeenth century, Europe had nearly 9,000,000 printed books compared with less than 100,000 handwrought copies fifty years before.

As far as the Church was concerned, the discovery of America opened up new mission territory. For the next 200 years zealous missionaries were part of almost every venture into the "New World," and pockets of Christianity were established in North America, Canada, Mexico, and the coastal regions of central and South America.* However, this is a story by itself. The most important historical event in Western Christendom at this time was the rise of Protestantism.

Copernicus BROWN BROTHERS

THE ST. LOUIS ART MUSEUM

Kepler EDITORIAL PHOTOCOLOR ARCHIVES

Galileo
BROWN BROTHERS

Reform of the Church, Stage I

For a thousand years Western Christendom had been Rome-dominated. Christianity in the West had one single expression, one form of faith. No matter what "heretical" movements had arisen or what developments history took, the norm of faith and Christian worship had been Roman, specifically, the papacy. It was taken for granted that it would always be so. To Western people Europe was the center of the world—the "true faith" was there. They saw the world consisting of Catholic Europe, the "heretics" on the perimeter, and the "pagans" and "savages" in distant lands. They saw it as their duty to punish the heretics and convert the pagans. They were not generally aware of the cancer that was eating away at their own situation; they could not appreciate that history was on the move and that drastic surgery was needed to rid Western Christendom of the disease that was destroying it from within.

The disease was the political use of religion by the corrupt hierarchy and the secular princes who named these bishops; the surgeon was the intent, fiery, concerned Augustinian friar-priest, Martin Luther. He was the man Christianity needed; for if he had not appeared, reform within the Church might have been delayed for centuries.

It was not that the realization of the need for reform had not been present before Luther. Those who sought to reform the Church had directed their attention to the problem as they saw it. Some tried to reform

---

* Meanwhile, of course, missionary activity continued in other areas. In Russia, for example, Roman bishoprics were established in 1318 A.D. even though Russia was in the Eastern sphere of influence. Dioceses were established in India in 1330 after extensive work by missionary priests in the principal cities.

the spiritual lives of the mass of Christians through a return to what they conceived as a primitive piety; some tried for reform through attempts to have a Council; some tried to reform Christianity through an intense study of the New Testament, which study, they believed, would cause Christians to return to the simplicity that characterized the early Church. *The problem was that the reforms proposed rarely touched the area where reform was most needed: in the political institution and expression of Christianity.*

Those who pressed for a reform through a general Council were blocked in their efforts by the popes, who feared that many who urged a Council had selfish, nationalistic, or personal gains in mind. The popes knew that bishops appointed by the powerful rulers of Europe would be subject to severe political pressures and would press for reforms that would benefit local political considerations at the expense of the entire body of Christians. They knew that those who had genuine reform in mind would be in a minority; hence, they delayed calling a Council, hoping the fever would die down.

Those who sought reform through education hoped that by educating Christians in the principles of the New Testament they would rid Christianity of the superstitions and the dogmatic and liturgical abuses that were prevalent at the time. Most of those who sought this kind of reform were humanists, raised in the tradition of the Renaissance. Typical of these was the outstanding humanist of the century, Desiderius Erasmus (1466–1536).

Erasmus was a Dutch scholar, deeply devoted to learning and to the Church. He was the most admired and respected man of his time, and his advice was sought by popes and kings, reformers and scholars, statesmen and common people. Well before Luther's demands came to light, Erasmus took issue with the power of the papacy and the corruption of some local bishops. He urged a lessening of the Church's official emphasis on such matters as fasting, indulgences, relics, pilgrimages, celibacy, confession, and the burning of heretics. "Truly," said Erasmus, "the yoke of Christ would be sweet and his burden light, if petty human institutions added nothing to what he himself imposed. He commanded us nothing save love for one another." Erasmus tried by every peaceful means to reform the Church, but he could reach only a few—the intellectual elite.

Those who tried for reform through spiritual, conciliar, and humanist approaches did not succeed. Most reformers of the past had had a profound effect upon the Christianity of their time, but, in the main, a *system* was being perpetuated which was corrupting the very essence of Christianity. How is it then that Martin Luther, this one among many, could so alter the historical situation that he could force reform when even the most powerful and reform-minded popes could not?

The answer, probably, lies in the mystery of the evolution of history. Every radical change in history is produced when three things are present at the same time:

(1) An historic situation that cries out for change,

(2) A charismatic person to lead the way,

(3) A popular appeal.

In other words when the time is ripe and the right person comes along, civilization is affected. History is full of such events; but history is also full of evidence, that, if the three are not present together, radical change does not take place. How then did Luther succeed where so many had failed?

First of all, the circumstances were right for a reform within Christendom. The situation was religiously bad and historically opportune. Two things in Christianity were so emphasized that they could shift completely the true Christian message. The one was the popular and widely taught interpretation of the means to salvation; the other was the authoritarian stance of the papacy.

Spiritual individualism had progressed to such a stage in Western Christendom that *individual works*—"meritorious acts," as they were called—were viewed as the pledge of salvation. The emphasis was upon earning salvation through works done for the sake of merit. So common had this become that it was widely believed, and theologically defended in most universities, that a person could ensure his salvation and the remission of what was known as "temporal punishment for sin" by performing some good works. So outrageous had the situation become that many practices such as pilgrimages, visits to the tabernacle, the contribution of money for a "good cause," fighting in the pope's army, or hunting down heretics took on an aura of magic: a good deed automatically got its reward.

The condition is best summed up in the preaching of John Tetzel, a Dominican preacher of the fund-raising campaign for St. Peter's Basilica (the Vatican), who allegedly boasted that the particular indulgence he was preaching would apply even beyond the grave to "the souls in purgatory." "As soon as the coin in the coffer rings," he is supposed to have said, "a soul from purgatory springs!"

Although this "indulgence problem" is the most notorious example of the bad theology that was being preached at the time, it is only one of many items that caused serious theologians and philosophers to press for reform in doctrinal presentation. Perhaps two causes can be cited to explain the poor quality of the theology: the idea that a person's earthly life was nothing more than a testing ground for his entrance into heaven, and the social conditions resulting from the

Hundred Years' War between England and France and from the Black Death (1347–1349) which wiped out at least a third of Europe's population. The plague and the war shattered the economic base upon which society was built and left the religious houses and universities in France with seriously reduced numbers. In an attempt to provide enough priests for the people, bishops sometimes ordained uneducated men (hoping that their education would improve as they went along) or untested men who later proved to be unworthy of their mission. With the universities all but inactive and the clergy poorly prepared theologically, it is no wonder that the content and the quality of preaching deteriorated.

The theological situation at this time was so poor that people lived in fear of hell. Punishment for sins committed was the incentive to lead a good life. God was preached as a God of vengeance, who would "even" put his own Son to death, and who would exact terrible punishments for even the slightest fault. Salvation through Jesus, God's care for His People, community faith, and love of neighbor took a backseat to making up for one's personal sins, doing penance for real or imagined sins, fasting to ward off the devil, and gaining indulgences to pay for sins committed. Fear was the order of the day. People were intent on buying off an angry God.

This was the theological atmosphere into which Martin Luther was born in Eisleben, Saxony, in November 1483. His father, Hans, had risen from peasant to middle-class merchant and had decreed that his second son, Martin, study for a career in law. However, when he was twenty-two years old, Martin entered the Augustinian monastery at Erfurt.

Luther was a complicated man. On the one hand he was cheerful, lively, outgoing, and fond of song and companionship. On

Lucas Cranach: *Martin Luther*   THE BETTMANN ARCHIVE

justice with eternal condemnation of the damned, Luther had lived in constant fear of his own eternal damnation. His whole philosophy of life changed when he came across St. Paul's famous analysis of the meaning of faith:

> . . . the Good News . . . is the power of God saving all who have faith . . . or as scripture says: *The upright man finds life through faith.*
>
> Romans 1:16–17

Suddenly, as he told his friends, Luther realized that it was *not* through his own actions that he was to be saved (from hell). He would be saved solely through the goodness of God. Luther's teaching and preaching were from that time based upon what he thought he found in Scripture and were centered on the importance of *faith* rather than works performed to "buy God off." His teaching and preaching became even more popular, and consequently caused a stir in central Germany.

Luther's teaching was so radical by the accepted standard of the day that one of his fellow Augustinian professors is supposed to have said: "This monk will confuse all the doctors. He will start a new religion and reform the whole Roman Church, for he bases his theology on the writings of the Prophets and the Apostles. He stands on the words of Christ, which no philosophy or sophistry can upset or oppose."** He didn't realize how

the other he was severe, intense, stubborn, introspective, and filled with fear of the wrath of God. He was preeminently, a man of his times. When he entered the monastery he gave himself with unflagging zeal to the practices of prayer, fasting, physical penance, and the gaining of indulgences. But he found no peace for his troubled soul.*

Luther studied as intently as he prayed and soon became an outstanding intellectual of his order. Within a short time he was teaching moral philosophy and theology at the University of Wittenburg and was attracting great crowds by his powerful preaching in the town church.

After Luther had earned his doctorate in theology, he began his intensive study of the Scripture, as much in search of personal peace as in the interest of theology. One day, while studying St. Paul's epistle to the Romans, Luther had an insight which was to change his own life and the lives of all Christians for centuries. Raised in the theological tradition which had equated God's

---

* Luther never did anything by halves. Almost everything was a crisis with him. Of his early days as a friar, Luther says he drove himself to the extremes in austerity, sometimes fasting for three days at a time or sleeping without a blanket in freezing weather. "I observed the rule so strictly," he wrote, "that I may say that if ever a monk got to heaven by sheer monkery, it was I."

** *The Reformation* by Edith Simon and the Editors of TIME-LIFE Books (New York: Time, Inc., 1966), p. 20.

right he was; nor did Luther foresee what would result from his teaching. He was interested in the truth of what he believed, and, convinced that he was right (he did seek advice and had long discussions with other theologians), he taught the truth as he saw it.

The second thing that made reform at this time both opportune and necessary was the political use of the papacy by the men who were bishops of Rome. Because the bishop of Rome was a religious *and* political leader, he was the most powerful man in Europe. Because the papacy was not hereditary, it was possible to have a man elected who could be controlled by the most powerful rulers of the time. The papacy was a prize well worth seeking; it soon became a political football. For a long period of time the papacy was occupied, with few exceptions, by politically opportunistic men who used their moral position to enforce their imperialistic designs. Under the guise of protecting the faith, they were, in reality, clinging to a political advantage for themselves and their families. The time was indeed ripe for a reform of the politico-religious situation. So low had the papacy and the papal court sunk that purely religious interests were rarely a prime concern of those in the establishment: the cardinals, curial officials, bishops, and powerful religious orders.

The men who controlled the administration of the Catholic Church were not all morally corrupt men, but they were skilled in the political arts of the day. Many, no doubt, were motivated by selfish gain for themselves and their families, but many others were convinced that the way the Church was administered and the way theology was taught were absolutely *the* correct way. They saw the Church as the one way of salvation and were convinced that it had to be preserved as it was regardless of the hardships it provoked on individuals. They had been raised in the belief that "this is the way

it always was," and in their view whatever means were necessary to continue it were lawful and just. For this reason those who sought genuine reform within the administration of the Church were easily controlled by those who gave more attention to politics than they did to religious affairs.

The papal court had become the richest, most ornate and probably most corrupt court in all of the West. Pope Adrian VI (1522–1523), a pious, intelligent cardinal from Utrecht in Holland, who was a compromise candidate between two factions in the election, told the assembled Roman cardinals that "the Roman scandals are the talk of the world." So worldly had the papal scene become that this same pope, upon his arrival in Rome, had to have the cardinals pointed out to him, "for in dress and manner they were simply Renaissance princes."* The concern in Rome was political, for "the faith was secure; everyone believes."

The "Roman situation," the rise of nationalism, and bad theology created a situ-

* Philip Hughes, *A Popular History of the Church* (New York: Macmillan Paperbacks, 1962), p. 183.

Luther's House at Eisenach DEAN, FREDERIC LEWIS

BROWN BROTHERS

Historic Wittenberg Cathedral, on whose
door Martin Luther nailed his 95 theses

BROWN BROTHERS

ation into which a powerful man could step
and have an effect. If the much needed reform could not be secured from within, it
had to be achieved from without. It was.

Martin Luther is one of the top four or
five religious personalities of history. He is
ranked by some scholars with Moses, Mohammed, Buddha, St. Paul, and Gandhi. Dr.
Jerald Brauer, the Lutheran dean of the
University of Chicago Divinity School, believes that Luther is one of the three or four
greatest figures in the history of Christianity.
He says that Luther is "perhaps the greatest
prophetic figure in Post-Apostolic Western
Christendom."

The irony of the Luther revolt is that
*Luther himself had absolutely no intention
of breaking away from the Catholic expression of Christianity,* and the furthest thing
from his intentions was to catapult into history a division of the Christian faith that
would necessitate separate denominational
names for various Christian sects.* "One
should help and cling to the Church," wrote
Luther at the beginning of his troubles.
"Conditions will not be improved by
separation."

Luther was seeking genuine reform of theological expression. He was a doctor of theology, a professor of Sacred Scripture, an
Augustinian monk, and a sincere, intensely
religious man who was appalled by the theology being propagated by the popular
preachers of the time. His electrifying
preaching, his recognized qualities of leadership, and his popularity as a teacher made
him a man of great stature in his university,
his town, his monastery, and his order.

Alarmed by the bad theology, which he
found contrary to his personal experience
and to the fruit of his studies, he reacted as
many theologians did in his time; he taught,
he preached, and he wrote against the

---

* Karl Adam, the respected German Catholic
theologian and author of *The Christ of Faith,
Christ our Brother,* and other famous books,
and a man who exerted great influence on Vatican Council II, suggests that Luther did not
leave the Church—the Church left him. Had
Luther remained within the Roman Church, he
says, "we would be his grateful debtors today
. . . and he would have been the greatest saint
of our people, the refounder of the Church in
Germany, a second St. Boniface." (*U.S.
CATHOLIC,* January 1975, page 29.)

164

abuses. The upshot was that, when he was denounced by the Dominicans in Rome who were seeking to protect their own preacher John Tetzel, he offered to debate the issue by posting the now famous 95 theses or propositions. These were theological statements of his opposition to some of the currently preached theology.

Roman authority reacted in the only way it knew how. (It must be understood, of course, that the "Luther thing" was a very minor item in the political complexities of the time.) Dissidents had been handled before and, they thought, Luther was no different from the many that had appeared in previous Christian history. Rome's reaction, while not swift, was typical of the times: condemnation of the ideas, persuasion to win back the "heretic," excommunication if there was no renunciation, and banishment and/or punishment by the state.

When Luther was confronted by the papal delegates he was only concerned with discussion of the issues; the Roman delegates were only concerned with his renouncing his "novel theories."* They would not discuss with Luther; they insisted on submission. In conscience Luther could not renounce what he believed in. The reply he is alleged to have given to papal and imperial orders to renounce his teachings—"Here I stand, I cannot do otherwise. God help me. Amen."—has become one of the most famous phrases in all religious history.

Luther's stand, however, does not explain the success of his movement. His firmness resulted in his condemnation (1521). All that was left was for him to be punished by the state. That he was not was due to the rise of nationalism, the political development that brought the countries of Europe into being, and the refusal of Frederick, the ruler of Saxony (in the East Germany of today), to impose the papal punishment on the popular and convincing preacher.

For twenty-five years, Luther continued his work, excommunicated, it is true, but not separated from his Christian belief. He wrote and taught and preached. Because of the improvement in printing processes, Luther's ideas were quickly spread throughout Germany. His books, the best-sellers of his day, were the chief force in bringing about the cultural changes that were to affect all of Christendom. His translation of the Bible into German not only made the Bible popular reading, but it transformed the German language. His hymns, many of which are used in Catholic liturgy today, his pamphlets, his books, his sermons, his total literary output as well as his powerful personality make him, in the words of a famous biographer, "not an individual but a phenomenon." Luther died in 1546, just when the Council of Trent was assembling to consider needed reforms in the Church.

What Luther did was to trigger a movement long latent in Western Christendom. There was more and more dissatisfaction with the imperialism of the papacy, more and more pressure for self-determination within the sovereignty of the kingdoms within the Holy Roman Empire, and more and more unrest among the people. It was not long after Luther's defiance of Rome that other religious reformers, seeing that they would probably escape the torture of the rack and execution by burning, became increasingly outspoken. Most of them lacked the magic of Luther, and many of them lacked his learning. Literally hundreds of "protest movements" sprang up; most of them died almost within the lifetime of their originators.

---

* It is significant that many of Luther's novel theories: vernacular liturgy, priority of Scripture, the Church as the People of God, the priesthood of the laity, the importance of faith, the priority of conscience, and the like, were adopted by the bishops of Vatican II.

Consciences in Conflict: Luther and Rome

In view of Martin Luther's conviction that theology is a practical, not a speculative discipline, it is not surprising that we do not find in his works the kind of systematic treatment of "conscience" that can be found, for example, in Thomas Aquinas. We find instead, both in his writings and in his life, not simply a keen sense of the importance of conscience, but such a sense of fidelity to conscience that he expressed his willingness to "lose [his] life and head" rather than abandon what he conscientiously held to be the Word of God. That this was not the rhetoric of an academician disengaged from life or from a real threat on his own life is well known. That this perception of the absolute obligation to follow one's conscience was not a Reformation discovery of Luther but an inheritance he had received from the previous Christian tradition is not as well known but, hopefully, will become so in the course of this paper.

There can be no thought, in a paper as brief as this, of offering even a reasonably complete survey of the meaning of conscience for Luther and for the Church of Rome in his day. I therefore feel at liberty in my conscience to focus upon just a few representative utterances and upon just one celebrated event where the conscience of Luther and the conscience of the Roman Church come into conflict, namely, at the Diet of Worms. Despite this narrowing of the focus I am confident that no significant episode in this drama of conscience will be omitted.

I

It is well established that, as a young Augustinian friar, Luther's conscience was wracked with anxiety and guilt over his inability to live up not only to his monastic profession, but to his Christian baptismal profession as well. Neither daily confession of his sins nor increasing quantities of ascetical and penitential exercises were able to calm his anxieties. Indeed, it seems that these practices served only to heighten his torment. What we are describing, of course, is Luther's early Catholic experience of a troubled, burdened conscience, if not his full-blown scrupulosity. Luther was able to overcome this anxiety of conscience only by rejecting what he came to regard as the totally false premise on which his conscience had been formed: the semi-Pelagian doctrine of William of Ockham and Gabriel Biel that the grace of justification or forgiveness of sin is normally only given to those who do all that is within their natural powers of reason and free will.

Like so many Catholics before and after him, Luther was never sure that he had done everything in his power or, if he did, that he did it with a sufficiently pure intention. In fact, he was sure he *never* did enough. It was while simultaneously studying St. Augustine's anti-Pelagian writings and lecturing on St. Paul's Epistle to the Romans in the years 1515–1516 that

Luther came to a shocking awareness that his teachers from the Ockham-Biel tradition—representatives of the *via moderna*—had duped him, had given him a distorted view of Christianity and had infected him with a modified version of the error that had been so energetically challenged by St. Augustine more than a thousand years before: Pelagianism.

From this time on Luther was convinced that relief from his anxious conscience and the acquisition of a peaceful conscience could only come about through a trusting, confident faith in Jesus Christ and his grace. This discovery led Luther to begin his campaign of sharing the good news with the other Catholics of his day, many of whom he regarded as still living in anxiety and slavery to the law by thinking that their salvation depended primarily on their own effort, not on their faith in Christ. Before taking his case to the people, Luther first began to attack the Pelagian tendencies he found in the Late Scholastic theologians. He did so by means of ever more sharply formulated, sometime hyperbolic theses. It was these early verbal challenges to the Scholastics, not just his theses on indulgences, that aroused the ire of theologians such as John Eck and Cardinal Cajetan, who ultimately were involved in drawing up the bull *Exsurge Domine* (1520), in which Pope Leo X threatened to excommunicate Luther unless he retracted 41 propositions that were directly—albeit extra-contextually—extracted from Luther's writings. Luther interpreted this as nothing less than a demand to retract the Gospel itself and accordingly consigned the papal document to the flames in

December 1520, thereby setting the stage for his summons to the Diet of Worms in April of the following year.

It is at Worms that one can see how Luther relates his primary Reformation concern—the preaching of grace and faith as a means of consoling and unburdening consciences (Conscience I)—to his conviction that one must always be faithful to one's own conscience (Conscience II). When asked at Worms if he would revoke any of the things he had written, Luther replied that, in attacking the papacy and the papists he was attacking those "who, by their doctrines and their example, were ruining the Christian world, both spiritually and temporally. For no one can either deny or dissimulate, since the experience and the complaints of everyone are the witnesses, that through the laws of the pope and the doctrines of men the consciences of the faithful are most deplorably vexed and torn to pieces . . . especially in this illustrious German nation. . . . If, therefore, I should revoke these [writings] I would be doing nothing else than giving support to tyranny. . . . However, since I am a man and not God . . . I ought to both desire and expect someone to give testimony against my doctrine."

When pressed by the official interrogator, John von der Ecken, with indirect arguments for retracting, Luther responded with a demand for direct arguments in his celebrated words: "Unless I be convicted by the testimonies of the Scriptures or by evident reason (for I believe neither the pope nor councils by themselves, since it is clear they have often erred and contradicted themselves), I am overcome by the Scriptures I have cited and, since my conscience is held fast in the words of God, I am neither able nor willing to revoke anything, since to act against conscience is neither safe nor blameless."

At Worms, then, we see two fundamental aspects of conscience coming into play for Luther. He insisted he would be violating his conscience (Conscience II) if he were to retract his reformation teaching, a teaching directed above all at liberating, by means of the Word of God, consciences that had been ensnared by papal decrees and teachings (Conscience I).

II

One would surely be engaging in a "good guys versus bad guys" kind of historicizing were one to imagine that Luther had a monopoly on conscience in his struggle with Rome. In the first place, Luther did not invent the doctrine that one can never act against one's conscience. This was part of the biblical and Scholastic tradition he had inherited. The Franciscan Rule of 1223, for example, charges the friars "to obey their ministers in all things which they have promised God to observe, and which are not contrary to their conscience and to our Rule." Another witness says: "Were the pope to command anything against Holy Scripture, or the articles of faith, or the truth of the sacraments, or the commands of the natural or divine law, he ought not to be obeyed, but in such commands to be disregarded *(despiciendus)*." These are not the words of Wycliffe or Huss or some anti-papal conciliarist, but of Cardinal John de Torquemada, uncle of the Spanish Grand-Inquisitor.

Moreover, since the time of Thomas Aquinas, the radical view began to spread that it was wrong to act against even an erroneous conscience. At Worms, however, the official, von der Ecken, responded to Luther's appeal to conscience by saying: "Set aside your conscience, Martin, which you are bound to do, because it is erroneous, and it will be safe and blameless for you to revoke it. For Aquinas, on the contrary, one ought to set aside one's conscience, be it true or erroneous, only when the conscience is not at least probably certain. . . ." Had such a concept of conscience been operative at Worms, the official would not simply have *told* Luther his conscience was erroneous and then have expected him to retract. He would have had to furnish Luther with reasons sufficient for him to see the error of his ways. The Diet of Worms was simply not equipped for this sort of procedure.

Secondly, despite the criticism that the jurist von der Ecken deserves for his unnuanced handling of Luther's appeal to conscience, one must nevertheless note that part of his indirect argument against Luther was based on the fact that he thought Luther was calling into doubt the "most holy orthodox faith . . . which has been confirmed by the blood of martyrs." In other words, he is invoking as testimony to the truth of the traditional faith precisely those persons who have been heroically faithful to their consciences in holding to that faith.

What I am suggesting here is that both sides—Luther and Rome—are appealing to conscience, and that the ultimate question is not who is taking a firm stand on the basis of conscience, but: What is the truth? What is the Christian faith? Who is affirming it? Further, are either, or perhaps both, of the parties operating with a conscience that is to some extent erroneous? Luther, at least, realizes that this is a possibility for him. That is why he asks for someone to oppose him at the Diet by stating sound reasons or the clear testimony of Scripture against his teaching, if that is possible. As we know, such an adversary never came forth at the Diet of Worms. . . .

Harry McSorley, from *The Ecumenist*, March–April 1974, pp. 43–45.

Cathedral at Worms   DEAN, FREDERIC LEWIS

This Reformation monument at Geneva, Switzerland, honors
Calvin, Farel, Beza, and Knox.

BROWN BROTHERS

One religious reformer who stands almost as tall as Luther is John Calvin (1509–1564). His doctrine of predestination (some will be saved; some lost) put fear into the hearts of many. Where Luther cried "I have to rebel with all the heart that is in me against any man's being submerged in this world," Calvin preached a harsh, unremitting doctrine that everyone faces an inexorable fate: heaven or hell, regardless of his actions. His insistence upon the justice (that is, for him, vengeance) of God led him right back to what had caused Luther all his trouble: how can a person stand up against a tyrannous, whimsical God? Calvin, like Luther, precipitated a break from Rome and started a whole new trend in theology which was to affect not only Roman Catholicism but Protestant theology as well.

A third major break from the Roman Church came in England.* The essential issue was different, but the cause was the same: throwing off the "shackles" of Roman domination. At this time there was no general break in the Christian faith. There were problems, of course, but no one anywhere considered the unity of faith destroyed. No one could possibly see that God was leading His Church to a new understanding of itself —an understanding that was necessary if the Christian Faith was to survive in a world where the dominant civilizing influence was to be the dignity of the individual.

Once again the human side of the Church had to learn the hard way that it was not the super-state, the overriding, dominant, all-encompassing force in the state. It had to learn that Christianity is more than a political organ with religious motivation, more than a political system, more than a "guardian of faith and morals." It had to learn, at the cost of much suffering, that the Mystery of Christ was "super" natural; it belonged to no one in particular, to no special group, society, culture, or era. It had to learn that

---

* Luther had drawn most of Germany and Scandinavia away from Roman control; Calvinism swept through France, the Low Countries, and Scotland.

Christ was all things to all men and that the expression of Christ, as in the primitive church, was universal, it was not Roman. The lesson was not learned immediately. It did, however, begin to be understood when England declared itself free from the rule of Rome and set up an English Christian Church.

Like the Germanic revolt, the English revolt was political, based upon what seemed to be a very simple request. Henry VIII, King of England from 1509 to 1547 A.D., had petitioned the pope for an annulment of his marriage to Catherine (the Spanish niece of Emperor Charles V), who had been married to his older brother Arthur. Henry had married Catherine with a papal dispensation.

Such a request was rather routine, and certainly not new. Other sovereigns had requested it before him; some had been suc-

cessful, some not. Henry and Catherine did not have any male heirs, and hence the succession to the English throne was in jeopardy. To Henry the solution was simple; to the pope it was not. He was indebted to Charles V, the Spanish Emperor of Western Christendom, and was in hot debate with Francis I, King of France. He could hardly grant an annulment to Henry without displeasing Charles, and would not grant permission for Henry to marry Anne Boleyn, a favorite of the French court. What seemed to be a routine political-ecclesiastical matter turned out to be a nightmare.

The attempt by Henry to secure an annulment dragged on and on. The issue soon became strictly political and Henry, who had been given the title "Defender of the Faith" for his famous work "The Defense of the Seven Sacraments" (a reply to Luther's allegation that there were only two sacraments,

Henry VIII

Anne Boleyn

Henry VIII and his Council ordaining the translation of
the Bible into English.

baptism and the Lord's Supper), turned against the Roman system and asked for a judgment to be made in his own land. It was granted, but intrigue and delay infuriated Henry. Finally he took matters into his own hands. He divorced Catherine, married Anne, and took over the authority of the Church in England.

The history of papal relations with England are summed up in this one incident. A prominent Catholic historian writing of the separation of England from Roman ecclesiastical authority says:

[Henry] reflected the opinion of an entire nation, which though faithful to Catholicism, had little love for the face which the Church presented to the world . . . The centralized monarchy headed by the Pope of Rome, the taxes levied by Rome, the courts whose system of appeals led eventually to Rome, the Church's preoccupation with Italian politics—all these were things which English Catholics found extremely repugnant.*

Henry's excommunication in July, 1535, resulted in one of the sorriest episodes in the history of Western Christendom. Not only did the affair cause the beheading of St. Thomas More, one of history's most brilliant and beloved men, it precipitated a half century of violent persecution and the ultimate separation of the Church of England from the Church of Rome. Not since the days of Imperial Rome was Christianity at such a low tide. Twelve hundred years of mixing religion and politics had finally run its course. Christianity had survived in spite of politics, not because of it. Only because there were good people always working for the true mission of the Church did Western Christendom retain, at its core, its basic

faith. It was because of these people that the Roman Church was to rise from its sixteenth century defeat and take on the new life which would enable it to meet the challenge of the twentieth century.

The revolt against Roman Catholicism soon moved away from its political-theological center and became religious. Many divergent expressions of Christianity developed. These many Protestant groups can be divided into four general categories, depending upon how they relate to Roman Catholicism against which they were protesting.

1. The **Lutheran** groups followed Martin Luther's rejection of those parts of Roman Catholicism which he felt contradicted the Bible.

2. The **Reformed** Protestants retained in their religions only those things in Roman Catholicism which they believed were expressly contained in the Bible. Such groups as the Calvinists, Presbyterians, and Puritans, reflecting austere simplicity in their religious services, are outstanding examples of these groups.

3. The **Radical** Protestants departed even further from Roman Catholicism and rejected those aspects of Lutheranism and Calvinism which had any resemblance to Rome. They rejected all formulas, insisted on "a new birth in the Spirit" as shown by strict adherence to rigid moral laws and the rejection of infant baptism as valid. They tended to take Scripture very literally and tried to form ideal communities with common ownership of all goods. The Baptists, Anabaptists, Mennonites, Unitarians, Quakers, and Congregationalists are typical of the Radical Protestant groups.

4. The **English** Protestants retained almost all of the externals of Roman Cathol-

---

* Cf. Daniel-Rops, *The Protestant Reformation,* Vol. II, p. 231.

A Man for All Seasons*

Many people, unfortunately, have a faulty notion of what it means to be a saint. They often think of saints as not really human beings who live in a dream world far removed from the realities of human existence, almost totally removed from society, who spend their days praying, eating little or nothing, and experiencing none of the passion, turmoil, and concerns that most people experience. They seem to be puppets, dangled before the world by a god who works magical effects through them to dazzle people.

Nothing could be further from the truth. Men like Paul and Augustine, and Andrew and Francis, and women like Cecelia and Catherine, and Teresa and Elizabeth Seton were highly involved in the affairs of the world in which they lived. Perhaps the most famous of these "involved" saints was Thomas More, who lived and worked in the toughest arena of them all—politics, in a period of history when intrigue, double dealing, bribery, forgery, and the use of raw, naked power were the order of the day.

Thomas More was born in London in 1478. He was a brilliant student at

---

* The name of a prize-winning play which became an Academy Award winning movie written by Thomas Bolt, one of England's great living playwrights. *A Man for All Seasons* is the story of the conflict between St. Thomas More and Henry VIII, King of England.

Oxford and received his law degree from the Inn of Courts, one of England's most famous law schools of the sixteenth century. When he was twenty-four, he was elected to the House of Commons where he got a reputation for being bright, witty, sharp in debate, and a strong pleader of causes for the common people against the power of the government of Henry VII, father of Henry VIII. When Henry VIII became king in 1509, he appointed More, in succession, to knighthood, the king's cabinet, special minister, treasurer of the kingdom, and chancellor of one of the great states near London. In 1529 he appointed More as his chief executive officer (Lord High Chancellor). More was, after the king, England's most powerful man. It was as chief executive officer that he ran head on into conflict with the king.

Henry had married Catherine of Spain, but because they had no male children, Henry wanted to marry Anne Boleyn, to have, as he said, a legitimate male heir to the throne. Expecting to have his way, Henry sued for divorce from Catherine. After long and involved negotiations, the divorce was denied by the pope. Henry was furious—he decided to take matters into his own hands and declare himself head of the Church in England. He wanted More to approve his actions (they were political, not religious), but More refused, not principally because of the divorce, but because he believed the pope to be the head of the universal Church with final say in religious matters. When he ordered More as chief executive officer to approve his actions and spearhead the move, getting it through the House of Lords and approved by the House of Commons, More resigned. This was in 1532.

More's resignation did not end his involvement. Although he returned to his home and kept his views to himself, his reputation was so great that the king insisted that More make a statement approving his actions. Again More refused. For nearly two years the game of cat and mouse continued. Finally the king ordered More arrested and placed in the Tower of London, England's famous jail for political prisoners. For fourteen months More resisted every promise and threat to himself and his family. Finally he was brought to trial for high treason, and on July 1, 1535, he was condemned to death.

Thomas More, perhaps the most loved and respected saint outside of St. Francis of Assisi—and the apostles, of course—was a statesman, author, scholar, and humorist whose reputation extended beyond England. He was gentle and kind, honest and straightforward, sincere, and deeply religious. He was known as England's fairest judge and best Chancellor. He was loved by the nobles and the common people alike and respected by all because he was fair and honest. And before "the trouble" he was Henry VIII's best friend. He died because he refused to compromise on the unity aspect of the Church. In his last response to the prosecutor who accused him of being a traitor, More replied, ". . . I call and appeal to God . . . the Church is one and indivisible, and you have no authority to make a law which infringes on Christian unity." It was for his opposition to Henry's attempted takeover of the Church in England that Thomas More was beheaded on July 5, 1535.

icism except papal authority and the Latin language until King Edward VI (1547–1553) and Elizabeth (1558–1603) moved the English Church more and more toward Continental Protestantism. The Anglicans and the Methodists represent the two forms of English Protestantism; one nearly "Roman" in its worship, the other clearly anti-Roman in its practice.

As Protestant groups moved further and further from the Roman position, they expressed an entire spectrum of belief and practice ranging from nearly exact copies of Romanism to total rejection of Roman traditions. Many Protestant groups were formed in protest to existing Protestant practices, but all of them retained two basic elements of protest against Rome: opposition to the papacy and to the Roman interpretation of the faith. These two remain characteristic of all Protestant groups.

Not all of these Protestant groups, of course, arose in the sixteenth century. The successful development of these divergent expressions of the meaning of Christ took many years and drew more and more people away from the expression of Christianity that was peculiar to the Roman Church, which had been "The Faith" for twelve hundred years. Where once Western Civilization had been unified in its religious expression —however inadequate it had been from time to time—now this civilization was fragmented into dozens of expressions of faith, each reflecting the special theological and cultural peculiarities of its adherents.

Typical of the times, differences in religion (and politics) precipitated religious wars. Religious dissidents, wherever they arose, were suppressed or tortured or put to death in crude and, to us, inhuman ways. Wherever the dissent arose—in Catholic or Protestant countries—the treatment of "heretics" was the same. If the Spanish Inquisition is notorious in history for its treatment of non-Catholics, then so is much of the record of Protestantism. Luther's condemnation of the peasants in their uprising against his protector, Calvin's espousal of burning at the stake, Zwingli's going into battle, Henry's torturing, the Huguenots' degrading torture of opponents, and the shameful treatment of "other" groups by particular Protestant sects in early American history are a shameful record of religious fanaticism. Such reaction was typical of the times. It was to be a long while before religious toleration would become part of the political scene in Europe and America.

Recent Developments

The political, social, economic, and religious effects of the Protestant movement directly affected the lives and liberty of people in Europe (and America) for 400 years. In spite of the bitterness that resulted from the political-religious upheavals of the period, there were Christians who spoke out against the separation and worked to restore the unity that had existed in Christendom. It was not until the 1800s in the United States, however, that organized efforts were made to promote interdenominational organizations whose primary concern was Christian unity. The first efforts were made by Protestant groups which were somewhat similar in philosophy and practice.

During the 1950s this movement, which came to be called Ecumenism, gained momentum and took on worldwide proportions. Protestant groups formed a World Council of Churches, and after many attempts, persuaded Roman Catholics to at least be observers and advise the World Council on Catholic concerns. In the past five or six years, the Ecumenical Movement has produced great results. Dialogues between scholars and commissions set up by both Protestant and Roman Catholic authorities have come to many agreements, the most important being that they all have the

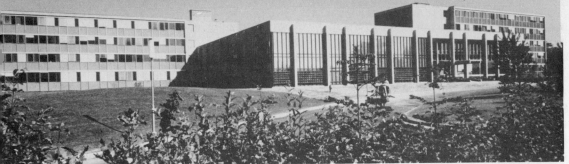

World Council of Churches' Headquarters, Geneva

same goal: bringing the message of Christ to all people and establishing the kingdom of God on earth.

Not all problems, of course, can be solved immediately, but major breakthroughs are in evidence. Lutheran and Catholic theological study groups, for example, agree basically on the Eucharist (Catholic and Lutheran Eucharistic celebrations are somewhat similar in form) and Catholic and Lutheran scripture scholars are working to produce Bibles and Biblical materials that are common to both. Catholic and Anglican study commissions, set up jointly by Pope Paul VI and Archbishop Ramsey of Canterbury, agree on the validity of the Anglican priesthood and on the Eucharist. Although these are preliminary agreements only (the findings of these groups must be submitted to and be approved or modified as necessary by appropriate Church authorities on both sides), they move the Catholic/Lutheran and Catholic/Anglican communities closer to unity in other matters also.

In a historic statement presented by the joint commission of Lutheran and Catholic theologians meeting to discuss the role of the papacy in the reunion of Lutheran and Catholic expressions of Christianity, the commission stated that "papal primacy need no longer be a barrier to reconciliation." For Catholics, the papacy would hold its traditional role; for Lutherans, the papacy would be a visible symbol of the underlying unity of all Christians.

Not all Protestant groups join in the Lutheran-Catholic and Anglican-Catholic agreements, of course, and not all agreements among Lutherans, Anglicans, and Catholics will be total. The important point

in all this is not total unity, however, but that a different tone in religious attitudes among divergent sects of Christianity is present. Various Christian expressions of the meaning of Christ for people are beginning to come together and explore their common concerns. They are not stressing differences; they are seeking similarities. This is the first and most important step in restoring unity to Christ's Church which is found not in conformity but in charity.

The Reform, Stage II

The external forces which stripped the Roman Church of its power in the civil world forced the Roman Church to purge itself internally. This it tried to do, and in a measure succeeded, at the very height of its external troubles.

Luther and Henry VIII had attacked the authority structure of the Church, and Calvin had attacked the concept of salvation. Others had attacked on both these fronts before, but none had been so successful in drawing large segments of the Church away from Rome. The attacks on the very heart of the sixteenth century expression of Catholicism and the success of the reformers resulted in a reexamination of the principles of Roman Catholicism and how these principles were expressed. **Doctrinal statements** (often the "preached" doctrine had veered away from the core idea), **disciplinary practices** (some governmental and moral stances were very questionable) and **worship** (the conduct of the liturgy and the devotional life had become routine, almost magical) received a complete overhaul in the council discussion held at Trent, on the border between Northern Italy and Germany, in three major sessions, 1545–1547, 1551–1552, and 1562–1563 A.D. During the long intervals between sessions specialists worked almost constantly, addressing themselves to doctrinal questions and the reform of Catholic life generally.*

There is no doubt that the principal characters in the drama of revolt considered themselves members of the Catholic Church, but they resented, and therefore resisted, the autocratic control of the Church by the papacy. More often than not at this time, the papacy was under the control of the curial (governmental) cardinals and their lackeys, and bishops who held their positions as favors from local rulers. As hostility grew between each faction and the "Roman condition," statements were made which continued to widen the gap. These in turn led to doctrinal and liturgical stances which made Protestantism (in its many expressions) a separate Christian community.

The comparison between the doctrinal and liturgical formulations of early Protestantism and Roman Catholicism at the time of Trent illustrates a basic point about the way in which positions were formulated. *The Protestant positions were generally the product of a single person's theology; the Catholic positions were the result of a consensus generally approved by the pope.* Many Protestant positions were a reaction (and a justified reaction) to Catholic abuses. Protestants generally relied upon Scripture; Catholics relied upon Tradition.** It is, of course, an oversimplification to say that Protestants relied only on Scripture and Catholics relied only on Tradition, though the *stress* was as indicated. Similarly, it is false to say that Protestants teach that faith alone is necessary—without good works. As

---

* Political upheavals, war, and disease interrupted the Council, once for four years and once for ten years.

** Tradition, Thomas More had said, is the adaptation to changing kinds of society of the one single fundamental message.

Council of Trent

a matter of fact, *good works* have always been the hallmark of most sincere Protestants.

Nevertheless, Catholic theologians must always test their ideas against the ideas of other Catholic theologians; Protestant theologians do not. Thus, there is a unity of expression in Catholic theology that is lacking in Protestant circles. This does not mean to say that Catholics are always right or that Protestants are always wrong! What it does imply is that there is a basic unity in Catholicism that is lacking in Protestantism, though denominations do have unity within their own churches. This unity in Roman Catholic theology is focused in the Pope, even when the papal prerogative of infallibility is not in question.

The practice of calling together experts to lay the groundwork for the bishop's discussions was most in evidence at the Council of Trent. Luther's attacks upon cherished traditions (and other reformers' expressions of doctrine) led the theologians to take a long hard look at everything Catholic. When the Council finally closed and the decrees were given papal approval, a new era began in the Church which was to last until the Second Vatican Council of 1962–1965.

The bishops at the Council of Trent and the popes who ruled during the critical years of Trent so reformed Catholic life that never again would the cardinals and bishops as a group be princes in the secular sphere. They expressed doctrine in statements that left no doubt as to what the Roman Catholic Church at that time considered true doctrine. They legislated about liturgical worship to bring the Mass into central focus again in Catholic life. Most of all, they did away with so-called "Catholic practices," which had taken on an air of magic, and did away with abuses which exploited the simple faith of many uneducated Christians. They cut away years of faulty preaching and practice and established beliefs on sound principles.

The whole body of Catholic doctrine and practice was discussed at Trent in the light of Protestant criticism of it at the time, and decrees were published and regulations laid down to clarify the Catholic view and to regulate Catholic life. Special decrees on Sacred Scripture, salvation, the sacraments in general, and the sacraments in particular (Baptism, Penance, Confirmation, Anointing of the Sick, and the Eucharist), and on original sin were published. Laws, with strict enforcement measures were promulgated on the episcopal and priestly life as well as on the collection of fees and on preaching. Special rules for the study of Scripture and theology were published and particular attention was given to the Mass as sacrifice.

While it is true that the Council of Trent came as a reaction to Protestant criticism of the Church, its function was not that of an agency trying to state new doctrines in opposition to Protestant views. **It was the official teaching authority of the Church attempting to express Catholic doctrine as it came to be understood in the long tradition of the Church.** There was no question of forcing belief to "Trent" doctrines; it was a question of trying to state what the Church had believed about basic Christian doctrine for centuries. The role of the theologians was, as always, to explore, to examine, to restate, and to clarify (some of the hottest debates in the history of the Church took place at this time). The role of the bishops, on the other hand, was not to engage in theological debate but to preserve traditional belief as it was understood through the ages. The triple sources of Scripture, the Fathers of the early Church, and the statements on various topics as accepted by the popes through the ages, were the test of what the Church believed up to that time and what it believed at the moment. Thus,

the decrees of the Council of Trent attempted to restate doctrine as it was traditionally understood; they were not simply a refutation of Luther's viewpoints or those of other Protestant critics.

Although the official Church was deeply involved in the politics and the religious protests of the time, general Catholic life moved in the mainstream of history. Catholics were deeply affected by the political and religious issues, but Catholic life did not grind to a halt while the political and religious issues were being resolved.

The reform of Roman Catholicism within its own ranks was not confined to official positions or to statements of doctrine. At the same time when many were being drawn from the Roman Church, Catholic preachers and teachers were intensifying their efforts to bring reform to the Catholic people, and Catholic missionaries were going out to the newly discovered lands outside of the European perimeter.

Typical of the reform of Catholic life from within were the emergence of several new religious orders and the appearance of a number of well-educated and holy people who worked to improve the spiritual and moral expression of Roman Catholicism. Persons like St. Teresa of Avila (1515–1582), and St. John of the Cross (1542–1605), St. Charles Borromeo (1538–1584), St. Philip Neri (1515–1595), St. Vincent de Paul (1580–1660), St. Francis de Sales (1567–1622), and St. John de la Salle (1651–1719) were typical of the leadership in the Catholic Church which sought to reform Catholic life without separating from Catholic unity. Perhaps the greatest influence for reform, however, came from one of the new religious orders which developed to meet the contemporary needs. This religious order was the Society of Jesus, popularly known as the Jesuits, founded by St. Ignatius of Loyola.

Ignatius appeared on the historical scene at the very height of the sixteenth century turmoil (1491–1556). He had been an officer in the Spanish army during the wars against France, and in one of them he was so badly crippled that he had to give up his military ambitions. After long and careful thought he decided to become a priest and work toward improving the conditions of the poor people in his native Basque territory. He began his studies for the priesthood at the age of thirty-three in Paris. While there, he and some of his close friends formed a kind of religious society for the purpose of educating people and helping them to be better Christians. They called themselves the Company of Jesus.

The Jesuits were not the only religious order which came into existence at that time, but they are the most famous. Dedicated to scholarship, vowed to service "wherever needed by the Pope," they really led the way in the Catholic reform of the next three centuries. The Jesuits were to the Church of the sixteenth and following centuries what the Benedictines had been in the early Church and the Franciscans and Dominicans in the Middle Ages. Their life reflected the changing conditions and the continued understanding of the Church's mission to the world.

Religious orders in the early Church were monastic; in the medieval Church they were mendicant. In the "modern" age they were "free-lance," bound by vows, but dedicated to go where the action is. For this reason, the Jesuits were found in the universities, in parishes, in social action, or in the missions. They set the style for religious orders for succeeding generations.

Pictured together are Fathers Robert T. Cornell and Robert F. Drinan, who are concurrently serving terms in the House of Representatives.

181

The Church and the Missions During the Renaissance

As we have said, Catholic life did not grind to a halt during the political-religious troubles in Germany, Switzerland, and England. Not everyone in those countries joined the reformers, and in France, Spain, Portugal, Italy, Ireland, Poland, and Austria, Catholic life went on virtually undisturbed. Furthermore, there was a whole world outside of Western Europe which had opened its vistas to Western Civilization. The Crusades had whetted the appetites of Europeans, and the stories of merchant seamen who had pushed ever further from the shores of Europe, stirred the imagination—and the greed—of kings and commercial giants in all of Western Europe.

The Crusades helped to move Western European civilization from its insular position and brought both the government and the Church into contact, not only with the Eastern Mediterranean cultures, but with Far Eastern and African civilizations. Among the plunder brought back from the expeditions "to win back the Holy Places," were spices, cloth, precious gems and metal, and works of art. There was a rise of interest in the East, especially India, among the sea-

faring nations, and one of the first orders of business in each of these nations was the establishing of trade routes and controlled ports. Portugal, England, Spain, France, and the various independent states of Italy each staked out territory and guarded it carefully. A new business was born which would soon be a deciding factor in many a nation's history. When these ventures began, these countries were one in Christianity; where they went, the faith went with them. Priests

Columbus at the
Court of Ferdinand and Isabella

(both religious and secular) accompanied the merchant ships, first as chaplains, then as missioners. From the conversion of the barbarians (about 500–800 A.D.) until the discovery of "new lands" (about 1500), the work of conversion had taken place on the perimeter of the old Roman Empire. Now, however, a whole new mission endeavor began.*

A typical example of the effect of this stress was what happened in Paraguay, in the very center of South America. The Jesuit missioners had established settlements of natives in what they called "reductions," or areas whose center was the church, the school, and the hospital. The entire population worked the settlement, each person contributing to the good of the small city. Well over 100,000 Indians lived in these villages, and the territory was Christian in the very best sense.

When the government took over, expelling the Jesuits and the nuns who ran the school and the hospital, the "reductions" became slave camps—and one of the worst periods in human history ensued. What happened here was rather typical of the treatment of natives everywhere, and soon the Church representatives were forced by government decree to limit their activities to caring for the families of the Europeans only. A kind of church-caste system developed, and the emphasis upon services for the rich —first for the Europeans, later for the landed aristocracy of each nation—became the pattern of activity of the Church in South America.**

Once the merchants of Europe had established themselves in foreign lands, the rush was on. Between 1493 and 1560 the Spanish and Portuguese had virtual control of southern North America, Central and South America. The French had Canada for their territory, and by 1664 England firmly controlled the eastern seaboard of what was to be the United States. The Portuguese, Italian, and Spanish fleets had control of the African coastal territories, India, and Japan, and had made inroads in China. Wherever they went, priests established small Christian settlements and the work of conversion went on.

In almost all of the expeditions three kinds of people were present: representatives of the government and trading companies, soldiers and sailors, and missionaries. In spite of the good work of the missionaries, the other two groups established the final impression that Western civilization was to leave on the natives. In the last analysis, though the governments proclaimed their desire to establish the faith in the native lands, their first interest was financial; they stopped at nothing to make sure that their ventures were profitable.

The ever-present question remains: Why go to foreign lands when there is so much to be done at home? It is simplistic to say that "the Church" ought to work among its

----

* In spite of the emphasis on politics during that 1000 year period, the missionary thrust in the Church had never been lost. The first, or central, emphasis was always on the bringing of the Christ-event to those who did not have it. In this next mission venture the old zeal was present, but a very important aspect of mission work was forgotten. In the new effort, the Latin (or Roman) Church with its developed dogmas, its complicated moral systems, and its "medieval court" liturgy was brought *en masse* to the natives of each land. Although there was tremendous success due to the saintliness of individual missioners, the over-emphasis on Western Catholicism (which was associated with Western governments) was to wreak havoc when the corruption of a government became linked with the Western Church.

** Brazil is typical of the development. Today Brazil is a "Catholic country" with 98 percent of the people Catholic. But the pitiful condition of most Brazilians testifies to the social structure bred 300 years ago.

L. MANNING, VAN CLEVE PHOTOGRAPHY

RELIGIOUS NEWS SERVICE

own (of course, it ought to), for there is an imperative inherent in the faith of Christians which impels the Church to bring the knowledge of the Christ-event to everyone. The very nature of *what* is believed makes it necessary that everyone at least *hear* this belief.

Missionary work must involve more than "converting" people to a cultural expression of Christianity. There is the important "not yet" aspect of creation which Christianity and Judaism have at the very heart of their salvation history.

For Christians, this "not yet" aspect has been interpreted in various ways at various times leading, as we have already pointed out, to new self-understanding. In St. Paul's day, for example, the "new creation" was believed to be imminent: Christ was soon to reappear.* Later it was envisioned as the City of God as St. Augustine presented it. Still later, when Christians realized that there was no immediate City of God, this "not yet" element came to be understood as the need for making *this* world better. This thrust toward achieving the "not yet" has

_____

* This is evident from the very last words of the Christian Bible: "Come, Lord Jesus."

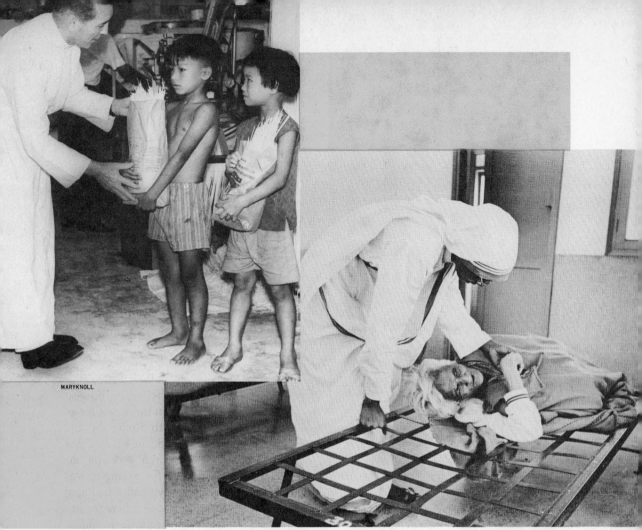

MARYKNOLL

RELIGIOUS NEWS SERVICE

impelled Christians to fulfill their prophetic mission of bringing their interpretation of the mystery of life to all people.

There are, then, two aspects to missionary work: 1) the need to let others know of the Christ-event and what this means in each age, and 2) the need for the now-Christians to be truly the People of God, and by their lives to testify that the human condition can (and must) be better in this present life, for this life is the place where Christianity is meant to have its impact. Christians who truly understand the meaning of Christ realize that they must go beyond the practical here and now (but not ignore the practical

here and now) and assume the risks inherent in being ahead of civilization in ideals, words, and actions. This is the "penance" of modern Christianity; to renounce the "what's in it for me" in favor of "what must be done for humanity."

This is essentially the motivation of missionaries. In contrast to the self-interested privateers who set out for foreign lands *to take* what they want, the missionary goes out *to give* what is most precious to him: his faith. This missionary thrust has continued throughout the history of Christendom. This explains why there are over one billion Christians in the world today.

18th Century French statesman, Talleyrand

The End of the Fifth Era

While religious turmoil was dominating the history of the Church in the sixteenth century, civilization continued to move forward at ever increasing speeds. When the emphasis of people's interests was shifted from the eternal world to the world in which they lived, every aspect of life developed a new force. The economic side of life improved with exploration, with the inventions for improving productivity, and with the improved science of banking. The political side of life saw the development of new countries, the rise of new power blocs and new forms of statesmanship, and the development of self-determination within each state. The cultural side of life also responded to this new emphasis, with literature, operas, plays, music, art, architecture, and the social mores of every country reflecting the new humanism and the new politics.

By 1750 Western Europe had changed radically from the Europe of the late medieval period. Change was no longer slow and nearly imperceptible; too many things were happening in too many places too rapidly for gradualism to be a workable scheme. Once the religious reform movement had set in, once the countries outside of Europe had been explored, once the new age of science and freedom of inquiry had begun, a new stage in the development of human history began.

This tumultuous 250 year period closed with the Church in an entirely new position. The long period of Western European history in which the pope was the central political and moral force in Europe was over. The heads of states no longer even consulted the papal authority, much less let it influence policy. The general religious life also reflected this trend. Only in those territories which were still "loyal" to Rome did the Church have any say—and in many cases only indirectly. The Church was still involved in politics (Italy, for example, was not yet a unified country, and the Papal States exerted a strong influence here for another two hundred years), but it no longer controlled the practical destiny of civil government.

The Church in Europe was no longer *the* Church, but *a* Church, often struggling for survival in an era when the religion of the ruler was the religion of his people.

This new position was not necessarily a bad thing. Many, of course, considered it a tragedy, but in reality it freed the Church from virtual enslavement to political pressure, enabled it to give most of its attention to spiritual matters, and permitted it to be flexible enough to adjust to the age of freedom that was about to develop all over the world.

1. Summarize the political, economic, and cultural changes taking place in Western civilization as it moved into its fourth five hundred years.

2. What political changes affected the Church at this period of its history?

3. What is meant by "humanism"? How did it affect the life and culture of western Europe?

4. Prepare a brief report on the invention of movable type for printing.

5. What seemed to be the underlying cause for a need for reform in the Christian Church in the West?

6. What things seem to be needed to make a reform or revolution successful? Explain.

7. Why was the papacy under attack during the Renaissance?

8. Why was the preached theology of the late 1400 and early 1500s so wide of the mark of true Christianity?

9. What aspect of salvation, as preached by so many, disturbed Luther? What was his view about salvation?

10. Was Luther qualified to discuss theological and scriptural matters? Why? Why not? What was his most important Biblical contribution?

11. What were some of the reforms Luther advocated that were made a part of Roman Catholic practice during Vatican II?

12. What was the heart of Luther's stand against the pope?

13. What was Luther really seeking in his opposition to Catholic theology and practices current in his day?

14. What was the political reason for Luther's success?

15. Prepare brief reports on John Calvin, John Knox, John Hus, John Wyclif, John Wesley, and Huldreich Zwingli.

16. What caused the break between Henry VIII and the pope?

17. Why did Thomas More oppose Henry VIII? Why was he put to death?

18. Be prepared to make a distinction among the various kinds of Protestantism. Discuss why some are more able to begin discussions on unity with Rome than others.

19. Find out what Protestant denominations are represented in your general neighborhood.

Without causing embarrassment to your Protestant friends, find out how much they know about the basic beliefs of their denomination and of the origin of their form of Protestantism.

20. What is ecumenism? What are some recent moves toward unity initiated by Lutherans, Anglicans, and Catholics?

21. What aspects of Catholic life did the Council of Trent address itself to? What principal abuse did it do away with?

22. What is the main difference between the way Catholic and Protestant doctrinal statements come about?

23. What is "tradition" in the Roman Catholic Church? Why is it important to Roman Catholics?

24. How did the religious orders founded in the sixteenth and seventeenth centuries differ from those of earlier periods?

25. What contribution to Catholic reform did St. Vincent de Paul and St. John de la Salle make? Prepare a brief report on each.

26. Prepare a brief report on St. Ignatius Loyola and the Jesuits.

27. Was the "Reformation Episode" all there was to Catholic life in this period of Church history? Explain.

28. Prepare a map indicating the lands to which missionaries went during the period of exploration.

29. What was the difference between the philosophy and purpose of the missionaries and the governments and trading companies who went to newly discovered lands?

30. What caused the failure of so many missionary efforts in many promising areas of the newly discovered lands?

RELIGIOUS NEWS SERVICE

Modern Christianity

12

The Church Enters an Age of Scientific Development

In the 400 years between the end of the Council of Trent (1565) and the conclusion to Vatican Council II (1965), the Church lived a reformed life. Stripped of its political and economic power, and wielding less and less influence in philosophy, culture, and art, the Church concentrated on its own internal religious affairs. The reforms initiated at Trent gradually changed the liturgical, doctrinal, and moral emphases of the fourteenth and fifteenth centuries, and led to a distinctive "Catholic" religious life-style. As Protestantism moved further and further away from "Roman" practices, the distinctions between Roman Catholic and Protestant Christianity became more noticeable. Catholics had their religious way of life, and Protestants had theirs—the two lived in different religious spheres. There was the "Catholic" religion and the "Protestant" religion, and for all practical purposes, neither thought of the other as Christian. The effect, of course, was to create a kind of Christian isolationism, and Christians began to live in two worlds: the world of their own religion and the world of their secular affairs.

But God had not intended Christianity to be insular. So Christians believe He set in motion the human forces that would move Christianity from its preoccupation with itself—from its "self" consciousness—to concern for the world in which it lived. These forces were the revolutions in science, philosophy, and politics which were to usher in the New Age of the Twentieth Century.

The Scientific Revolution

From the time people emerged from their prehuman existence, progress toward a more sophisticated mode of living has been inevitable. People have emerged from their near-animal stage to the present period of civilization—the modern era when most people have learned to control and manipulate their environment to suit their needs. But the development of people from primitive conditions to modern sophistication has been uneven—forging ahead swiftly at one time; leveling off at another. In some places the development came early; in others it lagged behind.

As slow as the cilivizing process seems, it has progressed with amazing speed when it is compared with other evolutionary developments in the process of fulfilling the creative dynamics implanted in the universe when God first called matter into being. The forming process of the universe, for example, took at least five billion years, and maybe as much as fifteen or even fifty billion years according to some scientific speculation. And after the earth was ready to support life, a billion years, at least, passed before evolution began to shape and form animals and people. Over a million years went by before people could live on this earth in relative security and begin to cultivate crops and raise animals for their own use. But once the forces of evolution brought the dynamics of the civilizing process into focus, like a magnifying glass focusing the rays of the sun, progress in the civilizing process accelerated with amazing speed—each generation, building on the accomplish-

ments of the past, has brought civilization to its present stage.

The developments in science, philosophy, and politics in the West which ushered in the New Age started slowly, but increasingly gained momentum so that at the present time, the rate of change almost staggers the mind. And the changes went on almost simultaneously—each one affecting the others and all three moving civilization ever more swiftly toward its created goal.

The movement of civilization in the West toward the New Age had its roots in the economic and cultural developments which were accelerated by the Renaissance. When the focus of people's attention was centered upon themselves and the world in which they lived, the stage was set for an entirely new civilization to emerge.

Perhaps no period of civilization illustrates the influence of one culture upon another and the importance of tradition than the period following the revival of interest in Greek thought, the period we call the Renaissance. When the philosophy, art, architecture, and literature of ancient Greece influenced late medieval thought, a knowledge explosion occurred which affected the economics, politics, and culture of succeeding generations, not only in Europe but around the world. Once the Renaissance impact was felt, people with particular genius in every field came to contribute increasingly to the advance of others in their own field.

A striking example of this is the effect that Copernicus (1473–1543), the famous Polish astronomer, had on Galileo (1564–1642), the Italian scientist who revolutionized people's concept of the universe, and on the two scientific philosophers, Francis Bacon of England (1561–1626) and Rene Descartes of France (1596–1650). The scientific geniuses of this age created a whole new period of history sometimes referred to as the "Scientific Revolution."

The scientific revolution stressed independent inquiry and knowledge from observable data as opposed to speculative thought and hypothetical conclusions. This new approach to knowledge affected the philosophers of the age and spurred inventions for the improvement of the human condition ranging from a seed planting drill (1701) which improved crops, to chlorine bleach (1785). Almost every facet of economic life improved as a result of the scientific revolution. Mechanical weaving (1733), mill-rolled iron (1784), the steam engine (1796), beet-sugar extraction (1747), the modern toilet (1778), and some fifty other major inventions or practical improvements appeared on the human scene in the eighteenth century.

As civilization moved into the nineteenth century, more and more inventions changed the economic and cultural life of people, and when the twentieth century explosion of science took place, the period of transcivilization began.

The Philosophical Revolution

Perhaps the most far-reaching effect on human culture, however, came in the field of philosophy. So important was this effect that the eighteenth century is often referred to as the "Age of Enlightenment." Scientists, mathematicians, and inventors had popularized the scientific method; philosophers adopted their method and created a whole new approach to the study of philosophy. They stressed the importance of the human reasoning capacity and rejected whatever could not be "proved" by reason.

The working principle of these philosophers was summed up by Immanuel Kant (1724–1804), the German philosopher, who wrote: "Enlightenment is man's emergence from non-age [which is not] lack of intelligence but a lack of determination and

Immanuel Kant   BROWN BROTHERS

courage to use that intelligence without another's guidance. Dare to know! Have courage to use your own intelligence!"

Every aspect of human experience was examined by these scholars and intellectuals, but no area got more attention—or was affected more by their sharp wit and biting criticism—than politics and religion. Every European country produced a whole school of these radical philosophers, whose common bond was a critical attitude toward the existing authoritative stance of government and religion, which, they contended, interfered with people's basic freedom and the use of their intelligence. They believed in freedom of speech and the press, and in personal liberty; they wrote vehemently against cruel legal procedures and arbitrary enforcement of law; and they were openly hostile to organized Christianity and subjected it to piercing sarcasm and disdainful wit.

To replace organized Christianity—a religion of "magic and marble" as they caricatured it—they proposed a new religion

Something Happened

Everyone experiences unique, even strange, inexplicable things in his life. Who hasn't had a disturbing dream, a "sixth sense" experience, a "feeling" about something, a sense that someone was watching, an impression of something preternatural, something eerie, something that defies immediate, physical explanation? People accept these experiences, often shrug them off, give, perhaps, an easy "natural" explanation, or dismiss them as coincidental, lucky, or weird.

In addition to these common experiences, some people experience extraordinary events which affect their lives profoundly. (We are not speaking here of feats of magic, once-in-a-lifetime opportunities, or the narrations of charlatans, psychotics, or hysterical people.) Skeptics may scoff, and experts may give "explanations," but the fact remains that some people do experience something that cannot be dismissed or explained away. How do we explain, for example, the sudden turn-around (conversion, if you will) of St. Paul? Something happened to him. He said he saw Christ. How do you explain Moses' sudden determination to return to the Egypt he fled in panic and confront the pharaoh about the slavery of the Hebrews? Something changed his mind. And what was it that made Joan of Arc "do her thing"?

One such extraordinary experience which defies physical explanation is the phenomenon of Lourdes, a small town in southwest France in the foothills of the Pyrenees mountains. It was in Lourdes that Bernadette Soubirous was born in 1844. She was a frail girl, too often too sick to go to school. When she was able, she took care of some sheep in the pasture areas around Lourdes, but generally she was home, doing small jobs for her mother because her asthma kept her from exerting herself. She seemed to be an average girl, prayerful, it's true, but not much out of the ordinary.

One day, when she was fourteen, her mother sent her to get some firewood from the driftwood along the river outside of town. Her sister and a friend went with her because she was too frail to bring much wood home. As she was getting ready to walk through the small river to the other side (her

RELIGIOUS NEWS SERVICE

sister and friend had already gone across), she heard a strong wind, but felt nothing. She looked around, saw the trees were not moving, so she went about her business. But when the sound continued, she looked toward a kind of grotto in the rocky hills near the river. All of a sudden, she tells us, she saw a brilliant light and made out the form of, as she said, "a beautiful lady." She was, naturally, rooted to the spot. Her sister and her friend called to her, but she didn't respond. They went back to her and saw that she was experiencing something—an asthma attack, they thought. When she finally "came to," they pressed her for an explanation. When they got home, her sister told her mother who became very angry and told Bernadette to forget her daydreaming.

Seventeen times between that day, Februrary 11, and June 1858, Bernadette experienced the appearance of her beautiful lady, who finally told her, "I am the Immaculate Conception." Among other things, her Lady told her to tell the parish priest that he should build a chapel on the spot where the apparitions took place.

Naturally nobody believed Bernadette. Her parents were frightened and angry. The parish priest told her to forget it. The mayor of the town and the police threatened to put her in jail. The skeptics taunted her, and her friends laughed at her. Through it all she kept her composure and stuck to her story. Finally, the following October, her pastor, convinced that "something" had happened to Berna-

dette, asked the bishop to investigate. For three years a panel of experts (doctors, lawyers, clergymen) investigated the phenomenon and concluded that Bernadette had, really, experienced a visitation of the Blessed Virgin. But for twenty years, Bernadette experienced the doubts, derision, and contempt of people, even some of the nuns in whose convent she had entered. She died, finally, of the asthma she had suffered all her life, on April 16, 1878.

One of the most extraordinary Christian shrines in the world is located at Lourdes where, however it is explained, something happened that changed the life of Bernadette, the town of Lourdes, the people of France, and the devotional life of Catholics all over the world. Catholics believe that Mary, the Mother of Jesus, did appear to Bernadette that cold, damp day in the grotto above the river Gave.

EDITORIAL PHOTOCOLOR ARCHIVES

called *Deism*. They rejected miracles, revelation, God's acting in His world, dogmas not explainable by reason, and any sort of hierarchy that enslaved people's minds and lives. Most of them believed in God, but it was a mechanical God who had created the world with laws to govern it, but who like a watchmaker then left it to tick for itself. The effect of Deism was not so much an abandonment of religion as a reconsideration of the place religion should have in people's lives.

Some of the educated ceased to practice Christianity except in its more obvious cultural forms; some became more and more skeptical of Christianity's claim to be the one true faith (it had been shown that there were many other religions whose people believed just as firmly as Christians); some ignored religion as being completely irrelevant to people's earthly progress and comfort. The most serious result was that, from this time on, religion occupied a very secondary place in many people's lives and had little if any influence in the political and cultural arena. This effect has lasted well into the twentieth century.

The Political Revolutions

History is filled with incidents of heroic endeavors by fearless individuals to establish the principle of individual liberty and dignity. The Greek ideal, the Roman Republic, and the revolt of the gladiators are celebrated in song and story. No matter how ruthless the suppression of freedom was (for centuries, it was understood as a matter of course that the defeated would be killed or taken as slaves), the evolutionary thrust of people for self-determination always remained alive. Even in the days of "the divine right of kings," strong men tried to place limits on the inevitable grasp for total power by a single person. One of the most celebrated examples of this effort to limit the power of the ruler was the defeat of the English King John at Runnymeade, where the nobility forced him to sign the Magna Carta (1215 A.D.), which was a bill of

King John signing the Magna Carta   BROWN BROTHERS

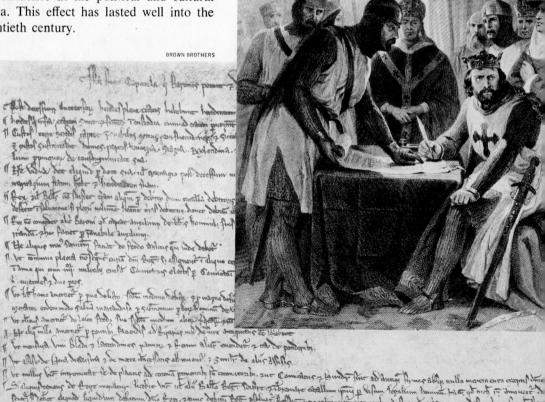

BROWN BROTHERS

rights for the English lords, guaranteeing them their rights and privileges.

It may have seemed a minor effort at the time, but it established a mode of action which was copied in the next several centuries when groups of lesser nobles resisted or fought against despotic power.

When the German princes were able to defy the Emperor at the time of Luther, and the English could successfully defy the pope, a pattern of striving for independence was set which led eventually to the American Revolution, which made possible the establishment of the first really democratic government (in which those who govern do so by the consent of the governed), and to the French Revolution (1789 A.D.). The success of these democratic movements ensured that the next era in civilization would be characterized by the theme of freedom: the right of the people to be governed by those whom they choose. This evolution toward individual liberty is still taking place.*

People's move toward personal freedom was heightened in Europe by the scientific and philosophical revolutions which came from the Renaissance. It was inevitable, therefore, that the political structure of Europe would change and that the old monarchic system of government which grew out of the abuses of feudalism would disappear.

Thinking people no longer accepted the principle of the divine right of kings or the concept of absolutism as these were represented by the civil and ecclesiastical governments of the time. They wanted a say in how government ordered their lives and a voice in choosing those who would govern them. Once again, the tensions between the forces for change and the forces for continuity came to a head; the resulting conflict produced an entirely different political picture in Europe and gave rise to what is known as constitutional government in almost every European nation.

The change in the political system which eventually made self-government throughout the world possible was most dramatically portrayed in the establishment of political democracy in the United States and in France toward the end of the eighteenth century (1776 and 1789).

We do not have the space here to discuss the American Revolution in detail. Let it be sufficient, therefore, to remark that the leaders of the American Revolution were in the main Deists and as such they were strong advocates of freedom of speech, of the press and of assembly. They felt that, given the proper circumstances and the proper structure, people could govern themselves. When the economic and political practices of En-

---

* The thrust toward self-determination, democratic forms of government, and individual liberty, like other evolutionary developments, is never smooth. It is over 2000 years since the promulgation of the Greek ideal, but only a handful of people seem able to govern themselves, or are given an opportunity to govern themselves.

gland forced a showdown in the American colonies, the framers of the *Declaration of Independence* and the *Constitution* were ready with the principles of self-government which they wrote into the American political system.

It was not long before the success of the American Revolution would have a far-reaching effect on all of Europe. Although there was a technical difference between the American Revolution and the revolutions in Europe, the effect on the political structures was the same.

The American Revolution was a *separation* of people *from* a government; the European revolutions of the succeeding periods were an *overthrow* of a government *within* a country. The first and most significant political revolution in Europe was the French Revolution (1789–1793). It had a serious effect upon the Roman Church, for it destroyed the last stronghold of the papacy outside of Italy, brought to an end direct papal influence in government, and forced a change in ecclesiastical thinking which af-

fected Church-State relationships down to the present day.

In their attempt to replace the existing government, the leaders of the French Revolution attacked everything that was even remotely connected with the government, and that meant the hierarchical Church with its vast array of titled bishops and princely abbots. Paradoxically, there were many good, zealous priests within the Church structure who were working for the people and against the existing conditions. But in the fanaticism of the Revolution, everything associated with Catholicism was attacked with a fury which is beyond description. Churches, shrines, universities, charitable institutions, and religious houses were destroyed, and a new "religion" of the state was set up.

It should not be concluded, however, that the French Revolution (or any of the attacks on the Church as a system) was a religious persecution as such. It was a revolution against the concept of *absolutism* ("I am the State," said Louis XIV, King of

The storming of the Bastille

France), and anything which stood for absolutism had to be destroyed.

By 1848 the liberal trend had reached almost every capital in Europe. It culminated in the establishment of the *country* of Italy (1861–70), which for centuries had been composed of independent states ruled over by separate "houses" and divided into North and South by the Papal States, which cut across the whole of Italy from Rome on the West to the Adriatic Sea on the East. After fierce civil war and the intervention of French, Austrian, and Spanish forces (now supporting the papacy, now turning against it), the Papal States, which had grown out of the gift of Charlemagne (c. 800 A.D.), were reduced to the present Vatican State (or Vatican City, as it is called), 108.7 acres of land within the city of Rome itself—one-sixth of a square mile.

After the period of political revolutions in Europe, the systems of government which had controlled people's lives for a thousand years disappeared. Civilization was moving into a new age which was to bring it ever nearer to the ideal of personal freedom and individual dignity toward which it had been moving since the dawn of history.

This growth toward personal freedom was not without its own problems and limitations, as we shall see. But the fact is that all the structures of society were affected by the scientific, philosophical, and political revolutions of the eighteenth and nineteenth centuries. Our concern here is with the structures of the Roman Church, which, like other human institutions, had to learn to adjust to the forces for change which were affecting all of civilization.

As we have said, by 1848 the political changes in Europe were all but completed. What remained was the need for those economic changes which would make the life of the common person more in keeping with the personal freedom and dignity which were rightfully his.

BROWN BROTHERS

The Economic Revolution

Once the political situation in Europe became somewhat stabilized, the social, economic, political, and intellectual changes that occurred gave rise to a period of Western imperialism and colonialism. By 1914 Europe had made itself the ruler of almost the entire world. The footholds established during the age of exploration were now expanded into military and economic dominance. Entire countries and cultures were subjected to forceful and often cruel subservience to those regimes from Europe that had but one controlling purpose: economic advantage for the home country. Such policies had disastrous effects upon religion, for Christianity, whether in its Protestant or Catholic form, was associated with the government dominating the territory, and the abuses of government were associated with the religion of the people who represented the government. Christianity made little headway.

At the same time in Europe, the Industrial Revolution, which had given rise to inventions for the benefit of society's material progress, created a problem at home that

BROWN BROTHERS

of people victimized by the Industrial Revolution was proposed in Europe. Karl Marx (1818–1883), often called "The Father of Communism," was horrified at the plight of the poor in England, and with his collaborator, Frederick Engels (1820–1885), he began to write pamphlets attacking the causes of the plight of the poor. They said that there were two principal causes for the conditions in which the poor were kept: capitalism as an economic system, and what they called the "tools of capitalism"—the government, the press, the schools, and religion. To relieve the situation, they said, a new system of ownership for the means of production and distribution was needed. Their system was communism.

When they published their famous *Communist Manifesto* (1848), they proposed an overthrow of capitalistic governments, the elimination of religion, and the temporary establishment of a super-state that would regulate every feature of life and eliminate the exploitation of the poor, who would, in effect, own the means of production.* The practical results of the Marxian political philosophy were not felt extensively until the

was even more serious than the problems abroad. The inventions that mechanized industry soon made possible the exploitation of the uneducated mass of people who were not prepared for the problems that an industrial economy forced upon them. Population shifted from the farm to the city, and the cities, ill-prepared to cope with the problem and ruled by those who helped create the problem, became slums where the people employed in industry lived in filth and squalor. The exploitation of the poor in the "new" society was as ruthless and cruel as it had ever been in the days of feudalism.

Writers, philosophers, and humanitarians in all countries, along with sensible ministers of all religions, worked hard to improve the living and working conditions of the poor. The great change however was not effected until the bishops of the United States supported the labor movement of the Catholic working man in America and Pope Leo XIII made the cause of the working man a paramount issue in Church thinking, and until the rise of labor unions to important political power in the United States.

A far different solution to the exploitation

---

* Marx and Engels did not advocate a permanent super-state. They looked upon the super-state as a means to destroy existing evils, which, when destroyed would allow people to live in small "classless," stateless communities.

Karl Marx   BROWN BROTHERS

Russian Revolution of 1917 under Nicholai Lenin (1870–1924) and Joseph Stalin (1879–1953), who made communism a fact in Russia.

The attitude of the Church toward communism was about the same as it had been to the anti-Christian philosophers at the time of the French Revolution. Both the Communists and the radical Deists had attacked organized religion as one of the principal tools of the ruling class in the enslavement of people. They had mistaken certain persons in religion for religion and directed their attacks against the abuses which they said were an essential part of religion. It was against this distortion that Christianity reacted—and in some cases overreacted. For some this made Christianity appear to be the enemy of human freedom and the dignity of labor. Subsequent history, however, has demonstrated that Christianity, whether in the Protestant or Catholic expression, not only was not opposed to humanitarian goals, but also actively promoted them with religion as their base.*

Teilhard de Chardin, Prophet of the New Age

The most significant change, as far as the Church is concerned, to come about as a result of the changes which developed in this period of human history was not political, economic, or social. It was a change in world view.

This change, which precipitated a major crisis in Christianity, came about because of the discoveries in biology. In 1871, Charles Darwin (1809–1892), an English natural scientist, published his famous *The Descent of Man* (in which he developed the idea originally presented in 1859 in his *On the Origin of Species*) stating the completely revolutionary idea that living things, especially people, were not the product of an immediate creation, as the Bible *seemed* to say and as Christians generally believed. They were, said Darwin, the result of a long evolutionary process.

A storm of protest arose in both Protestant and Catholic circles because the evolutionary theory apparently attacked the biblical foundations of Christianity. The early twentieth century battle between the "facts" of science and the "revelation" of Scripture began. This misunderstanding, which did much to drive sincere scientists from religious circles, has slowly been resolved in the 100 years since the initial furor. Much of the credit for resolving the issue must go to those scientists who attempted to show that science does not contradict religion but assists it. Among those who are chiefly responsible is a priest-scientist, Teilhard de Chardin** (1881–1955), who showed that the discoveries of science enable people to appreciate more deeply the glories of creation.

The work of Father Teilhard, summarized in his book *The Phenomenon of Man* (finished in 1947 and published after his death in 1955), broke down many of the barriers which had separated science and religion. Others before him had contributed to a relaxing of tensions, of course, but his work had a special brilliance and popularity which make him the favorite spokesman for many scientific-minded Catholics today. Perhaps he is the most popular Catholic representative in our time of the kind of faith-interpretation of new thought patterns which was seen in the work of St. Paul, St.

---

* The social encyclicals of Popes Leo XIII, Pius XI, John XXIII, and Paul VI and the less formal writings on social issues by Popes Benedict XV and Pius XII, as well as statements of principles by various Protestant leaders, indicate the awareness of Christian leaders of the economic and cultural problems of the last eighty years and of the political solutions proposed.

** Tay-ard·duh·Shar-dan (as in "man")

Augustine, and St. Thomas Aquinas.

For centuries (over 2500 years in Judeo-Christian circles), people had accepted as **fact** the mythological story of creation as related in *Genesis*. And why shouldn't they? There was no scientific data on which to base any other theory. What had been forgotten, of course, is that (a) the story told in *Genesis* was based upon much older myths of pre-Hebraic origin, and (b) the Hebrew authors were trying to show that, however this world began, it was YAH-WEH* who had created it.

When scientists began to make discoveries in the field of astronomy, physics, and biology which led them to question the accuracy of traditional theories, they were attacked by non-scientists who viewed their work as an attack on the Bible, hence upon God! It was an unfortunate conclusion, for science was on the move and no amount of uninformed opposition could overcome the facts which science continued to uncover.

Father Teilhard was ordained a priest in 1911, at the height of the science *vs.* religion controversy. He dedicated himself to the study of earth sciences, especially to paleontology.** His research took him to China (after a stint as army chaplain in World War I), where fossil study was at its height. In 1946 he returned to Paris, and in 1951 he went to New York where he died on Easter Sunday, 1955.

Father Teilhard was a man of international scientific reputation, and a priest very concerned with the problems science presented to religion. From the first years of his serious work in humanity's early history, he was concerned with the human and religious meaning of the data he unearthed. His masterful work presented a reconciliation between the biological data which science presented and religious phenomena. He proved that, far from being enemies, science and religion are twin endeavors helping people to understand themselves *as persons in the*

material world.

The basic insights of Father Teilhard led him to picture the dynamic evolution of the world in four stages each called a "genesis," or process of birth and development (prelife, life, thought, and future life, or the stage beyond life as we now understand it). We can summarize Teilhard's genesis theory in the following way:

1. **Cosmogenesis.***** The period of time extending from creation-time (15 billion years ago?) during which the universe developed to its present state. This process of development is still going on.
2. **Biogenesis.***** The period of time from the appearance of primitive life forms (two billion years ago?) to the present. During this time, life forms became more and more sophisticated until the living species now on earth developed. This process continues, not simply at random, but also under such controls as the selective breeding of plants and animals.
3. **Noogenesis.***** The period of time extending from the point at which cre-

---

* A Hebrew name for God.

* The science which treats of the forms of life existing in past geological periods as represented by fossils.

*** From the Greek word *cosmos* meaning "universe," *bios* meaning "life," and *nous* meaning "conscious thought."

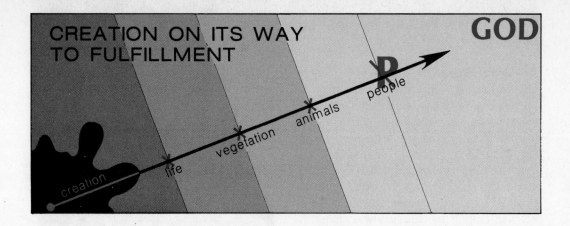

CREATION ON ITS WAY
TO FULFILLMENT

GOD

creation — life — vegetation — animals — people

ation became conscious of itself (1 million years ago?) and by reflection became human. As the process we call "intellectualization" continues, people's ability to reflect, to analyze and to create becomes more and more refined. It was during this time that the economic, political, and cultural roots of present society evolved.

4. **Christogenesis.** The period of time from the appearance of Jesus Christ to the present. This is the final era of the evolutionary process—creation on its way to fulfillment. Christians see the Incarnation of Jesus as the focus of creation's becoming divine through God's entry into creation's highest form, humanity. The "Christianization" of the universe is still going on, and like other processes in the attainment of the purpose of creation, it is slow and very gradual, depending on the limitations within people.*

Father Teilhard did not see people as a minor part of all of creation, as some scientists do, but as its final achievement, called by the very nature of creation to move toward that to which they are being called by their nature, because they are the most conscious of all beings.

For Father Teilhard, and for theologians who drew upon his basic insights to help them explain the relationship of people to their creator, evolution is another word for the creative dynamism of God, who is constantly creating—"making all things new," bringing all of creation to the fulfillment that is its own. They are attempting to understand doctrine, moral living, and worship in the light of this creative dynamism and to express the Christian understanding of life in the light of this new knowledge.

With Father Teilhard's monumental work in biology and the current work in economics, history, law, psychology, and the entire range of learning, *Christians are beginning to appreciate the ongoing nature of all of creation and to see that people, as they are now, are the product of their entire evolutionary history and that their future carries as much promise as their past permits and as their courage to face the risks of the evolutionary process allows.*

---

* This view, which we have taken from Teilhard, and which we might call a phenomenology of Christianity, complements the theology of St. Paul. It would be good here to read again in its entirety the quote from *Ephesians* appearing on page 48. Note that in St. Paul the view is from the forethought in the mind of God, whereas in Teilhard we see the plan not as forethought but as fulfilled in time.

Christianity Interprets Scientific Findings

What Teilhard de Chardin did was to give Christians a way to interpret creative phenomena religiously. Faced with a new world view (an evolutionary view as distinct from a static view), Christians could see Christ as the center of, or reason for, if you will, God's creative dynamic. The heart of the Christian message was not changed (the Son of God becoming a man to save people), only its human view was changed. Whereas people had understood the Christ-event as a curative intervention to save people from sin that had apparently upset God's original plan of creation, they could now understand it as part of a continuing process to bring creation to its preordained fulfillment —saving creation from a nondivine existence.

What makes this evolution of the universe towards fulfillment in Christ a work of God, and not just a product of blind chance?

Perhaps we can answer this question by distinguishing between *breakthrough* and *development* in the evolutionary process. "Development" means a predictable move forward—the direction in which a thing must go if its own laws are followed. It is this factor which allows scientists to predict what will develop if an experiment (in physics, chemistry, astronomy, biology, etc.) is conducted properly and if all of the negating factors are eliminated. "Breakthrough" indicates a completely different movement, which is totally unpredictable because an unknown factor is the cause of the breakthrough. It differs radically from what went before it and is explainable only *after the fact.* Thus we say that a breakthrough becomes intelligible in terms of its potential to develop; it becomes explainable only because of the unknown, or "X" factor.

Thus, in Teilhard's scheme, we can say

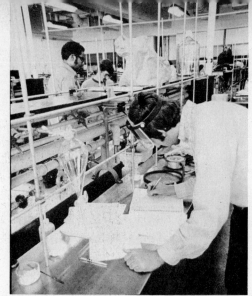

that **cosmogenesis** (the development of the universe) took place in an orderly fashion from the beginning because it followed the predictable patterns of its own potential. Cosmogenesis is a continuing process because the forces of nature continue to shape the universe: the winds, rain, earthquakes, chemical and magnetic forces, etc., change the shape and the development of the universe.

The first change in the direction of the evolutionary process apparently took place when life emerged (biogenesis) from the materials of the universe already in the process of change. **Biogenesis** can be partially explained in terms of the chemical, physical, and magnetic forces which brought the material to that place in evolution where a breakthrough was possible, but the breakthrough is explainable only in terms of the X factor *which caused the breakthrough in only one part of the cosmogenetic process.* If this were not so, the entire universe would have moved away from the lifeless condition and there would be no non-living organic matter. Biogenesis continues within the larger sphere of cosmogenesis, developing at its own rate and according to its own laws and potentialities. Once biogenesis occurred, the universe developed differently from the way it would have if no living matter were present.

A second breakthrough in the process occurred when matter became conscious of itself and this consciousness finally developed into "self" consciousness or introspection (noogenesis) and became human. As in the case of biogenesis, **noogenesis** was not predictable; it was a real breakthrough for it becomes explainable only in terms of its potential and the X factor which caused it. As in the case of biogenesis, noogenesis continues within the larger framework of cosmogenesis, but it also introduces a new aspect to evolution: controlled development, for choices were now possible. *Evolution was no longer simply unintelligent forces at work.*

A third major breakthrough, Christians say, occurred with the Incarnation. The entry of God into the universe was *totally unpredictable,* though, looking back at the event, Christians can find in the preaching of the Old Testament prophets a yearning for some climactic action on God's part to bring history to its fulfillment.

The Incarnation becomes an intelligible continuation of history in terms of what Christians believe about their God and his acting in history. Thus, **Christogenesis** is the fourth genetic development within the universe and, like the other breakthroughs, it continues within the area of the other three and is explainable only in terms of the X factor.

All four processes continue from their beginning in time, and all four change and develop and become more refined according to the potential of each and within the probables and the limitations imposed on each by the very nature of having been created. *This mystery of breakthrough—the X factor in the evolutionary process—is recognized by Christians as God acting in his universe to bring it to its fulfillment.* It is one reason why Christians believe that their interpretation of the mystery of life is more believable than other interpretations, which present this X factor as an Indifferent Power in the universe, an Impersonal Force outside the universe, or an Unconcerned Deity leaving the universe to its own fate; more believable than any interpretation which says that there is no cause for breakthrough. Christians also believe that their interpretation is more complete than the Jewish interpretation, which does not present God as having Personally entered his universe as a human being.

It is because of belief in this X factor (which makes the evolutionary process intelligible) that the Christian religion differs from science, philosophy, psychology, or humanism, all of which are dealing with data which is intelligible because it is predictable. For Christians, the X factor makes religion different from humanitarianism.

This understanding of God acting in his world is, essentially, the mystery of the Christian religion. Our intelligible explanation of the mystery of the universe is based on something *beyond* the universe becoming *present* and *focused* in it.

For Christians, the mystery of the universe is intelligible only in terms of Christ, the God whose entry into the universe as man, makes sense out of the universe. It is for this reason that Christians who accept the scientific story of evolution believe that this evolutionary process in all things reveals the Personal God who is bringing his creation to an intelligible future, totally unpredictable in its nature, which will be explainable only after it happens. *This final future breakthrough Christians call "heaven."*

Christianity, like all other breakthroughs in evolution, contains within itself potentialities to become more perfect, more refined, more sophisticated, according to the laws of potentiality within human endeavors. In other words, because intelligence brings with itself controlled development through choice, Christians can, by their conscious choices, make the potentialities of Christianity happen. They can make the condition of humanity better if they choose to do so (this is what is meant by Christian morality) by choosing those things in their economic, political and cultural world which will actually make the world better for people. This Christian potential to make a better world (to make the future happen) is called by Christians the *eschatological** potential of Christianity. Eschatology is the *theology of the future,* which Christians interpret as the better life to come because Christians have it within their Christ-given power to make a better life for humanity.

This Christian choice to make the world better, however, must always be made within the limitations of the real situation in which humanity finds itself at any given moment in history. Christians understand the tensions existing between the Christian ideal (which is potentially possible) and the immediately realizable (only so much progress can be made at any one time in history), and they learn to live with the problems of the moment, which develop because of human limitations. For this reason the history of Christianity (Church history) makes sense, for it is grounded in *faith* in the Personal God, whose activity in the past is a cause for *hope* in the future, if the *charity* of Christians puts into practice the ideals that Christ gave about achieving the ultimate destiny of people.

In contrast to this God-directed perfecting of an evolving universe, there is another view of the world, often called atheistic secularism, which sees the world as a place without God or where God is not necessary.

Atheistic secularism differs from Deism and secular Christianity because the Deists viewed the universe as created by God and left to its own resources, and secular Christianity, far from denying God, says that God is very active in this world. Secular Chris-

tians insist that it is precisely in the world as we know it that Christianity lives.

Atheistic secularists argue that, because many of the things religionists attributed to God are explainable in natural terms or because older explanations about the role of God in the universe are inadequate or apparently false, it is not necessary to have a God to explain the universe. They prefer to interpret the mystery of life without resorting to a God idea.

Christian secularists, on the other hand, see God as the answer to the mystery of life which atheistic secularists avoid or deny exists. Whereas atheistic secularists say there is no answer or that an answer is not necessary or that in some future time we shall have a "god-less" answer, Christian secularists say that there is an answer but that we do not experience it fully now.

Atheistic secularists would reduce God to non-God because in their view of the world God is not necessary. Christian secularists would return to the concept of the world that is inherent in the Jewish roots of Christianity: a person experiences himself in the world as a created, finite human being placed in a free and sovereign position relative to the rest of creation, free to accept his position and to work in the world, in history, in society for the true future of that which is already in the world. Christian secularists, as opposed to atheistic secularists, view this world as God's creation and people as having the potential to make themselves better in this world. They view this world as the proper place of people as they are and see Jesus as God's sign that this sonship is to be extended to all people. Secular Christianity, far from being a religionless humanism, is the Christian response to people's interest in human nature and its condition in this world. It is the Christianity of this world,

---

* From the Greek word *eschaton* meaning "end" or "fulfillment."

the understanding of the Mystery of Christ in the world in which modern people live.

The Church and the Modern World

The developments of the New Age resulted in profound changes within the Roman Catholic community, which culminated in the vast meeting of bishops called the Ecumenical Council of 1962–1965 or Vatican Council II, called by Pope John XXIII, who, some believe, was the greatest pope since the Renaissance.

Pope John saw that the Roman Catholic Church had more or less shut itself off from the mainstream of civilization and was becoming less and less of an influence in the lives of even its own thinking members. Before becoming Pope he had had wide experience in various capitals of the world, and his sensitivity to the needs of people and his love for the Church moved him to call all of the bishops of the world together to reaffirm the meaning of the Church for all. He attempted through the Council "to open the windows and let a bit of fresh air in—" to update the Church in all of its expressions.

From this Council a whole new look for the Church emerged. The Council Fathers rejected the image of the Church which often in the past had pictured it simply as a depository of truth and a "guardian of the faith," and declared it *an historical living reality of the saving event of Christ.* The Church, they said, was "The New People of

God" living out in the present time the saving actions of Christ. The Church is not a *structure,* the bishops said; it is *people who believe* that Jesus is the Son of God and who express this belief in their lives and in their worship. As Pope John put it in his opening speech:

> This being so, the Catholic Church raises the torch of religious truth by means of this Ecumenical Council. She desires to show herself as the loving mother of all; benign; patient, full of mercy and goodness to the children separated from her. As Peter of old said to the poor man who begged alms from him, she says to the human race which is oppressed by so many difficulties: Silver and gold I have none, but what I have I will give thee: in the name of Jesus Christ of Nazareth, arise and walk.
>
> In other words, the Council does not offer modern men riches that perish nor promise them mere earthly happiness. Rather she distributes to them the goodness of divine grace. This raises them to the dignity of the sons of God.*

Most of all the Council considered itself not the end and final arbiter of Catholic truth but a beginning, a dawn for a new day when the Mystery of Christ will be intelligible to all people. Once the documents which were prepared by experts in respective fields were discussed and approved by the bishops and enacted into Church practice by being promulgated as official by the pope, a new life and vigor took over the Roman Catholic Church. Not only did the Church present a whole new image to the non-Catholic world community; it afforded Christians within the Church a new flexibility and responsibility —it gave them a means to live the Christ-life in this New Age.

---

* *The Teachings of the Second Vatican Council* (Westminister: Newman Press, 1966), pp. 8–9.

Why Didn't God Make Me More Photogenic?

One day, when Cardinal Angelo Roncalli was walking into the Vatican for the election of a pope to succeed Pope Pius XII, he heard a woman remark about him: "My, look at how fat he is!" Turning to the woman and laughing with her, he said: "Madam, this conclave is not a beauty contest!" After he had been elected pope (much to everyone's surprise), he said, on seeing the official photographs, "God knew for seventy years that I would be pope some day; why didn't he make me at least a little photogenic?"

This extraordinary man, who took the name John,* was born in 1888. After he was ordained, he became secretary to the bishop of Bergamo where he became deeply involved with the social conditions of the Italian workers and the plight of the poor, and where he received his indoctrination in the delicate tasks of church and international diplomacy. He was, at one time or another, apostolic delegate in Turkey, papal nuncio in Paris, and Patriarch in Venice. Wherever he went as representative of the pope and usually in the most difficult posts, he distinguished himself as a priest and as a diplomat. "He never really failed," said a man who was closely associated with him. "He might not have accomplished everything he set out to do, but the situation he faced always turned out for the better because of what he did and because of the kind of person he was."

Without exception, those who testified at the preliminary inquiries leading to his being included in the official list of canonized saints, all

RELIGIOUS NEWS SERVICE

agreed on the extraordinary virtue and humanity of Angelo Roncalli. The consensus about Pope John, from people of every country and every condition in life, from housewives, laborers, executives, priests, bishops, diplomats, heads of state, such as Charles De Gaulle, President of France, and Queen Giovanna of Bulgaria, and fellow workers who knew him best, is summed up in the words of his old friend and former secretary, Archbishop Loris Capovilla, who said: "I was edified by his deep religious piety, which was founded on the Gospel and the writings of the Fathers of the Church. I was edified by

---

* The last pope to add a new name to the papal list was Pope Lando (913 A.D.). All popes since that time have selected names from the 121 predecessors of Pope Lando.

his boundless charity towards all: he never distinguished between friend or enemy, Catholic or non-Catholic, rich or poor. He always maintained a kind disposition. He was humble. Above all, I was struck by his pastoral energy: he wanted to reach everyone. He served the liturgy, cared for priestly vocations, cultivated courteous, human relations with every member and sector of society. He was a man of deep faith. When he had problems, he would retire to his chapel, and come out moments later composed and smiling. He never wanted people to pity him."*

Pope John had three loves which motivated his entire life: Jesus Christ to whom he prayed fervently, the Church for what it is and does, and people whom he respected with a deep, abiding charity. In spite of his great diplomatic and Churchly accomplishments, he is remembered most for his love of people. "He always spoke kindly of everyone," said Archbishop Capovilla. And Father Antonio Cairoli, director of the investigation into Pope John's life, on being asked what was the most obvious virtue of Pope John, replied: "Charity, undoubtedly charity. It was certainly the distinctive virtue of his life. In my study and investigation of his writing, and listening to the testimony of witnesses, I have not come upon one decision or word that went against charity. On the contrary, he so directed his ways of thinking and acting that charity would always be uppermost."**

This great man, as Pope, set one course for the Church: to be Christ to the world in its liturgy, its daily life, and its concerns for the welfare of people. To accomplish these goals, Pope John called an ecumenical council held at the Vatican in 1963. Although he died before the council finished its work in 1965, Pope John, through his own life's example and the work of Vatican Council II, set the Church on the course that was to be the most momentous for the Church since the Reformation. Through it, he sent the Church into the world to sanctify the world.

* Reprinted with permission from *St. Anthony Messenger*, September, 1974.

** *Ibid*, p. 98.

1. What was the effect of Protestantism and the Council of Trent on Catholic life in the seventeenth and eighteenth centuries?

2. What effect did the lessening of the Church's influence in politics and culture have on the Church?

3. Discuss whether or not this effect was good or bad for the Church as institution and the Church as the people of God.

4. Describe and illustrate what is meant by "the scientific revolution." Discuss whether scientists have any moral obligations to society.

5. Why does your book call this period of Church history "The New Age"?

6. How did the philosophy of this modern period of history differ in method from the philosophy of previous ages? What was the effect on religion? Discuss whether this was good or bad for religion.

7. What is the difference between a Deist and an Atheist?

8. Discuss the "Something Happened" insert appearing on page 192. Is it believable? Why? Why not? Why did people finally believe Bernadette? Do you think she really saw the Blessed Virgin? Why? Why not? Can you give examples of nonreligious experiences which people say are "unbelievable"?

9. A noted astronomer from Harvard dismisses UFO's with a quip and not-so-veiled contempt for those who accept their reality. Do you think this is wise on his part? Why? Why not?

10. Prepare some research on Lourdes since the time of Bernadette.

11. What is the central idea in the political revolutions of the last three centuries? What is the difference between the American Revolution and other political revolutions of the day and of modern times?

12. What was the effect of the political revolutions on the Church? Discuss whether this effect was good or bad for the Church.

13. Prepare a report on the unification of Italy as a political state.

14. What was the effect of the political and industrial revolutions on the average person in

England, France, and Italy? Discuss whether this might have happened if the Church were as politically strong as it had been, say at the end of the Dark Ages. (Refer to pages 111–116.)

15. Contrast the solutions to the problems of the working class as proposed by the Church and labor unions of the West and those proposed by Karl Marx.

16. Why does your book call Teilhard de Chardin "The Prophet of the New Age"? Was he qualified to speak to the problem of evolution and religion? Why? Why not?

17. Prepare a report on the life and work of Teilhard de Chardin.

18. Be prepared to summarize and explain Teilhard's thesis about creation. Does it make sense to you? Why? Why not?

19. What was Teilhard's major contribution to Catholic theology?

20. What does your book mean by "breakthrough" in the creative process? Illustrate. Discuss the pros and cons of this idea as you understand it.

21. Define and explain "eschatology" as it is used in Catholic theology. According to your book, what is the role of Christians in the evolutionary process? Can you give examples from modern life and concerns which show how this role can best be fulfilled by Christians? In what way do Christian ecologists differ from secular humanist ecologists?

22. Discuss the difference between Christian secularism and atheistic secularism. What are both interested in? Which makes more sense to you?

23. Prepare some research on the data of Pope John's life. Be prepared to discuss his role in history in light of the kind of man he was.

24. Try to obtain a copy of the documents of Vatican Council II. Make a list of the various topics discussed and reported on. Which ones seem to be directed to the Catholic in the modern world? Which ones seem to be directed to a Catholic's spiritual life?

25. Contrast the role and influence of the Church in this period of history with the role and influence of the previous 500 years. Be sure to give examples.

The Catholic Church in the United States

13

Catholics of Various Cultures Express Their Catholicism in a Democratic Society

The Church in the United States is a near-perfect example of the principle that Christianity is at once transhistorical and transcultural. It is made up of people from every race and culture. It has lived through and grown with the political, philosophical, scientific, and economic revolutions of Europe and the United States. It has developed from a handful of missioners bringing the gospel to the Indians, through the immigration flood of European Catholics seeking political and economic freedom in the United States, to become the largest single religious group in the United States. Unlike the Church in Latin, Central, and South America, the Church in the United States was not tied to a specific political and cultural expression, did not select its ministers and representatives from specific ethnic and political groups, and did not associate itself with a particular European government.*

---
* The fate of the Church in Latin, Central, and South America cannot be paralleled with the growth of the Church in the United States because the historical, political, cultural, economic, and social conditions in these countries differed markedly from those in the United States. (See page 183 for one of the reasons the Church in these countries developed differently.)

Site of first Mass in Florida, St. Augustine, 1565
RELIGIOUS NEWS SERVICE

The growth of the Church in the United States, though indebted to the European countries which nourished it, was not dependent on those countries for its life. It developed a life, an expression, and a posture that is distinctly American.

The story of the Roman Catholic Church in the United States at once precedes and parallels the story of American Democracy. The Church established roots in this country some 273 years prior to the actual founding of the United States; its growth here has kept pace with the emergence of the American ideal.

The Catholic Church came to America via three separate routes: the Spanish establishments were begun the year after Columbus "claimed" the New World for Spain; the French Catholic influence was established in Canada and throughout the Middle West (the Mississippi valley); and the English Catholics came to the colonies where the English sovereign was declared ruler.

Students of American history generally assume that United States history (and consequently American culture) begins with the story of the thirteen colonies that revolted from England. Although American culture and the American Catholic expression of Christianity are predominantly Anglo-Saxon, American culture has a heritage that goes far deeper and is much more all-inclusive than the English culture that is assumed to be American by adoption.

The history of the Church in the United States begins, really with the discovery of the New World by Columbus in 1492. Once the news of the discovery (mistakenly thought to be India)* reached Europe, governments sent out explorers, merchant seamen, soldiers, and government officials "to bring back the treasures from the East." Those countries that were Catholic (this was at the very beginning of the Protestant revolt) sent missionaries—mostly Francis-

cans, Dominicans, Carmelites, and Jesuits—with their expeditions.** Spain was the most aggressive exploratory country in the sixteenth century; hence its conquistadores established the rule of Spain in almost every part of the New World, except Canada, Eastern United States, and Brazil.

The Spanish Missions in North America

By the middle of the eighteenth century, Spain had established missions in the entire southern part of what was to become the United States from Florida (1513) through all the lands of the south (Texas, 1519) and up the west coast as far as San Francisco.***

In their explorations in the New World, the Spanish conquistadores were directed by the king "to contact the native peoples so that he might observe the manner in which may be undertaken their conversion to the Faith."† Charles V, Spanish King and Emperor of Europe at the same period when Luther was revolting in Germany and Henry VIII was preparing to break from Rome, wrote to his famous captain De Allyon (in

---

* Even after some European countries had Protestant rulers they did not, generally, send missionaries on expeditions to the new territories. Luther thought that the principal missionary effort should be spent on "converting" Europe; Calvin believed that God would provide for the "heathens" in his own way since they were not "predestined" to be Christian.

** That is why the islands southeast of Florida are called the "West Indies," and that the inhabitants were called "Indians."

*** The Spanish missioners gave Southwestern and Western America its distinctive architecture and many of its romantic names like San Antonio, San Diego, Los Angeles, San Francisco, etc.

† From Columbus' sea journal.

Mission Santa Cruz

1523) that "the chief motive you are to bear and hold in this affair" (the conquest of Florida) is the conversion of the Indians to Catholicism "and to this end it is proper that a religious person should accompany you." * For this reason, literally hundreds of missioners came to the Southern United States during the critical years from 1500 to 1750.

The system that the Spanish missioners used to convert the Indians to the Faith was the "mission system." Wherever they settled, usually one day's journey from the previous settlement**), the missioners established a school, a church, a place of refuge, and a market place, and trading center. To each they brought the Indians, whom they tried to teach how to live an ordered life. They taught the women how to sew, spin, weave, and cook. They trained the men to plant crops, carpenter, tan leather, run a forge, tend cattle, shear sheep, make irrigation ditches, and dig permanent wells. They brought an ordered existence into the lives of the nomadic, warlike Indians and had flourishing settlements.***

So successful were these missions that the less successful civil establishments coveted the wealth of the Franciscan, Jesuit, and secular priest missions. They succeeded in ousting the missionaries and gaining control of the mission by convincing the Spanish king that the priests and their helpers were defrauding the king and corrupting the Indians. When they gained control of the missions, they turned Indians into slaves and completely destroyed whatever faith the missioners had implanted. The result was suspicion and hatred for the white man that has carried down to the present day.

---

* From the Spanish archives of events of this date.
** For example, *La Quinta* Country Club in Indio, California, is the site of the fifth "station" from San Diego in Southern California.
*** The Spanish Franciscans had at least 35,000 Indians living in ninety settlements in New Mexico by 1630!

One Among Many

The bells that ring out from Mission San Diego de Alcala in Mission Valley, east of the city of San Diego, California, are the bells installed in the mission church in 1769 by Father Junipero Serra, the most famous of the many missioners who came from Spain to the New World.

Junipero Serra, a Franciscan monk, was born on the island of Majorca in 1713. Although he was a distinguished professor of theology at the University of Palma, he resigned and asked to be sent to the Indian missions. He was refused because he was lame and rather frail—"he couldn't stand the rigors of the mission life." He persisted in his demand, however, and was finally sent to the missions in New Spain in 1749. After learning the ropes from Franciscans who lived in Mexico and Texas, he set out from Santa Fe, New Mexico, across the Sangre de Cristo mountain range to San Diego, nearly 900 miles, on foot.

For the next thirty-five years he worked among the Indians of California, establishing missions from San Diego to San Francisco. In the twenty-one missions he founded, at least 40,000 Indians lived, raising 400,000 cattle, 300,000 hogs, sheep, and goats, 120,000 bushels of grain, fruit in hundreds of orchards, and vegetables in thousands of small gardens. They had thriving businesses, looms, shops, forges, wine presses, and the dozens of other occupations which are part of living in a village or town complex. Contrary to the accepted image of the American Indian, the Indians were able to be taught how to live in organized complexes, and were industrious, religious, and responsible. In their missions, the Franciscans made "contributions the like of which could be duplicated in no other area of colonial America, and it was no romantic impulse when [Herbert] Bolton spoke of the missions of the Spanish Jesuits and Franciscans as 'a force which made for the preservation of the Indians, as opposed to their destruction, so characteristic of the Anglo-American frontier.' "*

Father Junipero Serra died in 1784. In 1921, President Coolidge had a statue of Father Serra placed in the Capitol in Washington, D.C. among "the fathers and founders of the American homeland."

---

*John Tracy Ellis, *American Catholicism,* (Chicago: University of Chicago Press, 1956), page 6.

213

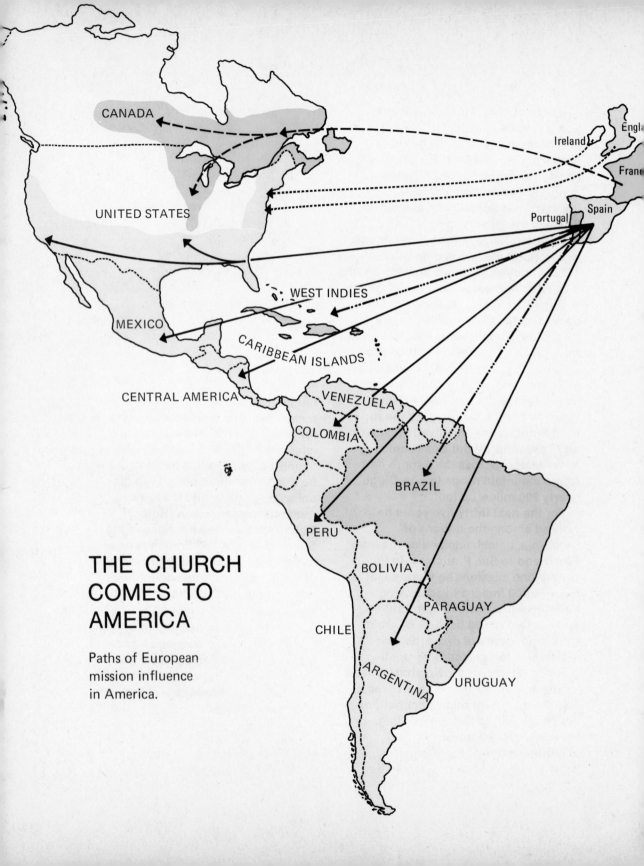

CANADA

Ireland

Engla

UNITED STATES

France

Spain

Portugal

WEST INDIES

MEXICO

CARIBBEAN ISLANDS

CENTRAL AMERICA

VENEZUELA

COLOMBIA

BRAZIL

PERU

THE CHURCH
COMES TO
AMERICA

BOLIVIA

Paths of European
mission influence
in America.

PARAGUAY

CHILE

ARGENTINA

URUGUAY

The French Missions in North America

To the historian, place names are almost as important as the names of people and events which shape a nation's growth. They tell him something about the place, and give him clues to events, to unfolding history, and to meaning.

Just as the place names of the south and southwest tell us of the Spanish missioners' unfolding history in America, so do the place names that dot the Mississippi Valley and the Great Lakes regions tell us the story of the French missioners. Names like Sault Sainte Marie, Detroit, Eau Claire, Dubuque, La Salle, St. Louis, Baton Rouge, New Orleans, and hundreds of others from Duluth to the Gulf of Mexico, from the Appalachians to the Rockies attest to the activity of the French government and the French missioners in the New World.

The Catholic faith brought by the French missioners to the Indians of this region was the second major Christian influence in the New World. The French government may have had territory, wealth, and power as its objectives, but the thousands of priests, religious brothers, and laymen who brought the faith to this area had the same view as their counterparts in the south and southwest. To them, "the Indian was a man whose soul has equal value in the sight of God with that of the white man," and they set out to bring the faith to him.

From the time of the French settlement in Canada in the sixteenth century until the Louisiana Purchase in the nineteenth (1803), Jesuit, Capuchin, Recollects and diocesan priests trained in the seminaries in Quebec and Montreal, lived and worked among the Indians "teaching them crafts and skills, and the Holy Faith."*

---

* At the height of the mission effort, more than 300 Jesuits were active in the Indian territories.

THE BETTMANN ARCHIVE

For a century and a half [these missioners] traversed the heart of the continent in pursuit of a goal that often eluded them. If the souls of these steadfast priests had not been kindled by a deep and abiding faith, they would soon have despaired; the story of the sufferings of the Jesuits alone during the 1640s at the hands of the savages remains one of the most heroic tales in our colonial past. From the time that Isaac Jogues, after incredible tortures, was felled beneath the ax of an Iroquois near the little village of Auriesville, New York, in October 1646, to the murder of Brebeuf and Gabriel Lalemant on Georgian Bay in March 1649, the slaughter continued. . . .

The Huron mission, it is true, had failed, but the Blackrobes did not quit New France. Instead they directed their eyes westward toward Lake Superior where Isaac Jogues had traveled as early as 1641. . . . by 1673 there were 1,800 refugee Ottawas and Hurons resident at St. Ignace Mission on the north shore of the Straits of Mackinac. South and west from these northern bases, the Blackrobes fanned out into the future states of Michigan, Wisconsin, and Illinois . . . [and] reaching down to the borders of the southwest . . . affording religious ministrations to the white settlers in the wilderness and [seeking] converts among the red men. . . . After the French had established the new colony of Louisiana in the early years of the eighteenth century, an agreement in May, 1722, brought the Capuchins, who endured throughout the century and beyond the time of Louisiana's purchase by the United States." *

The French mission effort in Middle America was not as lastingly successful in the Great Lakes region as the Spanish was in the south, southwest, and California for several reasons.** The Indians in Middle America were more savage and more nomadic, the French government was more authoritarian, the mission approach was slightly different, and the geography and climate more hostile. Very few permanent religious settlements were made, although the site of some of the missions became important settlements from which Middle America grew to its present strength. Some areas, notably southeastern Canada and Louisiana, however, were known as "Catholic" and have remained so to the present time.

It must be remembered that even though it was the Spanish missioners who were chiefly responsible for bringing the Catholic faith to the south and southwest, and the French missioners who were chiefly responsible for bringing the Catholic faith to the midwest, it was not the Spanish national church nor the French national church that brought Christianity to the United States; it was the Roman Catholic Church. The Catholic faith of the missionaries and their converts was expressed through Spanish or French cultural patterns, but it was the same faith. It had the same philosophy, moral stance, and liturgical practices. This was far different from the religious situation on the eastern seaboard where national Protestant churches established footholds and controlled the politics and the religion of the territory they claimed.

* *Ibid.,* pp. 12 to 16.

** It is estimated that one-fourth of the Catholic population in the United States is of Spanish heritage and that most of these have Spanish as their basic language.

The First Settlement,
Jamestown, Virginia

The Catholic Church in the English Colonies

The story of the Catholic Church in the original colonies along the east coast of the United States is far different from the history of the Church in the south, southwest, west, and Central Plains areas in the sixteenth, seventeenth, and eighteenth centuries. On the one hand, the missioners in the rest of the North American continent had come to land where the people were non-Christian Indians. The land was, as it were, virgin territory. On the east coast, however, settled early by the English and the Dutch, the people were refugees from religious persecution. What settlements there were, were religious settlements, and the people in them were fanatically bent on preserving their own religion.

The political-religious wars of Europe in the sixteenth and seventeenth centuries had spawned a cancer that was completely anti-Christian: the "enemy" was Christians of any other sect. The only common bond among Protestants of the period was their suspicion of and hatred for the "papists." The sectarianism of the Protestants and their hatred for Catholics was carried over to the New World.

At the time of the great English explorations and their claiming of "the New World" for the English sovereign, Catholics in England lived a persecuted, hunted life. Priests were systematically hunted down, tortured, and put to death. Consequently, when the few Catholics who were able to flee from England came to the colonies, they, too, were hounded, hunted out, persecuted, and in many cases jailed, or murdered.

For over 200 years in the colonies, Catholics were "the enemy" and suffered systematic discrimination and active persecution. It was not until the Revolutionary War succeeded in separating the colonies from England and religious toleration became the law of the land that Catholics were allowed to live in relative peace—even though a kind of passive discrimination, punctuated by active hostility, continued well into the Twentieth Century.

William Penn in Philadelphia

What is surprising in this persecution of Catholics in the colonies is that most of the people who came to the colonies were victims of religious persecution. They sought for religious freedom to practice their religion in peace, yet, once they were settled, they were as intolerant as the people from whom they had fled. In all of the colonial territory only two settlements actually practiced religious tolerance: the Maryland Colony, founded by a Catholic family, and Pennsylvania, founded by William Penn as a Quaker refuge. The irony of the Maryland settlement was that it was later taken over by some Puritans who had been given refuge there from persecution by other Protestants. The Puritans gained political power with the help of the Catholics who befriended them, but once they had power, they launched a campaign against the Catholics who had helped them!

To the English colonists, however, a century of official hostility had made Catholicism more hated than any other Christian faith. In fact, so thoroughly had the job been done that, as a student of English expansion remarks, "With such conviction did they preach this doctrine that Englishmen at length accepted it as their imperial destiny."

For present purposes the history of the Catholic Church in colonial English America may be reduced without too great simplification to four main points. First, a universal anti-Catholic bias was brought to Jamestown in 1607 and vigilantly cultivated in all the thirteen colonies from Massachusetts to Georgia. Second, the small body of Catholics, mostly English and Irish, who settled on the Atlantic seaboard after more than a century of active persecution and handicap clung to their religious faith. Third, the Catholic minority in their brief tenure of power in two colonies introduced the principle of religious toleration. Finally, the absence of domination by any one of the different Protestant churches fostered the principle of religious freedom for all, a principle to which the Catholics gave full assent.

The first point scarcely needs much documentation, since the proscription against Catholics in the colonial charters and laws is too well known to require emphasis, and the sermons, religious tracts, books, and gazettes of the period with monotonous regularity bore the same spirit and intent. The Anglican ministers of Virginia and the Puritan divines of Massachusetts Bay were often worlds apart in their theology, but there was nothing that would cause them to close ranks more quickly than a supposed threat from the Church of Rome. That is why one finds so much similarity between Virginia's law against Catholics of March, 1642, and the enactment at Massachusetts Bay five years later. It may be said that this transplantation of English religious prejudice to America thrived, though carried thousands of miles from its place of origin, and struck such enduring roots in new soil that it became one of the major traditions in a people's religious life. In a recent work Louis Wright states that, for better or for worse, Americans have inherited the basic qualities of their culture from the British. The thought prompts him to say: "For that reason we need to take a long perspective of our history, a perspective which views America from at least the period of the first Tudor monarchs and lets us see the gradual development of our common civilization, its transmission across the Atlantic, and its expansion and modification as it was adapted to conditions in the Western Hemisphere." Apace with the influences exercised by other national strains in the generation of American

civilization, the British has yet remained the strongest and has assimilated most of the others. Americans are not Englishmen, but, as Wright concludes, "we cannot escape an inheritance which has given us some of our sturdiest and most lasting qualities." Certainly the anti-Catholic bias brought to this country with the first English settlers has proved one of the sturdiest and most lasting of these qualities. The viability of that tradition would have astonished even Edmund Burke, who understood so well how the hatred of Catholics had operated in his native land. It was Burke who in a famous letter on the

THE ORIGINAL THIRTEEN COLONIES

penal laws against the Catholics of Ireland remarked:

You abhorred it, as I did, for its vicious perfection. For I must do it justice; it was a complete system, full of coherence and consistency, well digested and well composed in all its parts. It was a machine of wise and elaborate contrivance, and as well fitted for the oppression, impoverishment, and degradation of a people, and the debasement, in them, of human nature itself as ever proceeded from the perverted ingenuity of man.

That the penal codes of the American colonies did not reach the tyrannical perfection noticed by Burke elsewhere was no hindrance to holding the few colonial Catholics in thorough subjection.

What made the laws against Catholics in colonial America seem so absurdly harsh was the fact that at no time was more than an insignificant minority of the population Catholic. Protestants outnumbered Catholics among the 200 to 300 colonists who settled Maryland in 1634, and a census of that colony in 1708 turned up only 2,974 Catholics in a total population of 33,833. In Pennsylvania, the other colony where Catholics were concentrated, the census of 1757 recorded about 200,000 inhabitants, of whom 1,365 were Catholics. Even as late as 1785, when the new United States contained nearly four million people, there were scarcely more than 25,000 Catholics. Catholics were lost to the faith during these years by reason of the lack of facilities for the practice of their religion in many areas, but for the

most part the colonial Catholics held tenaciously to their faith amid the most trying circumstances. There were even some conversions among the Protestants, as, for example, the Brooke and Taney families of Maryland from whom the later Chief Justice of the United States was descended.

Why did Catholics come to America in the first place? The predominant motive was the same as that which had prompted the Puritans to settle in Massachusetts and the Quakers in Pennsylvania, namely, the hope that they might worship God according to their consciences, free from the hampering restrictions of England's penal laws.*

Religious toleration was slow in coming to the English colonies. Three conditions led to a measure of toleration in the colonies in the years just before the Revolution and immediately following. The first was the total commitment of the very few American Catholics to the principles of the revolutionaries; the second was the need to stop hounding Catholics if Catholic France and Catholic Canada were to be allies in the Revolution; the third was the lack of any dominant Protestant sect in the colonies.

Religious toleration was brought into being by the force of necessity, and the idea of religious freedom was made actual by the *Constitution,* which declared all religions equal before the law and forbade the establishment of any official state religion.

Although the contribution of Catholics in the colonial public life is relatively small since no Catholic was allowed to hold public office for over 100 years, it was highly significant for the future of America. It was the

---

* *Ibid.,* pp. 18–21.

Catholics who, with such important Protestant leaders as William Penn (1644–1718) and Roger Williams (1603–1683), promulgated and practiced religious toleration even in the instances in which it meant being forced to give up what power they did have in the established politics.*

The Catholic colonial concern for total religious toleration in the colonies is well summed up in a brochure written in 1784 by John Carroll (the priest who had been sent to Canada to win the French Canadians to the American War): "If we have the wisdom and temper to preserve [religious liberty], America may come to exhibit a proof to the world, that general and equal toleration, by giving a free circulation to fair argument, is the most effectual method to bring all denominations of Christians to a unity of faith."

The Growth of the Catholic Church in the United States After the Revolution (1790–1850)

In spite of the vast Catholic influence in the Midwestern and Southern regions of the United States, it was not the Spanish or the French expression of Catholicism which determined the nature of American Catholicism. It was the Catholicism of the English seaboard which established the pattern of Catholicism in the period following the Revolution.

The colonial uprising which established the American way of life was confined for the most part to the Eastern coastal region, but the colonists assumed that much of the New World belonged to them once they were free of English dominance. The Spanish and French settlements had been claimed for "God and country" and remained attached to, and dependent upon, the home country for support and control. Once the colonies

were free, they thought in terms of total freedom, and began their westward push into territories claimed by the French and their southern expansion into the territory already under the Spanish crown. A series of small wars, a few treaties, some astute purchases** and sheer exploitation eventually brought all of the territory between Mexico and Canada under the control of the United States.

During this period (1790–1850) two things contributed to the image of Catholicism in the United States: the nativist movement among white Anglo-Saxon Protestants, and the Americanization of immigrant (and Spanish and French) Catholics.

The nativist movement which is best characterized by the slogan "America for Americans" was the most serious threat to the American ideal the United States has ever faced. Under the guise of what its adherents called true patriotism, it was in reality a vicious attack on "foreigners and Catholics." Significantly, its attacks in print, from the pulpit, and in action (in Philadelphia, for example, in 1844, nativist rioters burned two Catholic churches, killed thirteen people and injured scores) were directed at Catholics, although there were many foreigners of other faiths.

What lay behind these vicious attacks, of course, was the hostility which English

---

* See the famous Toleration Act of 1649 enacted by Lord Baltimore and the guarantee for religious freedom in New York published in 1683 by Colonel Thomas Dongan, the Catholic governor. This last was short-lived, for a German-born Calvinist, Jacob Leisler, overthrew the government and started a reign of terror against Catholics. (Consult *American Catholicism*, John Tracy Ellis, University of Chicago Press, 1955, p. 30.)

** The Louisiana Purchase is one of the most significant deals ever made. In 1803, for $15,000,000 the United States bought, from France, all the land from the Mississippi River to the Rocky Mountains.

RELIGIOUS NEWS SERVICE

Gilbert Stuart: *Bishop John Carroll* RELIGIOUS NEWS SERVICE

Protestants had inherited from their forebears. The attacks centered around the Catholic "allegiance to a foreign power" (the pope), and the conclusion that Catholics could not be loyal Americans and remain true Catholics. (This thought was not finally laid to rest until John F. Kennedy became President in 1961 and demolished the unspoken rule that no Catholic could ever be President.) Historical data, of course, indicated the contrary, and no serious historian disputes the fact that American Catholics have been unswerving in their adherence to, and support of, the American democratic ideal.

The man chiefly responsible for the tone of Catholicism in the United States is Bishop John Carroll of the famous Maryland Carroll family. (Three relatives were signers of the *Declaration of Independence* and the *Constitution.*) It was he who enunciated the principle of religious toleration for all, and who defined the role of the Church in American life and the mission of the priest. He refused to be drawn into public controversy on purely civil issues and confined his public political statements to refuting the vicious rumors and violent attacks of the nativists. So highly respected was Bishop Carroll that, in the question of appointment of priests for the vacant Louisiana Purchase diocese (predominantly French-speaking), he received a communication from Secretary of State James Madison that "his [President Jefferson's] perfect confidence in your views and in the patriotism which will guide you in your selection of ecclesiastical individuals" made it unnecessary for Jefferson to suggest anything at all in view of "the scrupulous policy of the Constitution in guarding against a political interference with religious affairs."

In spite of the attacks on Catholics up to the Civil War, "on their religious beliefs, on the institutions of their church, and on their right to exist in the United States as citizens," the Catholic Church continued to grow until it became the single largest Christian denomination in the country. There were no more than 35,000 Catholics among the 3,929,214 people living in the Thirteen Colonies and and parts of the midwestern United States in 1790. But, because of the vast numbers of immigrants from Ireland, Germany, Poland, Spain, Italy, and France, the number of Catholics in these areas grew to 90,000 by 1820; to 800,000 by 1840; and to 2,000,000 by 1850. It is estimated that 1,710,000 Catholics came to America between 1790 and 1850.

This rapid influx of Catholics, most of whom were poor, disenfranchised, little educated and, in many cases, foreign-speaking, posed a problem for the small Church in the United States.* To meet the needs of these people, four distinctly Catholic responses were inaugurated: parochial schools, charitable organizations, the Catholic press, and the pastorial guidance of priests and bishops. These were the means used by American Catholics to "Americanize" the Catholics from foreign lands.

What these people had in common, of course, was their basic Catholic Faith. They could recognize "their Church" by its liturgy, its priesthood, its moral stance, and its sacramental life, which were the same whether the priest was native to their culture or not. What they needed was some indication of concern about their needs as human beings in a strange land. They found it in the Church structure for education, which eventually became the vast Catholic school system (there was one Catholic school in 1791; by 1840 there were 200 parochial schools); in the hospitals, orphanages, homes for the poor, and charitable lay organizations like the St. Vincent de Paul society; in the Catholic press, which was first organized to give the bishops a platform to defend Catholics since they could not get published in the secular press in America; and in the unselfish concern the bishops and the priests showed them in their poverty. The bishops were leaders of their people and reached them in the daily work of the parishes. The daily work of the priests and sisters was so effective that they were the principal agents in transforming the Catholics from Europe into American Catholics.

"I am not a Catholic," wrote Thomas Hamilton in *Men and Manners in America* (1833), "but I cannot suffer prejudice of any sort to prevent my doing justice to a body of Christian ministers, whose zeal can be animated by no hope of worldly reward, and whose humble lives are passed in diffusing the influence of divine truth, and communicating to the meanest and most despised of mankind the comforts of religion."**

What Catholics from foreign lands were to learn, and then to contribute to the total church understanding, was that religion was not tied to nationality, race, or political structure. Catholics found that the *best* possible climate for religious expression was the American democratic ideal. It is significant that this lesson was learned by the Church in the United States at the very onset of political upheavals throughout Western Europe which culminated in constitutional (that is, liberally-oriented) governments. It took the European Catholic Church a long time to learn the lessons of freedom; the American Church accepted freedom as its hallmark.

The single most distinctive characteristic of the Catholic Church in the United States was its willingness to accept the American way of life and what America stood for.

The Catholic Church in the United States After the Civil War

Although in many quarters Catholics were considered an alien force in the United States,*** their numbers and policy were well established by the Civil War period. If nothing so shattered American life as the Civil War, nothing so clearly demonstrated the solidarity of American Catholics in their

---

* The American Catholic Church was the most democratic of all churches, for, as one foreign writer observed (in 1831), Catholicism was the church of the masses; in it the poor man was equal to the rich, the slave was equal to the master, the Negro to the white, and the minister (priest) served all regardless of position.
** *Ibid.*, p. 60.
*** The Know-nothings and the American Protective Association revived the nativists' charges and persecutions in the period from 1860 to 1900.

religious faith and their diversity in politics.

The burning question in the United States in the 1850s was the slavery question; the great issue was the union of the states. American Catholics generally supported he cause of either the North or the South, not for political reasons of safety, but for ideological reasons: the Northern Catholics were for preserving the union; the Southerners were against the federal government's domination of states' rights.

Catholics, like most others, took slavery for granted and owned slaves when they lived in areas of the country where slaves were part of "the American way." Because the Church's moral conscience directed Catholics to insist on fair treatment, education, and the preservation of family rights, many Catholics spoke out against the abuses and cruelty which were a part of the system of slavery.

When Catholics owned slaves, the general attitude concerning their freedom is best expressed in Ellen Hart Smith's account of Charles Carroll's views:

"Charles Carroll . . . would no more have considered setting free his slaves, without

making elaborate provision for their future, than he would have thought it a kindness to open cousin Rachel's wicker cage of tropical finches, setting them at liberty to fend for and warm and feed themselves in the cold Maryland winter."*

When the Civil War broke out Catholics were on both sides, but the real story of American Catholics at this time is found in the charitable works of the sisters and priests who went into the war areas to help the poor and the suffering. Over 800 sisters left the parochial schools to volunteer as nurses in the hospitals, and countless priests served as volunteer chaplains on both sides. *The sorry side of the story is that the Church in the South, poor and alienated from society by public policy, was the victim of the war, and had not the manpower, the money, or the institutions at war's end to care for the Blacks as many as would have wished.** The southern bishops did what they could, but their efforts were frustrated, not only by ex-

---

* *Ibid.*, p. 169, note 10.
** There were barely 300,000 black Catholics among three million blacks in the South.

Two for the Schools

Elizabeth Ann Seton is recognized by American Roman Catholics as the pioneer of the parochial school system. She was born Elizabeth Ann Bayley in New York, August 28, 1774. Her father was a physician; her mother the daughter of an Episcopal minister. She was raised a Protestant. She became a Catholic after her husband died in Italy leaving her with five children.

In 1808 she opened a small parochial school in Baltimore, and a year later, in Emmitsburg, Maryland, she founded the Sisters of Charity of St. Joseph. She died in 1821, but her work lives on in the order she founded and in the schools they still conduct. She was canonized in 1975.

St. Frances Cabrini was born in Lodi, Italy in 1850. Although she had wanted to be a nun, she was refused because she was so small, frail, and sickly. After completing her education she taught in the public schools. When she was thirty, she organized a group of women, Missionary Sisters of the Sacred Heart of Jesus, for missionary work in China.

Pope Leo XIII asked her to go, instead, to the United States to help educate the immigrant Italians in the ghettos. She arrived in New York in 1889 and began a long, fruitful career as an educator, founding parochial schools in the poor sections of New York, Brooklyn, Scranton, Philadelphia, New Orleans, Chicago, Denver, Seattle, Burbank, and numerous other cities. Meanwhile she founded hospitals, orphanages, and homes for the elderly poor. She died in Chicago in 1917 after twenty-eight years in the United States during which she established sixty-seven religious houses and left an indelible mark on the parochial school system of the United States.

treme poverty, but by racial bigots who tried to keep the slaves in servitude "within the law."

The Civil War had demonstrated beyond a doubt that Catholics were not tools of the political thought of Rome, as the bitter enemies of the Catholic Church in America had maintained. It also demonstrated the vigor of the faith, for Catholics alone, of all the major religious groups, remained united in faith. Most Protestant groups formed "southern branches" (for example, the Southern Baptists), and the preaching of the various "circuit rider" preachers was deeply fundamentalist and completely southern in sympathy.

It was after the Civil War also that the Church in the United States became known as the Church of the working people and of the cities. Two major developments contributed to this image. The first was that a great number of immigrants from Southern and Eastern Europe came to the industrial centers of the North looking for work. They found the Church in the cities active and well-established. They crowded the schools and the parishes and joined clubs where they could find friends with similar religious and cultural interests.

The second development was the support the American bishops gave people in their efforts to correct labor abuses. It was not at all uncommon for the working man to be a virtual slave of industry: he often had to work twelve to fourteen hours a day, six days a week, in deplorable conditions for very small wages. The American bishops not only defended the working man at home by supporting his secret labor societies; they also defended him and his efforts against the suspicions of the Church in Rome, where the American labor movement had been grossly misrepresented.

So successful was this defense that the famous encyclical *Rerum Novarum* of Pope Leo XIII was the product of their defense.

This encyclical was the first major position paper on the rights and dignity of labor by any leading world figure. It represents a milestone in people's struggle for self-determination; it became the "Magna Carta" of most subsequent labor documents.

One of the by-products of the massive immigrant movement in the 1850s to 1900s was the growth of the parish school. For several years the Catholic bishops had pleaded for "equal time" in the predominantly Protestant public schools. They made no headway. After pleading their cause in vain, they adopted a policy in 1884 of having a school in every parish; by 1900 there were 4000 in the urban centers of America. The completely erroneous charge that Catholics wanted to take over the public schools and force Catholicism on America was revived and has made the Catholic school *versus* the public school a political football up to the present time. As in all cases of controversy, this cultural issue is influenced by the practical politics forced on society by economic realities.

Although the American ideal was a product of radical Protestantism and Deism, the Catholic Church was a strong force in the shaping of American democracy. From virtual enslavement in the years before the Revolution, it grew to a position of respect (and fear, of course) within 100 years. By 1900 there were over 12,000,000 Catholics who were both distinctly Catholic and distinctly American. The famous American historian and social analyst Henry S. Commager, writing of the influence of Catholicism in American life, says:

"It might, indeed, be maintained that the Catholic Church was, during this period, one of the most effective agencies for democracy and Americanization. Representing as it did a vast cross section of the American people, it could ignore class, section and race; peculiarly the church of the newcomer, of those who all too often were regarded as aliens, it could give them not only spiritual refuge but social security."*

The Catholic Church in the United States After 1900

Civilization's ongoing progress toward the fulfillment of human destiny reached a new plateau with the assured success of what historians call the "American Experiment." It was an experiment at the time it was launched, for no one knew for certain whether people could really, and not theoretically, govern themselves.

By 1900 the experiment was over. It was proved that people of good will could arrive at a consensus and live peaceably together under a self-government whose leaders share in the corporate authority of the community. No one disputed the need for a leader in whom the authority of the community would be focused. The problem was to build into the system of self-government those safeguards which would prevent authority from being vested in a single person; hence, the system of checks and balances incorporated into the American Constitution.

When the twentieth century began, the world realized that the American form of government could withstand selfish ambition, internal strife, and outside encroachment. Without really realizing it, civilization had moved into a new era, the era of personal and community freedom.

Three principal developments have emerged in the Catholic Church in the United States since 1900. The first is a gradual lessening of prejudice toward Catholics generally; the second is the unprecedented material growth of the Church; the third is the increasing emphasis on social action, experienced particularly since 1960.

After 1900 there were few concerted efforts to discredit Catholics which broke out in violence. Overt discrimination, a carry-over from the religious wars of Europe, was becoming more and more a thing of the past, but Catholics felt the discrimination in more subtle ways such as the "unwritten law" that no Catholic could be elected President, the "separation of Church and State" slogan which kept Catholics out of important federal positions and blocked United States representation at the Vatican, and the publication of a series of magazine and newspaper articles and some books which supposedly gave "the truth" about Catholics. The atmosphere of prejudice has all but disappeared since 1960, even though the problem of federal aid to non-public school children and the hiring of priests and religious for public aid programs still creates an attitude of hostility in many areas of the country. Prejudice is still experienced by Catholics in part of the country, but it is no longer a generally accepted mode of procedure.

After 1900, when the number of Catholics in the United States increased dramatically** and their financial condition was able to bear the burden, Catholics contributed vast sums of money to support the material growth of the Church. Churches and schools were built in record numbers; hospitals and institutions for specialized care, seminaries, convents and monasteries appeared in all parts of the country. Organizations under Catholic auspices sprang up in every major city, and large staffs were hired to administer the affairs of the Church. Bishops sponsored groups for nearly every aspect of American life—from child welfare agencies to homes for the aged and adult education—and financed these operations from the contribu-

---

* *The American Mind: An Interpretation of American Thought and Character since the 1880s* (New Haven: Yale University Press, 1950), p. 193.
** By 1975 there were nearly 49,000,000 Catholics in the United States in over 23,000 parishes and missions.

Why Do Catholics . . .

Differences between Catholic and Protestant interpretations of Christianity range from minor aspects of doctrine and ritual, to major understandings of worship and doctrinal meaning. It is impossible, of course, to give a complete list of distinctions between the doctrinal, moral, and liturgical expressions of Catholic and Protestant Christians. There are, however, several questions which many Protestants ask about Catholic Christianity which point up the differences between some Protestant groups and Catholics in the United States.* Among the common questions which Protestants ask Roman Catholics are the following. They are usually phrased, "Why do Catholics . . .

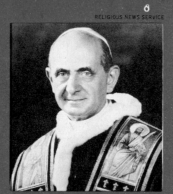

RELIGIOUS NEWS SERVICE

Have a pope? Catholics believe that the pope is the successor of St. Peter who was the "chief apostle." They believe that he is the supreme head of the Church. The growth of the authority of the pope in the Roman Catholic Church has been gradual and historically conditioned, but his primacy is rarely disputed by historians.

Honor Mary so much? The history of devotion to Mary goes back to the very early days of Christianity. Catholics (and many Protestants, of course) honor Mary because she is the Mother of God. Unlike other saints, Mary is the "universal" patron of Catholics; she is honored in all countries where Catholics are found.

RELIGIOUS NEWS SERVICE

* Most Catholics in the United States follow the "Roman rite" in their liturgy. There are other "Roman Catholics" who have their own rites, however, and in some cases their own bishops. The major non-Roman rites are: the Byzantine (Greek), Armenian, Chaldean, Coptic, Ethiopic, Malabar, Maronite, and Syrian.

Have saints? Saints are members of the Catholic "Hall of Fame." They are honored for their exemplary lives and for what they did. Canonization is not only a process for putting certain people on the official list, it is a process that weeds out myth from fact.

Have seven sacraments? For Catholics, sacraments are signs of the activity of Christ in his Church. Catholics have seven sacraments (all Protestants have baptism and many have "The Lord's Supper") because, historically, special rituals were used to signify specific moments of Christ's special activity in the lives of Christians.

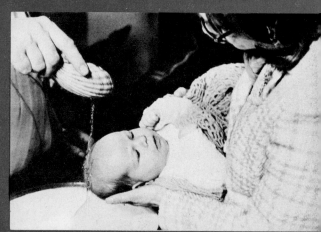

Go to Mass? For Catholics, the Mass is the community celebration of the Lord's Supper. For Catholics, it is the principal act of worship in the Church toward which every other action points and from which all actions flow. It is the solemn, official liturgical act of the Church.

SUSAN MC KINNEY, EDITORIAL PHOTOCOLOR ARCHIVES

ROHN ENGH

RELIGIOUS NEWS SERVICE

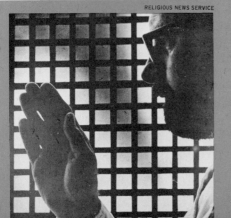

Have their own schools? Catholics believe that religious education is as important as any other education. Because religious studies are banned from public schools in the United States, Catholics have formed their own schools for those who can attend them, and provide special religious education programs for those who cannot.

Have nuns? From the days of the apostles, there have been men and women who have dedicated themselves to special work in the Church. Nuns are women who form a special type of community within the Church and vow themselves to the special work of the community.

Go to confession? Confession, or the Sacrament of Penance, or Reconciliation, is one of the seven sacraments of the Church. Its principal purpose is to reconcile Christians who may be alienated from God and their community with their fellow Catholics.

tions of Catholics from all over the country. The archdiocese of Chicago, for example, had over 100 agencies serving the Catholic population in Chicago, in addition to the regular parishes, schools, and hospitals.

This growth of the Church is reflected also in the number of missioners sent from the United States to care for the needs of people throughout the world. American missioners in Africa, Asia, Central and South America, and the Pacific islands now outnumber the missioners from any other country. American Catholics are the largest contributors to the Propagation of the Faith, the international organization with headquarters in Rome whose function is to administer the world-wide missions.

Once the Church in the United States could stand on its own feet, and suspicion and prejudice began to die down, the Church in America was able to give more and more attention to the social problems which plagued the country and the world. The National Council of Catholic Bishops set up agencies for caring for the poor of the world and those suffering from temporary difficulties. Catholic Action groups, whose purpose was to function in the world of social action, blossomed in all parts of the country. The Extension Society, whose purpose was to care for Catholics in rural America; the St. Vincent de Paul Society, organized to give direct aid to the poor in the cities; the Glenmary Society, whose work was directed to the underprivileged in the South; and organizations like PAVLA, CALM, the Association for International Development, Front Line, and the International Catholic Auxiliaries, are but a few of the many groups giving their attention to social problems.

These are not the things, however, that distinguish the Church in the United States from the Church in other parts of the world. The Catholic Church in the United States had a unique and distinct role to play in the total Church's continued growth in self-understanding.

The United States' Catholic Contribution to World Catholicism

The Catholic Church in the United States was destined to lead the whole Western Church in its expression of religious freedom. But first it had to be recognized as a distinctly American Catholic Church with its own style and corporate identity. It had to demonstrate its ability to exist on its own terms within the community of the Roman Catholic Church. That it can has been demonstrated by the history of the Church in the United States since 1900.

Just as it has taken the world a long time to realize that the thrust for freedom is real (and not just an isolated rebellion), so it has taken the Roman Church a long time to adjust to the thrust for freedom within its ranks. This aspect of the Church's developing self-understanding is still going on.

What is the Church in the United States teaching the Western Catholic Church about itself? It is teaching it that *there can be unity within diversity*. Unlike the Roman Catholic Church in Europe, Asia or Africa, the Church in the United States is made up of diverse cultural strains; yet there is unity of basic faith. The Western European Catholic Church did not have within its experience this particular challenge of diversity. The Church in France, for example, is made up of Frenchmen, the Church in Italy is made up of Italians, the Church in Poland has a strictly and uniquely Polish cultural expression.

Contrast this with the Church in the United States, which is largely urban-centered (about 80 percent of Catholics are

living in cities) and made up of large segments of varying nationalities. The Church population in the archdiocese of Chicago, for example, with well over 2,000,000 Catholics, has 56 "Polish" parishes making Chicago the largest Polish "city" outside of Warsaw, several Italian, Irish, and German parishes, some French, Hungarian, Serbian, Mexican, Puerto Rican, and Black parishes, at least one Chinese parish and many Catholics of Eastern Rite expression, together with "general American" Catholic parishes. It has innercity, city, suburban, and ultra-suburban parishes, missions, and chapels.

This diversity of cultural expressions and the great land mass encompassed by the Catholic Church in the United States necessitated machinery for the attainment of a certain amount of unity within the diversity. This machinery was found in the *national conference of bishops,* which was set up, not to control or override the independence of any diocese, but to provide a setting for dialogue in which the bishops could exchange ideas, express their common concerns, and have a means for some kind of national agency that could utilize the energy and skills of all areas of the country for the benefit of those who need its concern the most. This system was incorporated into the thinking of Vatican Council II, which urged all bishops of every region to adopt "the American scheme." It was also reflected in such

developments as the vernacular liturgy, the decentralization of Roman authority, and collegiality (shared responsibility), which are part of the life of Roman Catholicism in the new era of freedom.

Of course, not all problems of unity with diversity have been solved. There are no magic answers in the mystery of life. It takes a long time for habits and cultural attitudes to change, for people to be open to diverse expressions. The major contribution that American Catholics have made to the Church's self-understanding of its mission in the world must be supplemented by the true charity of the Gospel. Catholics in the United States must learn to live in harmony amid diversity and to respect not only those cultural expressions that are different from their own, but also the right of individuals to an expression of their own conscience-directives which may cause them to express their faith in a way that is somewhat different from all others.

There is no doubt that the Catholic Church is ready for the next era in its long history. It will have to live through the growing pangs of change. Whatever happens it will have to keep before its collective mind the advice of Pope John XXIII:

"In incidentals let us have diversity, in essentials let us have unity, but in all things let there be charity."

1. Discuss the differences in the conditions that faced the missioners in the Southern and Central United States and those that faced Catholics on the East Coast at the beginning of American history.

2. What three cultural strains shaped the formation of the expression of Catholicism in the United States? Discuss why Catholicism in the United States is predominantly "English."

3. Why does your book say that the Catholic Church in the United States is a "near-perfect example that Christianity is at once transhistorical and transcultural"?

4. What historical/political events caused the Church effort in Southern and Western United States to be predominantly Spanish?

5. Prepare a major report on the coming of Christianity to one country in Latin, Central, or South America. Include some general remarks on the coming of Christianity to other countries in those areas.

6. Why did missionaries go to the "New World"?

7. Prepare a report with pictures and/or charts on a typical Spanish mission in early American history.

8. What was the basic difference between the Spanish missioners' approach to the Indians and the Anglo-Saxon approach?

9. Why did the Spanish missions in the South and West have so little lasting effect in the history of the South and West?

10. In a map of the Southwest and West, find names of places that have Spanish names and mark them on the map on page 214.

11. In a map of the Great Lakes region find names of places that have French sounding names and put them on the map on page 214.

12. Look up some data on the French mission effort in the central areas of the United States. Include a report on St. Isaac Jogues and St. John de Brebeuf and their companions.

13. Why did Catholics who came to the eastern seaboard of America experience so much hostility?

14. What is so strange about the hostility of the eastern Protestant groups toward each other and toward Catholics?

15. What was the political cause for the lessening of open hostility toward Catholics in the colonies?

16. Why didn't Catholics make more of an impact on the early political fortunes of the United States?

17. What caused the growth in numbers of the Catholic Church after the Civil War?

18. What was the "nativist" movement?

19. How did the Catholic Church "Americanize" Catholics who came from Europe? What role did St. Frances Cabrini play in that process?

20. Prepare some research on the coming of Catholicism to your geographical region. In a separate part of your report, present some background on your ancestors' coming to the United States.

21. Why were parochial schools started in the United States?

22. What major contribution did the Roman Catholic Church in the United States make to world Catholicism?

23. Prepare a report on the origins of the Maryknoll missions.

24. Prepare a statistical report on Catholicism in your diocese.

25. Prepare some thoughts on whether religion ought to be taught in the public schools in the United States in preparation for a class discussion on the topic.

14 Your Church

The Church Attempts to Meet the Needs of Global Society

If Christianity is seen as the social expression of Christ in history, it becomes obvious that there has been a gradual devlopment of this expression from the time of Christ to the present day. The foundation for this development is the meaning of Jesus in God's plan for His creation. Its superstructure is the cultural influences that have conditioned the understanding of this meaning in each age. That is, Christianity is expressed culturally.

The development of its expression is illustrated by the Church's doctrinal formulations, by her forms of worship, and by her moral directives as they have come to us in the twentieth century. What forms these doctrinal, liturgical, and moral expressions take depend upon the Church's understanding of its mission at any time in history and upon the cultural sophistication of the society in which they are expressed.

The prophetic mission of the Church requires that it spell out for each age its own understanding of the meaning of Jesus for the world. We have already seen examples of this in the development of doctrine. This mission also requires that the Church call attention to what it considers society's shortcomings and make every effort to move society toward more human consideration of its disadvantaged citizens. Thus, for example, in the seventeenth century St. Vincent de Paul (1581–1660) began hospitals for the poor and St. John Baptist de la Salle (1651–1719) began schools to provide general education for the underprivileged. Today, Christian churches are calling on society to move ahead in civil rights and in respect for the dignity of individual freedom. The Christian Church thus keeps alive the vision of Christ. It reminds society that its first concern ought to be God, and that that concern is best expressed in how society worships and in how it treats its citizens.

This prophetic mission for the Church in the new global society made possible by modern technology (instant worldwide communication and one–day–or–less flights to any place on earth) was proclaimed by the Church for Catholic Christians in Vatican Council II (1962–1965). Speaking to the whole Church, the bishops of the world said:

It is the goal of this most sacred Council to intensify the daily growth of Catholics in Christian living; to make more responsive to the requirements of our times those Church observances which are open to adaptation; to nurture whatever can contribute to the unity of all who believe in Christ; and to strengthen those aspects of the Church which can help summon all of mankind into her embrace. Hence the Council has special reasons for judging it a duty to provide for the renewal and fostering of the liturgy.

For it is through the liturgy, especially the divine Eucharistic Sacrifice, that "the work of our redemption is exercised." The liturgy is thus the outstanding means by which the faithful can express in their lives, and manifest to others, the mystery of Christ and the real nature of the true Church. It is of the essence of the Church that she be both human and divine, visible and yet invisibly endowed, eager to act and yet devoted to contemplation, present in this world and yet not at home in it. She is all these things in such a way that in her the human is directed and and subordinated to the divine, the visible likewise to the invisible, action to contemplation, and this present world to that city yet to come, which we seek (cf. Heb. 13:14). Day by day the liturgy builds up those within the Church into the Lord's holy temple, into a spiritual dwelling for God (cf. Eph. 2:21–22)—an enterprise which will continue until Christ's full stature is achieved (cf. Eph. 4:13). At the same time the liturgy marvelously fortifies the faithful in their capacity to preach Christ. To outsiders the liturgy thereby reveals the Church as a sign raised above the nations (cf. Is. 11:12). Under this sign the scattered sons of God are being gathered into one (cf. Jn. 11:52) until there is one fold and one shepherd (cf. Jn. 10:16).*

The joys and the hopes, the griefs and the anxieties of the men of this age, especially those who are poor or in any way afflicted, these too are the joys and hopes, the griefs and anxieties of the followers of Christ. Indeed, nothing genuinely human fails to raise an echo in their hearts. For theirs is a community composed

---

* From "The Constitution on the Sacred Liturgy," points 1 and 2, *The Documents of Vatican II* (New York: America Press, 1966), p. 137, 138.

of men. United in Christ, they are led by the Holy Spirit in their journey to the kingdom of their Father and they have welcomed the news of salvation which is meant for every man. That is why this community realizes that it is truly and intimately linked with mankind and its history. . . .

Today, the human race is passing through a new stage of its history. Profound and rapid changes are spreading by degrees around the whole world. Triggered by the intelligence and creative energies of man, these changes recoil upon him, upon his decisions and desires, both individual and collective, and upon his manner of thinking and acting with respect to things and to people. Hence we can already speak of a true social and cultural transformation, one which has repercussions on man's religious life as well.

As happens in any crisis of growth, this transformation has brought serious difficulties in its wake. Thus while man extends his power in every direction, he does not always succeed in subjecting it to his own welfare. Striving to penetrate farther into the deeper recesses of his own mind, he frequently appears more unsure of himself. Gradually and more precisely he lays bare the laws of society, only to be paralyzed by uncertainty about the direction to give it.

Never has the human race enjoyed such an abundance of wealth, resources, and economic power. Yet a huge proportion of the world's citizens is still tormented by hunger and poverty, while countless numbers suffer from total illiteracy. Never before today has man been so keenly aware of freedom, yet at the same time, new forms of social and psychological slavery make their appearance.

Although the world of today has a very vivid sense of its unity and of how one man depends on another in needful solidarity, it is most grievously torn into opposing camps by conflicting forces. For political, social, economic, racial, and ideological disputes still continue bitterly, and with them the peril of a war which would reduce everything to ashes. True, there is a growing exchange of ideas, but the very words by which key concepts are expressed take on quite different meanings in diverse ideological systems. Finally, man painstakingly searches for a better world, without working with equal zeal for the betterment of his own spirit.

Caught up in such numerous complications, very many of our contemporaries are kept from accurately identifying permanent values and adjusting them properly to fresh discoveries. As a result, buffeted between hope and anxiety and pressing one another with questions about the present course of events, they are burdened down with uneasiness. This same course of events leads men to look for answers. Indeed, it forces them to do so.*

These twin concerns of the Church today (the worship of God and concern for other people) are older than the Church. When

* "Constitution on the Church in the Modern World," Vatican Council II, nos. 1 and 4, *The Documents of Vatican II* (New York: America Press, 1966), pp. 199–203.

ALAIN KELER, EDITORIAL PHOTOCOLOR ARCHIVES

RELIGIOUS NEWS SERVICE

Jesus was asked (Matthew 22:35–40) about the greatest commandment, he repeated the Jewish Law about love of God and love of neighbor, and wound up by saying: "On these two commandments the whole law is based." And they have been the central concern of the Church for 1900 years. What is important for Catholic Christians today is that now, as the bishops point out, they have a new dimension: they are global. Only in this age of human development is it possible for Catholics to extend their care for people on a truly world-wide basis.

The Needs of a Global Society

What is God telling Catholic Christians of this era through the media and their bishops? He is saying in unmistakable terms that human society needs a force to meet the problems of a global society head on, not for reward, political gain or expediency, or security, but because it is the right thing to do. It is the Christian thing to do. It is the Christian imperative. "How can you say you love God," St. John wrote to his early converts, "and hate your brother? . . . A person who has no love for the brother he sees, cannot love the God he has not seen." (1 John 4:20) And St. James told his Christian community: "My brothers, what good is it to profess faith without practicing it? Such faith has no power to save one, has it? If a brother or sister has nothing to wear or no food for the day, and you say to them, 'Goodbye and good luck! Keep warm and well fed,' but do not meet their bodily needs, what good is that? So it is with the faith that does nothing in practice. It is thoroughly lifeless." (James 2:14–17)

Catholic Christians in this global society are called to political and social action in three major areas: civil rights, poverty/hunger, and world peace.

Not everyone can effect profound changes in society, and no one person alone can conquer the triple scourges of modern civilization. But everyone can do his part. Achieving an effect in the social world is like dropping a pebble in still waters: it is felt in ever-widening circles. A Catholic with a sense of his Christian mission can, by his life, his words, and his actions, affect his home, his neighborhood, his parish, his diocese, his country, and the world. And if all Catholics respond to the call of God to establish His kingdom on earth, the 500 million could change the world. And if a billion Christians bring the message of Christ to the world . . .

The history of the world in the last quarter of the Twentieth Century is your history. The history of the Catholic Church in the last quarter of the Twentieth Century is your history, for you are the Church. It is your Church, because Christ called you to be a Catholic Christian through your baptism. He has given you his Spirit in Confirmation, he feeds you with his body, and provides his special graces for you to be him to the world. He calls you to be a Christian, not just to go to church on Sunday, but in everything you do: in your spiritual life, in your personal commitment to his values, in your personal life, in your giving to others of your material goods, your money, and your self. Christ hopes to act through you. Will you let him?

In the 1900 years since the apostles came alive at Pentecost, the believers in the Christ-event have come a long way. Each age has shown how it understood what the Christ-event meant for its Christians.

History has a future because people, having groped their way from primitive consciousness to sophisticated self-awareness, have a future. In this future, the Church's self-understanding will continue to grow.

The Church will continue to proclaim the Mystery of Christ in terms that people will understand because the Church of today, giving witness to the coming of God into the world in Christ, has the same urgency that moved St. Paul to write to the Christians of Colossae:

It makes me happy. . . . I became the servant of the Church. . . . for delivering God's message. . . . which was a mystery hidden for generations and centuries and has now been revealed to his saints. It was God's purpose to reveal it to them and to show all the rich glory of this mystery. . . . The mystery is Christ among you, your hope of glory: this is the Christ we proclaim, this is the wisdom in which we thoroughly train everyone and instruct everyone, to make them all perfect in Christ.

Colossians 1:24–28

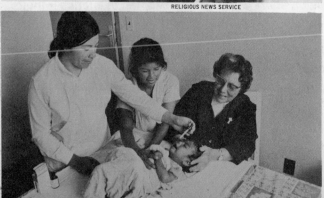

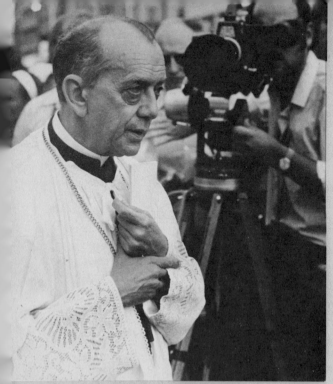

MARYKNOLL

Dom Helder:
a Prophet Besieged

A controversial man, Dom Helder Camara of Brazil arouses intense emotions. He is both loved and hated. Most of his fervent supporters are poor and underprivileged. Most of his bitter critics are in positions of influence or leadership.

Like prophets of the Old Testament, such as Amos and Isaiah, Dom Helder points to the disorders of society with a deep, personal sensitivity to human suffering. He also has the passion and courage to call for radical reform.

Like prophets of old, too, Dom Helder is not always understood. Rather, many of his critics apparently listen only to part of what he says. North Americans will applaud him when he denounces injustices committed under communism and ignore him when he condemns injustices from capitalistic practices.

Also like prophets of old, Dom Helder has been threatened with death. At least one direct attempt has been made on his life and his name appears on a list of 32 Catholic leaders marked for execution by a right-wing terrorist group in Brazil. One of his aides, Father Antonio Henrique Pereira Neto, was brutally murdered last year.

In the tradition of the prophets of old, Dom Helder is an independent thinker. He speaks the truth as he sees it regardless of personal consequences. He strongly criticizes his own country for allowing large numbers of people to live in poverty. He does not hesitate to point out areas in which his own Church needs reform. He is equally critical of the United States and Russia for what he calls their militarism and their policies toward the underdeveloped countries.

Dom Helder does more than criticize, however. With a passion for justice, he suggests positive policies. His statements have aroused the enmity of conservative interests in both Church and state who have tried to silence him.

Dom Helder has become a controversial political figure because he insists that the Christian Gospel involves not only men's souls but also their whole human existence—their right to work, to just wages, to decent housing and to political freedom. He contends that "all those who accept the truth of the Gospel in their lives are called to play their part in the defense of man and of justice."

For such views, Brazil's military government has denounced him as being "on the side of leftism." Dom Helder for his part points out, "The fight against communism provides a convenient pretext for dismissing the problems and maintaining the present situation."

This modern-day prophet is a small man physically, only 5 feet, 4 inches tall and weighing about 120 pounds. He usually wears a plain black cassock and simple wooden cross. As the Archbishop of Recife and Olinda in the Brazilian Northeast, he moved from a spacious residence to the dilapidated rectory of the Church of the Frontier.

The name of the church could not be more appropriate. Dom Helder is concerned with religious and economic frontiers. Brazil is the largest Catholic country in the world, with 90 percent of its 90 million people baptized, although probably no more than 15 percent go to church regularly. It also is a country where from one-third to one-half of the people know only subsistence living. The most extensive area of extreme poverty is the Brazilian Northeast.

Dom Helder and some other Church leaders are convinced that Brazil's society is in need of drastic reform. They point to economic inequalities, with 3 percent of the people owning 62 percent of the land. Great numbers of farmers live in semi-feudal bondage to landowners. Hundreds of thousands of families live entirely outside the money economy, and average per capita income is no more than $350 a year. The educational system caters to the rich, literacy is about 50 percent.

While he sees the Church as "the major moral force on the continent," Dom Helder also believes that it must share the blame for social and economic inequities as a defender of the status quo. He wants it now to take the lead in repudiating the past by working for change.

"We have accepted the ethic of slavery for three centuries," he argues. "We have acquiesced in the social order—really the social disorder —that keeps millions of human creatures living in subhuman conditions. We have preached patience and acceptance of suffering.

"With us, without us, or against us, the eyes of the masses will be opened. They must not associate the Church with their exploiters. The job of the Church is to open the eyes of the people."

Dom Helder is critical of all present societies—capitalist, communist or socialist. He charges that the U.S. grows fat on the wages of the Third

MARYKNOLL

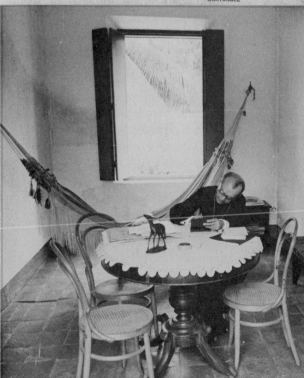

World's poor. For example, he maintains that money flowing to the U.S. from Latin America in recent years far exceeds U.S. investments in Latin America. In the world as a whole, he sees 85 percent of the people rotting in misery to make possible the excessive comfort of 15 percent of the population.

"This is serious because if in international relations we have injustices, there are injustices in the world scale," he emphasizes. "Without justice in the world scale, peace will be impossible. I think that we must try to obtain a great world movement of popular opinion to obtain justice as the way toward peace."

As for communism, Dom Helder denounces Moscow and Peking for invariably imposing dialectic materialism in blind obedience to the Communist Party. He argues that the best way to combat it is to tackle courageously and decisively "the most urgent problem of our days: the persistence and constant aggravation of the condition of two-thirds of humanity in underdevelopment and starvation."

Communism, he predicts, will disappear when spiritual leaders are moved by the crisis of humanity to concentrate their full influence on the defense of the human person. In so doing they will show that it is not necessary to deny God and eternal life in order to love man and fight for justice on earth.

"None of the present regimes, whether capitalist or socialist, can achieve a more human world," he explains. "Not capitalism because it is a system which creates misery. Neo-capitalism pursues simple solutions which do not go to the roots of the problem and lack justice.

"Socialist models are also inhuman because they want to impose their dogmas through force. The evil is not the dogmas, but the decision to impose them by force. Therefore, we have an atmosphere of dictatorship."

A man of strong faith, Dom Helder defines development as a deeply Christian event, the realization of man in his full human dimension and, by the grace of God, in his divine dimension. In his mind, the measures he proposes are Christian rather than political.

"The social revolution which the world needs will not come by an act of parliament, nor by guerilla warfare, nor by war," he predicts. "It is a radical transformation which presupposes divine grace."

The Church, he believes, has a duty to denounce unjust regimes. As he says, "There are spectacular miseries which give us no right to remain indifferent."

In support of Dom Helder's position that his views are more Christian than political is the fact that he has been expressing them for a long time. A Recife housewife who met him about 26 years ago, when she was a student preparing for social work, finds him little changed today.

"He was a young priest then, not very well known, but exactly as he is today," she recalls. "He had a firm belief, a deep belief in the goodness, love and brotherhood of men, and he found it difficult to believe that people couldn't understand it. I don't think his views are so political; with him I think it is a deep feeling, his own personal feeling. When he was speaking to about 20 students in our school, not to the public in general, he used to say the same thing, that development is absolutely indispensable for the people to have a decent life. He was supposed to teach anthropology, but all he did was try to make us understand the people in the slums where we were supposed to work after graduation.

"You could feel his great love for them, his great anxiety that they should improve. From that point, I think his feeling grew to the whole nation. It was a deep and sincere thing with him because what he said then is what he says now. To him it is so obvious that he does not understand how people fail to see his views."

Today Dom Helder is concerned not only with the poor of Brazil, but the poor of the entire world. Earlier this year he joined hands with the Rev. Ralph Abernathy, U.S. civil rights leader and president of the Southern Christian Leadership Conference, to launch "a worldwide campaign to awaken the conscience of the people to the great human cost of poverty, racism and war." Meeting in Recife, the two leaders of non-violent movements for justice declared:

"We are especially concerned with the widening gap between the poor of the world and the rich—not only in material goods as the rich get richer and the poor remain in misery—but the growing gap in understanding. The indifference of the well-to-do is perhaps the major obstacle in the world today."

Both leaders will take their message to the World Conference on Religion and Peace to be held in Kyoto, Japan, in October. They do not know the form that their movement will take, but foresee that it will include people from all religions who are seeking justice and love as the way of peace.

"There is hope, and there is a great dream of a world in which there will be no more misery, no more war, no more prejudice and all men will be free," the two leaders agreed. "This was the dream of Jesus Christ, of Mahatma Ghandi and of Martin Luther King. It is our dream, too."

To Dom Helder, such freedom necessarily includes economic independence. He denounces the international dictatorship of economic power as the real source of violence, and says that the whole world is in need of a structural revolution.

"The social order which we actually encounter, which consists in leaving millions of God's creatures in miserable poverty, should be called more appropriately the social disorder or systematized injustice," he contends.

Dom Helder would start by reforming international trade. Some poor countries lose more through trade than they receive in all forms of aid.

"If there are rich countries and poor countries, the problem is the absence of justice in the international policy of trade," he asserts. "Without changing the policy of trade of the United States and developed countries, the richest countries will grow more and more rich and the poor countries will become more and more poor."

Christian development as defined by Dom Helder avoids both extremes. "We must lift ourselves out of the subhuman situation of misery without falling into the inhumanity of super comfort and super luxury," he says. In achieving this goal he is opposed to violence. He points out that an armed revolution might well bring in the United States, determined not to permit a second Cuba on the continent, and the intervention of Russia and China.

"Between violence which might provoke an imperialist war," he explains, "and an attitude which consists in sitting on your hands, doing nothing except making declarations of compassion, we believe there is another road, that of liberating moral pressure."

On this point there is much disagreement. Many Christians in Brazil have concluded that moral pressure is not strong enough to change unjust social structures. As a teacher in Recife pointed out:

"Dom Helder is intelligent and shrewd. He believes that we can obtain reforms by a peaceful pressure on authorities. He says that he does not believe in violence but he respects the point of view of those who have chosen the way of violence to obtain social justice.

"On this point I don't agree with him. For me it seems almost impossible to obtain social justice without certain violence because the rich won't give up privileges peacefully, especially the privileges of not paying just salaries, of possessing large estates of land."

From a partner in a sugar plantation comes another opinion. This man says of Dom Helder:

"From what I know of him, from his behavior, his talks and acting, I have the impression that he is intelligent, clever, versatile and pliable. I consider him a kind of banner-bearer rather than a true leader. For a

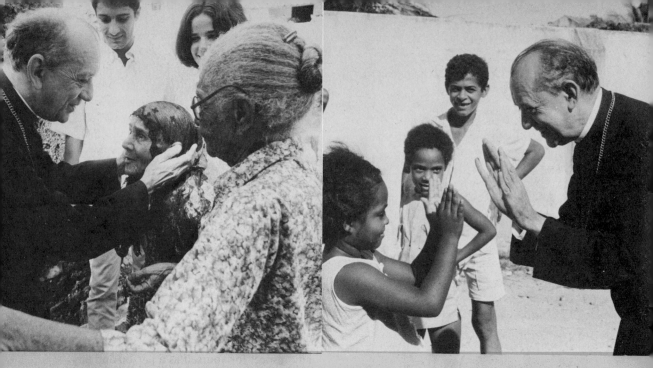

dignity of his rank, even if he is honest in his alleged desire to serve God by serving man, I think that a little more serenity and less demagoguery in his manners would not do any harm to the church."

Meanwhile, Dom Helder continues to speak his mind, to preach his controversial message that winning the battle against underdevelopment requires profound reforms in international commerce, agriculture, industry, finance, and labor. Only Christianity is independent enough and influential enough to make rich and powerful countries understand the value of selfless giving, so Christians must provide leadership.

"It is only those who achieve an inner unity within themselves and possess a worldwide vision and universal spirit who will be fit instruments to perform the miracle of combining the violence of the prophets, the truth of Christ, the revolutionary spirit of the Gospel—but without destroying love," says Dom Helder.

To him, non-violence means believing more passionately in the force of truth, justice and love than in the force of war, murder and hatred. "Love alone constructs," he insists, "hatred and violence serve to destroy."

That is the essence of Dom Helder's non-violent philosophy, that violence does not change mentalities, only love can. For himself, he will optimistically continue to do whatever he can to bring about conditions for peaceful human and social development.

"I hope not only in the help of God who will not abandon to destruction the chief work of creation," he says, "but also in man's intelligence and good sense."

Raymond M. Boyle, in *Maryknoll Magazine*, September 1970, pp. 2–13.

What of the Future?

What will your world be like in the year 2000? It will be the kind of world you make it, for then you and people like you will be world leaders. There will be technological advances we cannot even dream of now, but will there be justice for all? Will civil rights for all be a way of life? Will all people have enough to eat, and live in the light of peace instead of the shadow of war? We can live without technological advances, but can we live without justice for all in a world that makes it possible through technology for one to destroy many?

The world has tried political power to achieve its national goals, and it has tried military force to impose its will. When will it try Christian justice? As G. K. Chesterton, the famous English writer, said: "Christianity has not failed. It has never been tried!"

You have seen what the Mystery of Christ has meant to generations of Catholics, and you have seen how the understanding of this mystery has developed through the centuries. *The important question is: What does the Mystery of Christ mean to you?* Only you, as an individual, can answer it.

Your review of Christian history should have helped you to understand what it meant to be a Christian in the past. Your anchor in the Catholic Church, your maturity as an individual, and your understanding of your relationship to God can assist you in coming to a decision about what it will mean for you to be a Christian in the future.

If you really understand what is meant by salvation in Christ, you will be a Christian. If you really understand what the Catholic Church is, you may choose to remain a Catholic. The thing is, you must decide one way or another: positively by directing your future as a Catholic, or negatively by drifting on the fringes of belief or non-belief.

One thing you should not be, if you have any respect for yourself as a person and any respect for your own family of the future, is a *merely sociological* Catholic. That is, you should not be a Catholic by accident. You should not be a Catholic who happens to perform Catholic gestures (insofar as they are convenient) because you were born a Catholic, because your parents would be offended if you were not, because you need to be a Catholic for business or professional reasons. In other words, don't be a Catholic for any other reason than the right one: because you really understand what it means and intend to live up to the deepest convictions of that belief.

You are on the threshold of maturity. You live in a society that is constantly moving forward, constantly using the technological know-how of modern science that can help bring about a better world—if enough people have the vision and the prophetic energy to create a better world.

This is where the Christian Churches must find their mission. They must insist that the world must serve all people, that the Christ-event means that God is found in His creation, that the presence of Christ is in people, that the affairs of society—economics, politics, and culture—must focus their energy for the good of all people, so that they can live in dignity and honor in their own cultures.

But, as we said in the very first part of this book, the "Christian Church" is people. It is not buildings, not institutions, not a special group of professionals whose "business" is religion. It is the entire community of believers who accept Jesus as the Word of God. The Christian vision will not be kept alive among people unless these Christians understand its meaning in terms of the present human situation. Christians will have to shed their inclination to consider their religion as some kind of magic to placate a hostile God, some kind of ritual to please a friendly God, some kind of part-time contact with their God (a Sunday nod to the deity). They must understand that *all* of creation, *all* of their lives, *all* of their world has Christian meaning: that *this life* is the Christian life; that all they say reflects their understanding of the meaning of Christ for the world; that all they do reflects their understanding of how creation is related to their Christian God.

The mature Christian of the future will belong to a community of believers whose doctrinal, moral, and liturgical expression is centered in this present life, who express their understanding of Christianity by the way they live their total lives, whose first concern is for their fellow men. The mature Christian of the future will not belong primarily to a Christian denomination; he will belong to a community of people who believe in the Christian interpretation of life. This is not to say that the mature Christian will not be a member of a particular Church. He will be joined with those who believe as he does, but his belonging will be determined by how a particular Christian Church

RELIGIOUS NEWS SERVICE

Africa . . . Christian by the Year 2000

If present trends continue, Africa at the end of the century will be second to Asia in population and ahead of all continents in total Christians.

There is a widespread underestimation today of the magnitude of present Christian expansion in Africa. The fact is that since around 1910 Africa has been the only one of the world's six continents on which the entire Christian community has expanded uniformly at a rate over twice that of the population increase. By the year 2000, if existing trends continue, Africa will be the home of around 350 million Christians—the largest assorted Christian community then to be found on any continent in the world.

David B. Barrett, in *Maryknoll Magazine,* January 1970, pp. 3–7.

expresses for him the meaning of the Christ-event.

The mature Catholic will recognize his Christian fellows in the celebration of the Eucharist, in the bishops who are servants of the believing community, in the sacraments which are celebrations of the mysteries of life, and in the family which will be the heart of the Catholic community.

What will the Catholic Church in the United States look like in the future? No one knows the details, of course, because cultural expressions shift and change slowly, imperceptibly. But if the past is any indication of the future, the Catholic Church in the United States will continue to express the democratic principle within the framework of the universal Church. There will be unity with diversity, more regional autonomy, greater flexibility, and a concern for the expressions of a futuristic society.

What will the liturgy be like? How will church authority reflect its own understanding of democracy? Will ecumenism lead to better understanding and acceptance of others' religious beliefs and practices? Will the moral climate exhibit an emphasis on community consciousness? Will doctrinal explanations be open-ended? Will the Catholic school system shift its concern to adult religious education? How will the Catholic community express itself—in small parish groups, in congregations of people from the same sociological and professional avenues of life? What shall religious orders be doing in the future?

These and dozens of other questions will seek answers in the Catholic Church in the United States of the future. Its shape and form will be determined by the Catholics who are mature Christians. The way the Church meets the challenge of the future is up to you. When you are decision-making adults, the Church will reflect your understanding of its mission in the world. If one

of you understands the Mystery of Christ as St. Paul, St. Augustine, St. Thomas Aquinas, Teilhard de Chardin, and Dom Helder Camara understood it, he may be the prophet of the future. One of you may be the formulator of the meaning of Christ for your generation of Christians. But, whether you are or not, each of you can be a prophet in his own way. Each of you can be a witness, each of you can be a saint, each of you can be Christ to your world. All you have to do is try. Each of you can be the body of Christ. If you are, you are a member of the People of God, a social institution which, as pilgrim on this earth, attempts to make it a place where God's kingdom is a reality.

One thing is certain about the future. People will know more than they do now about many things; most of all, they will know more about themselves. *When people know more about themselves and the world in which they live, they will be able to formulate new answers to the ultimate question: What does it all mean?*

We Catholics think that we have a partial answer to that question. We invite you to explore its meaning with us, to share your interpretations, your convictions, and your concerns. If you do, you will join with the community of mankind which believes that

TO LIVE IS CHRIST!

1. On page 246 your book quotes G. K. Chesterton as saying: "Christianity has not failed. It has never been tried!" What does he mean by that?

2. Why is the future of the Church in your hands and not solely in the hands of priests and religious?

3. Describe in your own words the mission of the Church in this last quarter of the Twentieth Century.

4. According to your book, what are the three most important global challenges facing the world? In your view, what is the Christian approach to these problems? Discuss each in some detail.

5. If your own neighborhood is a microcosm of the world, to what extent are these problems present in your area? Discuss solutions to them, concentrating on what your peer group can do realistically.

6. Did the bishops of Vatican II display any foresight concerning the Church's future? Illustrate your answer. Find out what concrete proposals the Catholic Bishops of the United States have made to help solve world poverty and hunger problems.

7. What does your book mean by "sociological Catholics"? Do you think that most Catholics in your peer group are sociological Catholics? Why? Why not?

8. Be prepared to give a brief sketch of Dom Helder Camara. What does he think is the job facing the Church at this point in history?

9. What does your book mean by "Catholics are called to political and social action . . ."? To what extent are both open to your peer group? Be prepared to discuss this issue with your classmates.

10. Your book says that it is possible for you to be a saint. Do you agree or disagree? Why?

11. Many young people seem disenchanted with any institutional Christian church. Can you give reasons why? Discuss with your classmates whether or not noninvolvement with a Church is a good idea.

12. Five "major prophets" of the Catholic Church are mentioned in your book. By way of summary, give a brief sketch of each one's contribution to the Church's understanding of its mission.

13. Prepare a paper entitled "If I were the Pope" giving your ideas on what you would do about the Church at this moment in history. Discuss your ideas with your classmates.

14. What is the role of a bishop in a diocese? What is the role of the priest in the parish? If you do not know, find out what the name of your bishop is, and the geographical boundaries of your diocese.

15. In a short paragraph, give a reason why the title of your book is *The Emerging Church.*